ROYAL HISTORICAL SOCIETY
STUDIES IN HISTORY
SERIES
No. 17

THE PARLIAMENTARY AGENTS

A History

Other volumes in this series

Copies obtainable on order from
Swift Printers (Sales) Ltd, 1-7 Albion Place, Britton Street, London EC1M 5RE

THE PARLIAMENTARY AGENTS

A History

D. L. Rydz

LONDON
ROYAL HISTORICAL SOCIETY
1979

ISBN 0 901050 53 9

The Society records its gratitude to the following, whose generosity made possible the initiation of this series: The British Academy; The Pilgrim Trust; The Twenty-Seven Foundation; The United States Embassy Bicentennial funds; The Wolfson Trust; several private donors.

The Publication of this volume has been assisted by a further grant from the Twenty-Seven Foundation.

Printed in England
by Swift Printers (Sales) Ltd
London, E.C.1.

CONTENTS

PREFACE

The centre of gravity of this history lies somewhere in the second and third quarters of the nineteenth century, but it looks back to the rather informal origins of parliamentary agency and forward to when the importance of the profession was certainly not to be measured by its size. Chapter one calls for an explanation. I was not far into this study before I was being asked, "What is a parliamentary agent?". Chapter one is the result. It's first part, though historical in approach, I hope serves to indicate what private legislation is, as well as was, about, and I have introduced there more modern material than was appropriate to the rest of the work. In the second part I have tried to answer the question by describing what a parliamentary agent does. It may read strangely to a practitioner for, inevitably, it emphasises the procedural framework within which an agent works rather than his activities as an adviser and negotiator in matters of legislation and public policy. But the latter do not lend themselves to general explanation apart from particular cases.

I wish to thank the Society of Parliamentary Agents for making their records available, and especially Mr. H.W. Gamon, M.C., sometime honorary Secretary and now President of the Society, for much valuable advice and for reading the typescript. Mr. M. Pritchard, the Society's present honorary Secretary, has been unfailingly helpful, as have all the parliamentary agents I have turned to for information or advice. My many visits to Westminster were made pleasant by the cheerful helpfulness of the partners and clerks of Messrs. Sherwood & Co., and Sharpe, Pritchard & Co., and by the staff of the House of Lords Record Office. I record with thanks the co-operation of the Law Society.

I am indebted to Miss Sheila Lambert for helpful discussion, for reading part of the typescript, for her own researches, and for the quotation which heads chapter two. My thanks go to the University of Leicester for the honorary fellowship and the facilities made available to me there, and for much support and encouragement.

I am grateful for the generous assistance of the Nuffield Foundation, and the leave of absence which made this study possible, and I thank the Royal Historical Society for undertaking its publication.

Leicester

D.L. Rydz.

ABBREVIATIONS

BL	British Library
Bond	Maurice F. Bond: *Guide to the Records of Parliament* (1971)
CJ	Journal of the House of Commons
Clerical Organisation	O. C. Williams: *The Clerical Organisation of the House of Commons* (1954)
Clifford	F. Clifford: *History of Private Bill Legislation,* 2 vols. (1887)
HistPBProc.	O. C Williams: *Historical ,Development of Private Bill Procedure,* 2 vols. (1948)
HC	House of Commons
HL	House of Lords
HLRO	House of Lords Records Office
LJ	Journal of the House of Lords
May	T. Erskine May: *Treatise on the Law &c. of Parliament (Parliamentary Practice),* 18th. edn. except where otherwise indicated
Mins	Minutes
Mins of Evidence	Minutes of Evidence
MinSPA	Minutes of the Society of Parliamentary Agents
PRO	Public Record Office
Qn(s)	Question(s)
RecSPA	Records and documents in the possession of the Society of Parliamentary Agents, other than the Minutes of the Society
Rept	Report
SO(s)	Standing Order(s)

Parliamentary References

The numerous references to parliamentary papers are almost all to the Reports and Minutes of Evidence of Select Committees of the House of Commons, the House of Lords, or of Joint Select Committees. The titles of important committees are given and all committees are identified by their House, year and serial number in the following manner:-

> e.g. The Report of the Select Committee of the House of Lords upon Fees and Charges on Private Bills of 1827 is — HL(1827) 114.

References to parliamentary debates are distinguished from the above by the prefix "Parl.Deb.", and are identified by the House, year and column(s) —

> e.g. Parl.Deb. (HC 1844) c. 516.

1

PRIVATE LEGISLATION and PARLIAMENTARY AGENCY

'Lecturer to Expose Work of Mystery Agents' - *Leicester Mercury*.

Whatever unfulfilled expectations it may have excited that sub-editor's headline perhaps was less remarkable than the late O.C. Williams's observation that 'the position and functions of parliamentary agents in respect of private bill legislation are too well understood to need any enlargement'.[1] It would be difficult to think of a profession so little known and understood as parliamentary agency, or one concerned with affairs of comparable importance which has so few practitioners. In 1978-9 there were seventeen active members of the Society of Parliamentary Agents. They are often mistaken for political or election agents, those party political functionaries about whom we are not concerned here.

A parliamentary agent practises a profession with a number of paradoxes. First, his principal though not his only business is with private legislation the purposes of which are nearly always public. Second, though he needs legal knowledge (and nowadays is usually a solicitor), a highly specialised command of parliamentary procedures, and other less readily definable qualities, his qualifications are not formally prescribed by law or tested by examination. Third, he is both a servant of Parliament by a tradition which influences his attitudes and affects his responsibilities, and an independent professional man acting for clients who pay his fees.

Parliamentary agents owe their existence to the rights of individuals and bodies, official and private, to petition Parliament to consider and to enact their legislative proposals. For the consequent arrangements and measures, which in their basic features are virtually as old as statute law itself, the terms 'Private Legislation' and 'Private Bill' have always been used. In one very important sense those are not always apposite or enlightening terms. What for convenience may be described as the truly private bill, the bill that is not only privately promoted but also private or personal in purpose, had importance in the past and is not yet extinct. But the main historical significance

---

1 *Clerical Organisation*, p. 261.

of private legislation lies not in the opportunities it has afforded to promote bills of attainder or restitition in blood, divorce, naturalisation and estate bills, or bills for other private purposes. It is to be found, rather, in the extent to which it has been used as a legislative instrument for purposes such as inclosure which, initially private, became matters of great public importance, and for purposes essentially public though entertained by private individuals or bodies, or local public bodies - at the mention of which the sense of 'private' begins to be strained. 'Year by year', wrote Clifford in his *History of Private Bill Legislation,* 'the records of Parliament show that nearly every great industrial and social movement during the present century has stood in need of private legislation'. The bulk of Clifford's two volumes consists of a painstaking account of the largely public subjects of private bill legislation not only in his own but in earlier centuries. Bills for highways and bridges, tunnels, ferries, canals, railways, water, gas and electricity supplies, the regulation of trades and industries, of charities and churches, for inclosure and local improvement, and for a multitude of purposes inescapably of a public nature (however much in another sense the purpose might be private profit or advantage) dominate the picture. Clifford's observation, like that of O.C. Williams that 'since the industrial revolution, private bill legislation has provided the necessary powers for the expansion of our local government and the foundation and expansion of our public utilities', refers (broadly) to the nineteenth century.[1] This is not to imply that private legislation suddenly acquired a new public characteristic - the first recorded bill for a municipal water supply was that promoted by the Corporation of Gloucester in 1541-2 - but the scale, range and complexity of the projects for which legislative authority was sought and often given were new.

As Clifford put it, in a definition which showed a nice sense of what private bills were mainly about, and of the linguistic reservations possible: 'By private bills are commonly understood all bills affecting the interests of individuals or particular localities and not of a general public character'.[2] This was both an apt definition of much private legislation in Clifford's own day and one informed by considerable historic sense. Sharing with all parliamentary legislation an origin in

[1] Frederick Clifford's *History of Private Bill Legislation* (2 vols., 1887, reprinted Cass, 1968) is the most compendious account especially of the subject matter of private bill legislation up to the time it was written. O.C. Williams's *Historical Development of Private Bill Procedure,* (2 vols. 1948) deals adequately with its subject, has a summary account of private legislation and a chapter outlining procedure at the time the book was written.

[2] Clifford, I, 267.

petition to the King in Parliament for the remedy of grievances, the private bill of earlier centuries had no easily definable limits. So far as it was an endeavour to obtain peculiar rights or powers distinct from the general law it was 'not of a general public character', an expression which provides some loose justification for the appellation 'private'. But it is in another phrase used by Clifford, 'bills affecting the interests of individuals or particular localities', that we have the most significant indication of what gave a bill its 'private' quality.

Before there was much in the way of a distinctive procedure for private bills, and so long as all bills were ostensibly promoted and introduced by Members of Parliament or Peers, the existence of an identifiable beneficial interest afforded a practical test of what, for some or all parliamentary purposes, was a private bill - a test officers of Parliament from the Lord Chancellor down who enjoyed incomes from private bill fees were not reluctant to apply. Thus, we are told, officers of the sixteenth-century House of Commons distinguished between private and public bills 'in a very simply way. Could they extract fees from someone? If so it was a private bill'.[1]

Despite the development of distinctive private bill procedure and its formalisation in the early private business standing orders, officers of the House of Commons displayed considerable ingenuity in classifying bills as private, at least for fee-paying purposes, whenever there was an identifiable person or body from whom fees could be demanded. The increase in legislative business in the eighteenth century broadened the scope for ingenuity, and, with that talent for making the most of a good thing which is one of the more genial characteristics of eighteenth - century politicians and officials, the opportunities were vigorously exploited. The tendency found its clearest expression in the Commons' resolutions of 1751, the first of which laid down 'that every bill for the particular interest or benefit of any person or persons, whether the same be brought in upon petition, or motion, or report from a Committee, or brought from the House of Lords, hath been, and ought to be, deemed a private bill, within the meaning of the Table of Fees'.[2] This resolution paid scant regard to the more austere tradition that 'no private bill be brought into this House, but upon a petition', already formalised in the earliest of the Commons' private business standing orders,[3] and helped to place within the ambit of

1 J.E. Neale: *The Elizabethan House of Commons*, p. 336.
2 *Hist. PBProc.* II, 273.
3 CJ (1667-87) 719. The order was made in May 1685 and in its modern form is S.O. 2 (Commons' Private Business Standing Orders, 1969 edn.).

private legislation the widest possible range of legislative proposals. Clifford, when he came to give examples of what he called 'quasi-public measures' that were so treated,[1] resorted to the list of bills given by John Hatsell, Clerk of the Commons, 1768-1820, on which, in Hatsell's words, 'private persons and corporations had paid fees for the benefit they had derived from those Bills, whether in their nature public or private' between 1730 and 1747. Hatsell includes 'bills for encouraging trade in the sugar colonies . . . vesting printed copies of books in the authors or purchasers . . . to prevent frauds in gold and silver wares . . . relating to the insurance of ships . . . for laying an additional duty on foreign cambrics imported . . . to prevent brewers' servants stealing barrels . . . for regulating pawnbrokers . . .'.[2] He is careful not to say that these were private bills, or for that matter public bills, - just bills 'whether in their nature public or private' on which private bill fees had been exacted. The eighteenth century House of Commons and its officers did not invent the public character of private legislation, or rationalise it. They exploited the broad territory between the indisputably public and the truly private to maximise the employment of private bill procedure. So, by the late eighteenth century, there lay to hand an instrument deeply rooted in parliamentary history by which many of the multiplying needs, ambitions, and demands of that age and the following century could be provided for legislatively.

The greatly extended use of private legislation for diverse public purposes in the late eighteenth and the nineteenth centuries necessitated considerable reform and sophistication of procedure. An elaborate code of standing orders was developed, and Examiners appointed to oversee compliance with it. A Private Bill Office was established. Both Houses reformed the constitution of their private bill committees. Supervisory responsibilities were created, which in the Commons were placed upon the Chairman of Ways & Means gradually during the 1840s, and in the Lords had been assumed rather earlier by the Chairman of Committees. There were new regulatory devices, including model bills, Clauses Consolidation Acts, and the scrutiny of bills by government departments. The detailed history of these developments and innovations belongs essentially to the history of private bill procedure, but parliamentary agents were concerned with and in some cases had considerable influence on them which will be noticed in later parts of this work. As the significance of these changes lay not merely in

1 Clifford, II, 730-1.
2 J. Hatsell *Precedents and Proceedings in the House of Commons under Separate Titles: with Observations* (1818 edn.), pp. 284-5 .

the need to cope with an immense increase in private legislation but in the need to recognise and take account of the public quality of much of it, some notice of a few of them must be taken here.

The late eighteenth- and early nineteenth-century standing orders are from this point of view interesting in two respects. First, many of them were designed to protect the rights (or usually the property rights) of those who would be affected by a bill, or the interest of users of proposed services. Second, and more striking, the arrangement of the Commons standing orders in chapters by subject-matter, at a cost of considerable repetition, from the time they were first printed as a whole in 1810 down to 1836, vividly illustrates both the public nature of much of what they were providing for and its diversity. The 1836 edition, for example, contained nineteen chapters. Leaving aside the three chapters (67 orders) of general orders, those required, in Hatsell's words, to ensure 'that order, decency, and regularity should be preserved in a large, numerous and, consequently, sometimes tumultuous, assembly', those relating to the Private Bill Office and the short-lived Committee of Appeals on Private Bills, sixteen chapters (108 orders) were devoted to specific subjects, viz.:

Bills for Inclosing, draining, or improving lands (7 orders)
Bills for Turnpike Roads (12 orders)
Bills for Canals, water supply, river navigation (20 orders)
Bills for Railways (20 orders)
Bills for Archways and tunnels (1 order)
Bills for Ferries and docks (14 orders)
Bills for Piers, ports and harbours (5 orders)
Bills for Bridges (5 orders)
Bills for County rates, gaols, or Houses of Correction (4 orders)
Bills for Churches, chapels, burial grounds (1 order)
Bills for Paving, lighting, cleansing, or improving cities or towns (4 orders)
Bills for Town halls or market places (1 order)
Bills for Poor rates, maintenance or employment of the Poor, workhouses (7 orders)
Bills for Recovery of small debts (2 orders)
Bills for Letters Patent (4 orders)
Bills for Divorce (1 order)

Clearly to find a term expressive both of the public quality and the variety of such subject matter would be difficult; moreover, as Clifford observed in connection with the definition quoted earlier, it was 'commonly understood' what private bills were.[1]

1 From 1837 the Commons orders were gradually re-arranged, to avoid repeti-

In the decade between the publication of the edition of the standing orders just referred to and the enactment of the Clauses Consolidation Acts of 1845 and 1847, private legislation, particularly that related to railways, reached its zenith. Parliament may well have had cause to be 'alarmed . . . at the growth of powers which were of its own creation';[1] it certainly faced a pressing need for a device which would reduce the length of individual bills and their detailed consideration in the face of the torrent of railway bills which was pouring in by 1844. The 1845 Clauses Consolidation Acts[2] were intended primarily to cope with this practical problem, but it was not accidental that they introduced a measure of codification and standardisation in the public interest. The 1847 Acts[3] had behind them a much more positive regulatory intention, their protagonist, Joseph Hume, being concerned principally with 'the sacrifice of the public interests' and the lack of uniformity inherent in the use of private bill legislation for local purposes.[4]

Finally, in this necessarily selective reference to some of the procedural innovations of the 1840s, it may be noted that the supervisory arrangements in the House of Commons were intended to recognise the public character of most private legislation. The Chairman of Ways & Means told the Commons in 1851 that one of his functions in relation to private bills was 'to guard against injury to the public'[5] and his late Counsel told a select committee that he 'must be considered as perusing the bill on behalf of the public'.[6] It is interesting to note that evidence

---

tion and allow consecutive numbering, and bills placed first into three and then into two classes, depending on whether or not they involved the construction of works. Of course, the orders also underwent rapid elaboration and frequent revision. (See *Hist. PB Proc.* II, 4-6 and 11-14).

1   Clifford, I, 94.

2   Companies Clauses Consolidation Act, 8 Vic. c. 16, and (Scotland) Act, 8 Vic, c, 17; Land Clauses Consolidation Act, 8 Vic. c. 18, and (Scotland) Act, 8 Vic. c. 19; Railway Clauses Consolidation Act. 8 & 9 Vic. c. 20, and (Scotland) Act, 8 & 9 Vic. c. 33.

3   Markets & Fairs Clauses Act, 10 Vic. c. 14; Gasworks Clauses Act, 10 Vic. c. 15; Commissioners Clauses Act, 10 Vic. c. 16; Waterworks Clauses Act, 10 Vic. c. 17; Harbours Docks & Piers Clauses Act, 10 Vic. c. 27, Town Improvement Clauses Act, 10 & 11 Vic. c. 34; Cemeteries Clauses Act, 10 & 11 Vic. c. 56; Town Police Clauses Act, 10 & 11 Vic. c. 89.

4   Parl. Deb. (HC 1846) 85, cc. 670. For further details on the Clauses Acts see *Hist.PBProc.* I, 107-111, and Clifford I, 103, 221-223, 250 & II, ch.XV. Clifford considerably dilutes Hume's attitude by his use of the phrase 'public interests were occasionally prejudiced', though that may be a fair representation of the view taken by the committee for which Hume was moving in the speech referred to at the beginning of this note.

5   *HistPBProc.* I, 102.

6   HC (1851) 35, Qn.201.

was given to a select committee in 1846 that, after the first stage of that
scrutinising responsibility had been introduced in 1841 in respect of
unopposed bills only, some parliamentary agents had contrived to avoid
it by arranging for bogus petitions against their bills.[1]

Critics and champions of private legislation alike have grounded
their statements on its public quality. We have noted Joseph Hume's
concern that the process involved a sacrifice of the public interest.
Seventy years later when private business was at an ebb, a member
of the parliamentary bar, in terms more sour than temperate, wrote:
'Committees of Parliament often pass private bills which may benefit
the community and at any rate prove less harmful than the public
measures which bulk so large in the exaggerated estimates of the
public'.[2]

In the absence of a system of administrative courts, true legislative
devolution (if that is a logical possibility for the British Parliament), or
the extensive delegation of rule-making powers to an administration
capable of using them, private legislation played for a while the
principal part in facilitating piecemeal private and local enterprise in
matters of great public importance. Its heyday corresponded with the
period during which the provision of individual public utilities and
local powers was more urgent than the need for general public policies
about them; when railways rather than a railway policy (or system)
were in demand, and when the kind of public interest chiefly to be
considered was that of weighing the expediency of a particular scheme
against the property interests, or the vested interests of some prior or
rival scheme, which would be affected by it, rather than the public
interest in some much broader sense. By nature it was an instrument
better suited to do this than to be productive of uniformity, consistency, economy, tidiness, or coherent policy. It was this characteristic
of private legislation, and the vigour with which it was exploited, that
both provided the country with public services and did much to generate
the need for policies expressed in general public legislation and a demand
for scheme-sanctioning devices, hopefully less time-consuming and
costly, but above all more closely geared to the governmental and
administrative machinery where, as the nineteenth century moved into
its second half, policy was − or, it was thought, ought to be −
increasingly made.

In his preface, Clifford remarked with understandable pride in his
subject, but not in the most apt terms, that 'in bulk and number local

1 *HistPBProc.* I, 101.
2 J.H. Balfour Browne, *Forty Years at the Bar* (1916).

and personal enactments far exceed those of a public nature'.[1] The bulk and number has gone. Personal bills are now rarely necessary principally because of public legislation on naturalisation and divorce. And in the second half of the nineteenth century and subsequently a growing spate of constituent and enabling Acts, especially relating to local government and public health, for which private legislation had been 'the great laboratory',[2] endowed local authorities and public departments with duties and adoptive powers. These, and the power to make provisional orders, usually dated from the Public Health Act of 1848 but given to the Inclosure Commissioners in 1845, provided a system of delegated legislation which gradually reduced the need for private bills, and to which champions of private legislation uneasily reconciled themselves, despite 'its centralizing influences and other shortcomings', with the reflection that it was 'confined to projects relatively small and unimportant' and reserved to Parliament 'the right to review and amend or reject . . . even after sanction by the department'.[3] When Clifford wrote, in 1886-7, he noted that 'no fewer than eight departments in England, two in Scotland, and three in Ireland, acting independently of each other, now make and issue these quasi-statutory Orders'.[4] Approaching the end of his vast work he could not help remarking with disapproval upon the 'vague proposals' that were going about 'for allowing County Boards and other local authorities to decide at least upon some classes of private Bills'.[5] He was writing on the eve of the Local Government Act of 1888 (and when the out-and-out critics of private legislation were preparing one of their periodic attacks). At the present time, when the structure of local government has undergone its greatest change since 1888, it is interesting to recall the now-forgotten enthusiasm with which the authors of the 1888 Act dreamed of a great process of legislative devolution for which

1   Clifford, I, vii. He records that between 1800 and 1884 Public Acts totalled 9,556 and Private Acts, 18,497.

2   'Local legislation has been the great laboratory of local government law' – Ivor Jennings, *Parliament* (2nd. edn.), p. 462. Private legislation had performed a similar role before. Some of the public legislation of the first half of the nineteenth century – notably some of Brougham's legal reforms, the Poor Law Amendment and Tithe Commutation Acts, as well as general Inclosure legislation, had comparable backgrounds. See Clifford, I, 266-7.

3   Clifford, II, 676-7.

4   Clifford, II, 676. The orders were appropriately termed provisional, needing to be scheduled in a confirmation bill, which could be opposed like a private bill, before they could become operative. But some departments had already acquired powers to make orders which in certain circumstances were not provisional in this sense, for example the Board of Trade under the Railway Construction Facilities and Railway Companies Powers Acts, 1864, and the Local Government Board, in respect of the reconstitution of parishes, 1876.

5   Clifford, II, 913.

the Act was to be the principal instrument. Many of the powers of the Imperial Parliament were, according to the Prime Minister (an old critic of private bill legislation), to be devolved upon the new and financially self-sufficient County Councils. The devolutionary principle survived a parliamentary battering, in a 'provisional' form (see Local Government Act, 1888, s.10.), though devolution, like financial self-sufficiency, was a chimera. But the Act was a landmark in the long series of constituent and enabling Acts which in the longer run widened the scope of the provisional order system, though its immediate effect was to stimulate private bill promotion by new and more ambitious local authorities.

The decline in railway construction, the amalgamation into four companies of the railways by public Act in 1921 and their later nationalisation, and the re-organisation or nationalisation of other public utilities did much to reduce the bulk and number of private bills. Enabling Acts, especially in the field of local government, and the extensive delegation of rule-making and scheme-sanctioning powers to Government departments, first in the form of Provisional orders then (from 1919) of Special orders and other types of statutory instrument, and, from 1945, Special Procedure, have also made unnecessary or inappropriate the use of private bills for many of their former purposes.[1]   But these important developments have not brought with them any general restriction in principle on the right to approach Parliament directly. The most important exception is to be found in the Private Legislation Procedure (Scotland) Acts of 1899 and 1936.[2] In 1906, Speaker Lowther talked of prohibiting private bills where provisional order procedure was possible, and the Ministry of Health suggested, in 1930, the possibility of limiting the frequency with which local authorities could promote bills. In 1945 the Minister of Health appears to have thought that the provisions of the Water Act, 1945, to which Special procedure applied, would mark the end of Water Bills; that did not prove to be so. The Transport and Electricity Bills of 1946 had clauses requiring the prospective national authorities to get Ministerial consent before promoting a private bill. A local authority may require Ministerial consent to promote a bill, but the power is used to ensure compliance with certain preliminaries, not to prevent promotion.[3]   There is at least one instance of a Public Act conferring order-making powers including a saving clause for private bills.[4]

---

1   For Special procedure see Statutory Orders (Special Procedure Act, 1945, 9 & 10 Geo.6.c.18), *HistPBProc.*, I, 254-8, Jennings; *Parliament* (2nd. edn.) p. 489.

2   See below pp. 178-80 and *HistPBProc.*, I, 192-205.

3   Local Government Act, 1972, s.239.

4· Harbours Act, 1964, s.62.

However, gradually over the past century and more markedly since the middle of the first decade of the twentieth century, the private bill as an instrument of domestic - one might say special - legislation has moved from the centre to the periphery. The significance of the periphery is not as the place where the occasional essentially private legislative problem may be unravelled or the statutory rights or obligations of some old-established private body extinguished but principally as the scene of the complex, sometimes of the contentious, and the intrinsically important. The modern private bill is, typically, a measure promoted by a local authority, nationalised industry, statutory undertaker, or public company for purposes either clearly public or of public concern. A list of private (but not personal) bills deposited in the Sessions 1971-72 and 1972-73 is given in Appendix I.[1]

Subject to the references to public policy below, four principles are relevant to such private legislation, though none but the last can be said to have simple applicability. First, the promoters must have an interest or shared interest in what they are promoting; second, they must provide proof of expediency; third, the powers they seek should be such as are not obtainable in other ways, unless procedure by Ministerial order would be unduly complicated and/or the issues involved are exceptionally complex, controversial or important; fourth, the powers sought must be for, or in respect of, determinate, named persons, bodies or places.

The first two principles, especially the former, received much consideration after the promotion in 1958 by Kent County Council of a bill on its own behalf and that of 397 other Councils in Kent. Of the 442 Clauses and 6 Schedules in this vast bill (as deposited), 33 were concerned solely with the County Council; 136, in the words of the Lord Chairman of Committees, 'in part concern other authorities' and 238 'confer powers on other authorities exclusively'. The Chairman of Committees' view, in directing the attention of the Lords 'to any special circumstances relative to any Private Bill which may appear to him to require it' (Lords' private business S.0.91) was that the County Council had gone too far in a practice not unprecedented except in scale, and he announced his intention of striking out many of the clauses.[2] Considerable discussion followed (debate? - there was no motion). The same day, the Chairman of Ways & Means in a written report to the Commons indicated his agreement; he and the Lord Chairman had

1 Bills such as estate bills are properly called personal bills, if so certified: see May, pp. 842-3.
2 Parl.Deb. (HL) 209 (13 May 1958) cc.233-247.

concluded that 'a petitioner may petition Parliament only on his own behalf' and that 'a County Council Bill should not confer on local authorities or any other authority or person functions in which the County Council has no interest'. A week later a debate took place in the Lords on a motion in those terms.[1] The two Lords' interchanges, and the Report and Minutes of Evidence of the subsequent Joint Select Committee on Promotion of Private Bills[2] afford an extensive, sometimes enlightening, at times bewildering, exchange of views on the nature and problems of private bills, especially local authority bills, and the relative roles of private and public legislation - or what those should be. They cannot be examined in detail here and the reader who thinks he can stay the course must be referred to them. A few points must suffice. First, it is of historical interest, in view of what has been said above about the Local Government Act of 1888, that the Chairman of Committees in his first statement to the Lords observed that he could discover no intention of Parliament in 1888 'that County Councils should . . . become in effect miniature parliaments'.[3] Second, in its report the joint select committee, while sharing 'the concern of the two Chairmen at the prospect of a further substantial increase in legislation of this kind', considered that their rulings should be qualified in their application and that 'no objection on grounds of principle need in future to be raised to County Council Bills containing clauses of this type'.[4] The Committee took the view that there must be discretion and not a simple rule when it came to 'proof of need',[5] and, while upholding the principle of interest or joint interest as 'one of the two bases on which all private legislation is founded', considered that a liberal and flexible interpretation, not rigid demarcation, was desirable - 'The County Council have . . . a general interest in the good government of the county'.[6] In short, these were working principles, not rules of thumb. Finally, the part that regular, systematic public legislation might play in limiting the need for bills of the Kent type was very much in the committee's mind, though outside its order of reference. Its concluding words were 'that the true remedy lies . . . partly in the field of public legislation and partly in the restraint, moderation and good sense of all concerned in the promotion of Private Bills'.[7]

1   *Ibid.* (21 May 1953) cc.473-539.
2   HL (1959) 176, HC (1959) 262.
3   Parl. Deb. (HL) 209, c. 236.
4   HL (1959) 276, Rept, p.xi.
5   *Ibid.* p.vi.
6   *Ibid.* p.v.
7   *Ibid.* p.xii.

The third of the four principles mentioned in the last paragraph but one above is yet more empirical and imprecise in its application. It has already been remarked that the development of ministerial order-making powers has not, as a general principle, excluded the right to promote a private bill. There are two areas, by nature unamenable to clear demarcation, in which notwithstanding the possibility of procedure by other means a private bill may be deemed justified, preferable, or even necessary, First, though order-making powers and delegated legislation generally have been justified as procedures less cumbrous, simpler, and more flexible than parliamentary procedure, there is a point of complexity beyond which the reverse is true. The widest of order-making power is surrounded by restrictions, and in circumstances sufficiently complicated the number of orders required and their separate and different procedures, can result in a series of processes more protracted, expensive, and uncertain than an approach to Parliament. The uncertainty may reside not solely in the sheer complexity of the processes but also - as appears sometimes to be the case when projects involve the acquisition of common land - in the relationship of order-making powers to legislation requiring the sanction of Parliament for certain objects. It is partly for such reasons that the Water Act of 1945, and the availability of special parliamentary procedure did not in practice end private bill promotion by water undertakings. The second area (and, of course, in practice the two areas largely overlap) is that of the specially important or contentious, and here we meet another sense in which many modern private bills may be said to have a public quality. Bills for major schemes by public authorities and other statutory undertakers are not promoted without detailed consultation with government departments. Their views will be canvassed; advice, information, encouragement and hints will be sought (and sometimes offered) on a multitude of points, which may include the question of whether procedure by private bill or an application for an order is the course preferred by the department mainly concerned. The promoters are of course responsible for their scheme, therefore the department's official attitude must be non-committal, but in one way or another influential responses will be forthcoming. The department may well have, in a number of senses (apart from reporting on it should a bill be promoted), an interest in the project, which may be a local realisation of national policy or be based on investigations in which the department's officers have been involved. The background to the Great Ouse Water Bill, deposited in November 1960, exemplifies most of these points: its promoters were motivated, at least in part, by a belief that the Ministry of Housing & Local Government were giving consideration to a scheme resembling that which the promoters subsequently put forward; the technical working party responsible for the recommendations on which the bill was based was formed at a meeting held in that Ministry in February 1959, and chaired by one of the Ministry's engineering officers. In October 1959, in the course of seeking a meeting with the Ministry's Permanent Secretary, one of the promoters wrote emphasising their reluctance 'to pursue any course which would not have in principle the support of your Ministry';[1] and in the following month the promoters resolved to proceed by private bill and not by order only after having sounded the Ministry on that point. The importance of the project and the nature of the opposition expected had a good deal to do with that decision.[2]

The burden of the foregoing pages has been the public nature of much private legislation. It remains to ask wherein lies the 'privacy' of a bill. No one who troubles to scrutinise the long section in May entitled 'Difficulty in Determining whether certain Bills should be Public or Private' (17th ed. pp. 871-87) will expect a definitive answer. Though, as we have seen, modern private bills may be local applications of public policy, bills have been ruled to be not properly private when they have raised in a controversial way major questions of public policy. Interesting in this respect was the rejection by Mr. Speaker in 1939 of the London Rating (Site Values) Bill on the grounds, as the editors of May put it, 'that since the bill raised questions of public policy of great importance and affected interests of vast magnitude it ought to have been introduced as a public bill'. The sequel, which is not referred to in May, is of at least equal interest: 67 local authorities petitioned unsuccessfully for the introduction of site value rating by public Act. In short there was a public policy on rating, different from that which the promoters of the London Rating (Site Values) Bill desired. That a private bill is one 'affecting the interests of individuals or particular localities' will not suffice as an answer for much public general legislation does that. It is helpful to note that public general bills and private bills do this in different ways, the former by reference to some class or description of persons or places, the latter by naming or otherwise designating in a specific, definite and limiting way, the persons, institutions or localities affected. This observation brings us nearer to the fourth of the working principles already suggested — that the powers sought in a private bill must be for or in respect of determinate, named

---

1 Clerk, Beds. County Council to Permanent Secretary, Ministry of Housing & Local Government, 17 October 1959.

2 For a detailed account of the formation of the Great Ouse Water Authority see my study in *Public Administration* Summer & Autumn issues, 1971. The bill was enacted as The Great Ouse Water Act in August 1961, and with its 147 clauses and 7 schedules was considerably longer than the major public Act on water of that decade, the Water Resources Act, 1963.

persons, bodies or places. Thus, on the order for second reading (23 February 1959) of the National Association of Almshouses (Investment) Bill, the Speaker ruled that the bill was 'not proper to proceed as a Private Bill' because it extended 'the powers of an indefinite number of trust funds beyond those of the general law' and 'is promoted by an association on behalf of its members, the number of whom is not fixed'. We may note, too, the 'complete definition' of a private bill which the Lord Chairman of Committees offered to the Joint Select Committee on the Promotion of Private Bills, 1959:— 'The complete definition of a Private Bill . . . . . is a Petition to the Queen in Parliament, deposited by some person outside Parliament, and referring by name either to the persons, or to the areas, or to the institutions affected by the Bill'.[1] The principle of limited determinate application, it is suggested, is one quality a bill must have to enjoy 'privacy'.

If this be the primary characteristic of 'privacy' there are other characteristics which on this way of putting things must be termed secondary though they are of central importance to the parliamentary agents who are the subjects of this book. A private bill is an 'outside' bill. Its promotion, preparation, drafting, and, in part, its conduct through Parliament are the responsibility not of Parliament, or individual members, or the central government, but of individuals or bodies which in this context are private. Consequentially, it is procedurally private. It must be based upon petition, deposited, and conducted through Parliament in accordance with private business standing orders and parliamentary practices considerably more elaborate than those applying to public business, compliance with which requires expert knowledge and must be carefully proved. Its fate will (usually) be in the hands of private bill committees of both Houses who will not only consider its legislative merits but also apply their powers of judgment to the arguments of those opponents, if any, who (again on petition and subject to standing orders) are permitted by private bill procedure to oppose a bill on its merits as a whole, or on particular clauses; they may also hear petitioners against alterations. As a consequence of the strong judicial element in private bill procedure, an opposed private bill, during and before its progress through Parliament, will be surrounded by negotiation, often producing settlements 'out of court'. Lastly, its promoters (and any opponents) must pay parliamentary fees. In relation to all these matters parliamentary agents have functions and responsibilities, both to their clients and to Parliament.

---

1   HL (1959) 176, Mins. of Evidence, p.2.

Agents and agency

Entitlement to practise as a parliamentary agent is governed by rules issued in respect of the House of Commons by the Speaker and of the House of Lords by the Chairman of Committees. References in this section are to the rules as made by Speaker Morrison in 1952, and still current;[1] with the appropriate and obvious modifications of language they may be taken to represent the Lord Chairman's rules.

Having applied in writing for registration, the prospective parliamentary agent who wishes to engage on a permanent basis in both the promotion of and opposition to bills must satisfy the Speaker 'that he has practical knowledge of the standing orders and procedure of the House of Commons regulating private business' (Rule 8). The Speaker may if he thinks fit appoint an advisory committee on 'any question arising as to the qualifications of any applicant' (Rule 9), but this has never been done nor has any formal test or examination been imposed. The operation of this somewhat inscrutable process was referred to during the proceedings of a joint select committee in 1954, when the Chairman of Committees explained in evidence that he and the Speaker did not appoint anyone 'who has not, anyhow, considerable qualifications and is well recommended'.[2] The implication that he and Mr. Speaker relied much on the integrity of existing firms of agents and of the applicant, and the knowledge of them possessed by their Counsel and other officers of the two Houses, was brought out by the Lord Chairman's further observation — 'I would not like to say that I would not necessarily approve of some well-known member of a well-known firm applying to become a parliamentary agent'.[3] One member of the Committee who raised the question of 'any examining body, or any body with power to issue a certificate or diploma of skill or knowledge or experience', was told by the then President of the Society of Parliamentary Agents that the authority to admit to practice was in the hands of Mr. Speaker and the Lord Chairman; there was in fact no examining body; the manner in which he (Mr. Speaker) decided on fitness was a matter for him; nothing was laid down requiring him to examine the fitness of a person to act as an agent; 'he would merely satisfy himself'.[4]

1 *Rules to be Observed by the Officers of the House and by all Parliamentary Agents engaged in prosecuting Proceedings in the House of Commons upon any Petition or Bill:* 9 December, 1952. They do not differ greatly from the 1938 rules reproduced as Appendix H. See May, pp. 862-5.

2 Joint Select Committee on Private Bill Procedure, 1954-6. HC (1955) 139-1, Mins. of Evidence (1954) Qns. 204-6.

3 *Ibid.* Qn. 210.

4 *Ibid.* Qns. 929-37. The following exchange between the Chairman of this

The Speaker being satisfied as to his suitability, the applicant may be entered in the register of agents kept in the Private Bill Office, after subscribing to a declaration engaging 'to obey and observe the orders and practice of the House of Commons and any rules prescribed by the Speaker', and to pay the parliamentary fees and charges due from those for whom he may act (Rules 2 and 4). He may then practise as a parliamentary agent, if he wishes, as is commonly the case, under the name and style of any firm in which he is a partner (Rule 3). Nevertheless, the responsibilities just referred to and others that must ensue as soon as he practices are essentially personal and individual (Rule 21). The provisions under which other persons may, at the Speaker's discretion, be registered on a sessional basis for the purpose of conducting oppositions only need not be regarded as of much practical importance, for they hardly constitute an attractive invitation under modern conditions of practice. No one can qualify for registration in this way unless he actually has an opposition to conduct, (Rule 10), but anyone so permitted by the Speaker to register must subscribe to a declaration and assume the responsibilities already mentioned, so far as they are applicable. The historical reasons for these provisions will emerge in the course of this work and no more need be said of them here except this: the rules require those responsible for maintaining the register of agents in the Private Bill Office to distinguish between those agents entitled to practice permanently both in promoting and opposing and the class just referred to; hence the arrangements familiarly and conveniently referred to by agents and others concerned with private business as the 'A' and 'B' rolls, expressions which have no place in the current or any earlier rules. They originated in the documents circulated for discussion prior to the adoption of the 1938 rules.[1] At the discretion of the Speaker any parliamentary agent who acts 'in violation of the orders and practice of the House . . . ' or is guilty 'of professional misconduct of any kind as a parliamentary agent' is liable to an absolute or temporary prohibition to practise. No such person,

---

Committee and the President of the Society of Parliamentary Agents is of interest: 'How would a parliamentary agent be recruited? Would he go into a firm as a partner and . . . gradually take up parliamentary work? – It might work that way . . . perhaps more likely he would when he had passed his finals as a solicitor come on as an assistant . . . in parliamentary work. Then, having gained a certain amount of experience . . . would become a partner, and then . . . apply for admission to Roll A by applying to the Speaker'. *Ibid.* Qn. 868. All but one of the present parliamentary agents are solicitors; the exception is a Scottish Advocate.

[1] See pp. 152-4   They are however used on the two forms of application for registration. Parliamentary agents, 'entered in the register in either House of Parliament as agents, entitled to practise in promoting and in opposing Bills', have received statutory recognition as a distinct profession; see Fair Trading Act, 1973, schedule 4, para. 11.

and no one who has been compulsorily struck off the roll of solicitors or disbarred by any of the Inns of Court, may be entered or retained on the register without the Speaker's express authority. (Rules 22 & 23).

In the orders, procedures and practices which a parliamentary agent undertakes to observe and of which he has to show 'practical knowledge' the functions and responsibilities of agents — or rather those which Parliament recognises — are, of course, implicit and at places explicitly stated. Theoretically we could examine them systematically, deducing and extracting much of what the work of a parliamentary agent involves. But they constitute a somewhat formidable body and the exercise, if it is a practical posibility, would be lengthy. The purpose in this chapter is to indicate briefly, what a parliamentary agent does. I shall not, therefore, burden the reader with much reference to standing orders or nice distinctions between matters of order, procedure, and practice.[1] Let us, rather, note that in the pursuit of the principal part of his profession the parliamentary agent is concerned with the practical application of orders and procedure to particular bills — and with the drafting of those bills. He also advises his clients in relation thereto and negotiates on their behalf. It will be helpful to take brief notice of some of the characteristics of private bill procedure which most directly affect the working life of the parliamentary agent. From this point of view it has the following features:—

(i) It makes much detailed and circumstantial provision, notably in respect of the form and content, times and places, at which notices must be given and plans and other documents deposited, the general purpose of which is to ensure that parties who may be interested and Government departments are aware of the promoters' intentions. The same characteristic is noticeable in those standing orders dealing with clauses to be inserted, or not allowable, in certain types of bill;

(ii) It provides for the exercise of important discretionary and supervisory powers by the Chairman of Committees for the Lords and the Chairman of Ways & Means for the Commons;

(iii) It lays down a timetable. Petitions, bills, and other docu-

---

1 The reader desiring to follow the intricacies of private bill procedure must do so in an authoritative treatise (viz. May, pp. 817-1011.) and in the private business standing orders of both Houses. The latest published editions of the latter are of those in force in May 1977 (Lords) and May 1975 (Commons), they are not necessarily in every respect up to date. The less ambitious reader may turn with profit to O.C. Williams's chapter 'The Existing Procedure' (*Hist.PBPro.*, 1, chapter II), bearing in mind that some references to standing orders are now incorrect.

ments must be deposited and certain other procedures followed at or by specified times, as well as in the prescribed manner;

    (iv)   It makes the agent, and particularly the agent for the promoters of a bill, responsible for providing the initiative in carrying out the necessary procedures. It is the promoters' agent who must give the notices at the times and within the intervals stipulated without which (for the most part) a bill will not proceed through its different stages. In respect of other aspects of procedure the causes of the parties will not be advanced and may be jeopardised or lost unless the appropriate agent takes timely action;

    (v)   It places upon the committee on an opposed bill the task of adjudicating between the parties, as well as of considering the expediency of the measure.

With a bill of any complexity the preparatory stage may extend over many months and require a number of conferences and consultations among the promoters, their technical and financial advisers, the parliamentary agent and counsel. The principal duties of the agent during that period are to advise the promoters on the way they may best achieve their intentions, to draft the bill with due regard to the private business standing orders, practice and other legal requirements and the petition in consonance with it, in the knowledge that these must be deposited in the Private Bill Office on or before 27 November if the measure is to proceed in the current parliamentary session. The agent will determine the applicability to the bill of standing orders relating to the notices, advertisements, the deposit of plans, maps, books of reference, and in some cases other data, and copies of the bill, locally, in the office of the clerk of the Parliaments, the Private Bill Office, and with public departments. He will advise and assist the promoters in complying with these requirements (and, if the promoters are a local authority, certain statutory requirements), and see that they are complied with by the due dates. In fulfilling these requirements, and in other ways, the parliamentary agent has the co-operation of the promoters' local solicitor or legal officer.

During the preparatory period — for these are matters which may affect the drafting of the bill — the agent will advise and assist the promoters in negotiating with such opposition as has revealed itself, and with Government departments. Though opposition has not taken at this stage a procedural form some of it is likely to be known. In so far as it is not root-and-branch opposition but tactical and designed to secure protective or compensatory clauses it may be negotiable. Modern parliamentary agents must concern themselves much more than their predecessors needed to with public legislation and policy, and many private bills, especially those envisaging the construction of major works, are likely to raise directly or contingently issues of public policy. For example, the compensation provisions to be included in the Great Ouse Water Bill of 1960, previously referred to, raised an important issue of policy (for such provisions are liable to be treated as precedents); .the promoters relied mainly on their parliamentary agent to ascertain the most favourable provisions that would be acceptable to the (then) Ministry of Housing & Local Government. The reports of interested government departments stand referred to the committee on the bill, and though not necessarily fatal to the bill, if adverse, can well be so if an important issue of public policy is involved. Anticipation, inquiry, and negotiation in this respect can be therefore of great practical importance.

Standing orders having been, in the agent's judgment, properly complied with so far as is requisite by the time, the agent will deposit the petition and the bill by 27 November and enter an appearance as agent for it. The bill as deposited is amendable and likely to be amended but not, in the ordinary way, so as to increase the powers sought by the promoters. Late bills and petitions for additional provision are procedural possibilities, but these are discretionary matters, not to be regarded as remedies for mere dilatoriness or carelesness.[1] The orders relating to notices and deposits already referred to are the principal orders, though in some circumstances not the only ones, compliance with which has to be proved before the Examiners of Petitions on Private Bills, who begin their proceedings on 18 December. The parliamentary agent's duties in this respect ordinarily are to secure appropriate affidavits from those concerned in complying with the orders, complete a detailed Statement of Proof, attend the Examiners (who act simultaneously on behalf of both Houses), and give any explanations required. He could have to produce witnesses, and have something in the nature of a case to conduct if any party has deposited, by 17 December, a memorial complaining of non-compliance, but that is not now the common gambit it once was. The agent will also represent his client before the Standing Orders Committee(s), should the Examiners report non-compliance or make a special report because of doubt as to the construction of a standing order.

Whether or not a bill is opposed the agent for the promoters must ensure that the notice for second reading is given within the times and intervals laid down in standing orders.[2] He may have to attend the Lord

1 See May, pp. 859-61.
2 The promoters' agent has the responsibility of giving such timely notices for

Chairman and the Chairman of Ways & Means (or their Counsel) should they desire any explanations. The 'filled-up' bill (i.e. incorporating amendments made since the bill was orginally deposited, and in the form to be considered by the committee on the bill) must be prepared and deposited. If the bill is unopposed the parliamentary agent's function includes the representation of the promoters before the Committee on Unopposed Bills.

The deposit in the time allowed of a petition against a bill is of course the function of a parliamentary agent for any opponent. In advising an opponent of a private bill the latter will have regard not only to the technicalities of standing orders but also to the tactics best calculated to serve his clients' interests. In this connection two things may be noticed. First, 'no petition against a private bill shall be taken into consideration by the (select) committee on the bill, which does not distinctly specify the ground on which the petitioner objects to any of the provisions thereof; and the petitioner shall be heard only on the grounds so stated . . . ' (S.O. (Commons) 128, (Lords) 111). Second, as a bill proceeds through the first House it is liable to amendment; if the opponent now in mind desires to secure some modification rather than the defeat of the bill it may be advantageous to reserve petitioning rights for the second House. This is a tactical consideration to be weighed by the agent and advised upon according to the circumstances. One relevant circumstance may be whether other parties have petitioned against the bill and on what grounds; at the most, other petitioners may be attempting to do what is desired; at the least, they will have turned the bill into an opposed one and provided more time and new conditions for negotiation.

If a bill is petitioned against the promoters' parliamentary agent will advise his client on the implications of the petition(s) and the *locus standi* of the petitioners. If it is decided to challenge their *locus standi* he will proceed, possibly instructing counsel, in the Court of Referees (Commons procedure). Amidst the new outbreak of negotiation that is likely to happen when a bill becomes opposed, the promoter's agent may well be occupied drafting and agreeing amendments with agents for opposing petitioners, which will affect the preparation of the filled-up bill. This must be completed and deposited, as must copies for the

subsequent stages when the bill has to come before the House. The motions made in the first instance on the floor of the House at time of private business, in practice in the Commons by the Chairman of Ways & Means, reflect the notices given by the parliamentary agent in the Private Bill Office. This, of course, is not true of motions subsequently made by Members.

Chairman of Ways & Means and the Lord Chairman (as the case may be) and for the use of members of the committee on the bill, at the prescribed times. In preparation for the important committee stage counsel must be instructed, witnesses and their evidence prepared, and the parliamentary agents for all parties must assume a good deal of the responsibility for ensuring everyone is there when wanted. During the day-by-day committee proceedings counsel may have the limelight, but parliamentary agents are present to instruct counsel and generally to manage their clients' cases. They observe the trend of things, participate in conferences in the corridor or after the committee has risen for the day, and, with counsel, advise their clients in the light of what so far has gone on. New perspectives emerge; attitudes are influenced by the performance of witnesses under examination and cross-examination, and the view it is supposed the committee is taking. It begins to seem possible, expedient, or prudent to concede amendments and to offer new or revised clauses, which must be drafted and presented quickly. If, in finding that the promoters have proved the preamble to their bill, the committee desires to qualify its finding in some way involving amendment, parliamentary agents will have drafting tasks up to the last moments of committee proceedings. It remains for the agent to see the bill through the remaining stages in the first House, and, of course, through comparable stages in the second, though proof of compliance with standing orders has in the normal course been done once and for all, in the first House.

While we have been following, as it were, a notional bill along part of its progress a number of things demanding the parliamentary agent's attention may have happened. Two that certainly will have call for a close working relationship between the agent and the House authorities. On or before 8 January the Chairman of Ways & Means and the Lord Chairman, or their Counsel, will have held their conference to decide in which House particular bills shall originate, and agents will have assisted the Committee of Selection in their task of grouping bills and appointing the date on which the committee stage on each bill is to commence. In practice, for no one can foresee how long committee proceedings on a bill will last and how that will affect proceedings on others, arrangements and rearrangements at this busy time in the agents' year require close co-operation between the agents and the officers of the two Houses. We may conveniently notice here some other co-operative responsiblities. Agents are represented on the unofficial committee which from time to time, under the authority of the two Chairmen, revises model clauses — the preferred form in which certain clauses should be drafted if they are required in a bill. In less formal ways parliamentary agents have much influence on the revision of certain classes of standing order which experience or changing conditions show to be necessary or desirable.[1]

Before leaving the notional bill that has crept into these pages we must take heed that, notwithstanding the special character of private bills and the procedural provision made for them, they are passed, defeated or amended by a process which in principal is the same as that for public bills. They may be objected to by members on the floor of the House and become the subject of debate. Should that happen it would be surprising if interested parties, not necessarily parties to the bill, did not expect the assistance of their parliamentary agent. In those circumstances the agent would advise his clients on the handling of the debate and prepare a statement for circulating to all Members. The parliamentary agent, having entered an appearance as agent for a bill, bears a responsibility to the House for the accuracy of any written or printed statement relating to the bill and legitimately circulated within the precincts of the House.-

Some other aspects of the parliamentary agent's profession may be referred to briefly. In most circumstances when an individual or organisation has cause to approach Parliament, especially if proceedings are involved, he or it may turn to an agent for advice or representation. Many interests retain the services of an agent to watch the legislative scene on their behalf — perhaps one of the oldest senses in which the services of a parliamentary agent have been required and offered. In 1843 the agent J. St. George Burke confirmed that it was 'a common case that parties in the country send to you . . . that they may know what is going to be done', and he added, 'where they have important interests at stake, the usual course is to get us to send them a copy of the Bill, and then watch it in its progress'.[2] The Council of the Incorporated Law Society, in 1874, took notice of 'the expediency of appointing a parliamentary agent to report the progress of all bills affecting Solicitors to which it may be the duty of the Council ito give attention'.[3]

Parliamentary agents advise, draft, and act for petitioners for and against provisional orders under the terms of the Private Legislation Procedure (Scotland) Act, 1936, and in connection with the substituted

---

[1] It should be noticed that the editions of standing orders published by HMSO do not remain for long up to date. For example, every change in the departmental structure of government necessitates corresponding changes in the orders relating to deposits.

[2] HC (1843) 550, Qns. 308, 309.

[3] Mins. Council Incorporated Law Society, 20 March 1874.

bills provided for by that measure. They assist applicants for Ministerial orders and more particularly act on behalf of their clients in connection with orders involving parliamentary proceedings, of which the most important are Special Procedure orders made under the provisions of the Statutory Orders (Special Procedure) Acts, 1945 and 1965. They may also assist in the preparation and drafting of private Members' public bills.

Petitioners against those public bills deemed hybrid, to which certain private business standing orders and a procedure resembling but not identical with that on private bills are applicable, also may have the services of parliamentary agents. Being public bills, hybrid bills received no consideration in the first part of this chapter. Definition may be imprudent, but it may be said that a public bill is treated as hybrid when being a matter of public policy it is seen to affect the particular interests of individuals or groups, but not whole classes of such.[1] The uncertain frontier between private and hybrid bills is patrolled by public policy. The history of channel tunnel legislation provides an interesting commentary. The bill of 1874 proceeded as a private bill and was enacted as the South Eastern Railway Act, 1874. That of 1883 — the South Eastern and Channel Tunnel Railways Bill — also a private measure, was in effect blocked; in Clifford's words, 'Upon the works begun in anticipation of this bill, the Board of Trade, representing the rights of the Crown in the foreshore,[2] placed a veto, pending a decision of Parliament upon the general policy of the undertaking'.[3] Though re-introduced in 1884 it was abandoned after a Joint Select Committee, by a majority, had reported against a tunnel 'on the ground that it would diminish our present insular security'.[4] Implicitly, if done at all it were done more appropriately by public bill. In our own day, though 'insular security' in the sense considered in the 1880s may not loom so large, a channel tunnel project raises complex political, economic and environmental issues and the measure more recently brought forward was a government hybrid bill. Today, to put it blunty, no government would be content to see a private bill promoted for such a

---

1 We may note — 'I think a hybrid bill can be defined as a public bill which affects a particular interest in a manner different from the private interests of other persons or bodies of the same category or class'. Mr. Speaker Hylton-Foster, quoted May (17th edn.) pp. 871-2. For practice see *Ibid.* pp. 882-4.

2 It may be noted here that saving clauses for Crown rights and in these days for such considerations as Town & Country Planning appear in many private bills; their scope and character are an important matter for the parliamentary agent drafting a bill.

3 Clifford, I, 203.

4 *Ibid.*

purpose. But in contrast, and indicative of a boundary not clearly demarcated, we may notice the Thames Barrier & Flood Prevention Bill of 1971-72 which proceeded as a private bill on the promotion of the Greater London Council and was enacted, though it involved a large element of public policy, a strong government commitment, and had a somewhat political background.

Hybrid bills are one concern of the Parliamentary Agent for the Government, who is appointed by the Treasury on a sessional basis from amongst the parliamentary agents ordinarily in practice. He is called on to advise the officers of a Department or Ministry who have charge of a hybrid public bill on those aspects of the bill which make it hybrid, that is on the application to the bill of the standing orders of both Houses relating to private business and the related procedures and practices. He is responsible for seeing that the private business standing orders, so far as they are applicable or can be applied to the public bill, are complied with at the time of its introduction, for proof of compliance before the Examiners and, where necessary, the presentation to the Standing Orders Committee of any case seeking that compliance should be dispensed with. He will also advise the Department or Ministry on the *locus standi* of any petitioners, on the promotion of the bill at the select committee stage, including the instruction of counsel, on evidence and on other matters arising during select committee proceedings. Thereafter he will advise the Department or Ministry on the subsequent stages of the bill so far as they relate to its private business aspects. The government agent may also be consulted by a Department or Ministry in charge of an order to which the Statutory Orders (Special Procedure) Acts 1945 and 1965 apply. If so, he will advise on the steps they should take to represent the Department or Ministry's interests before any joint committee to which petitions may be referred for hearing, on questions concerning the *locus standi* of petitioners, and on the conduct of the Minister's case before the joint committee. He would also advise on matters affecting the order and arising under the Special Procedure Acts or the standing orders of both houses relating thereto, and on the parliamentary procedures and practices generally involved. A Department or Ministry may also consult the government parliamentary agent when it has charge of a Special Order as defined in the House of Lords standing orders relating to private business, that is an Order in Council, Departmental Order, Rules, Regulations, or other instrument laid before the House of Lords and requiring an affirmative resolution before becoming effective, which, if it were a bill, would be hybrid. Petitions may be presented against these in certain circumstances and stand referred to the Special Orders Committee of the House of Lords. The government agent may be required to advise and represent the Department in connection with proceedings before that committee.

In this survey we have seen a number of practical ways in which the parliamentary agent is 'a servant of the House'. The phrase also expresses a historical tradition, rooted in the fact that parliamentary agency was once undertaken by officers of the two Houses. When, towards the middle of the present century, members of the Society of Parliamentary Agents felt apprehension about certain developments that seemed imminent, it was agreed that the obligations of agents as 'officers of the House' should be the governing consideration. I have avoided that expression, not to deny the parliamentary agents a description they cherish but to avoid confusion: Officers of the two Houses and Members of Parliament are prohibited from acting as parliamentary agents. But as historical matters are approached the tradition and its origin are to be borne in mind. It is also helpful to notice that the modern parliamentary agent combines the functions of legal adviser, negotiator, and parliamentary draftsman with those of a manager of parliamentary procedure. The development of the private business standing orders and of the supervisory responsibilities of the two Chairmen did much to make that combination a practical necessity; the establishment of the Private Bill Office early in the nineteenth century much to make it practicable. And it is not difficult to perceive that when private bill committees were not fixed in size and their composition regulated in ways over which the parliamentary agent has no influence and when the proceedings of such committees were not ordered so as to ensure their quasi-judicial character, some of the activities of the parliamentary agent in serving his clients' interests are likely to have been quite different from those of an agent to-day.

2

THE EMERGENCE OF A PROFESSION

'The assistant clerk had a note in his book to notify 'Mr. John Bunbury, clerk to the Grocers . . . if a bill for the Apothecaries come in, he lieth at the Grocers' Hall in the Poultry', and similar reminders for those interested in other business of the House. In Elsyng's 'scribbled book' for 1621 there is a memorandum to inform Sir Charles Caesar of petitions or bills which might affect his family. Elsyng carried the Earl of Nottingham's bill on the agenda for several days before it was read, and specifically suggested the commitment of the silk throwsters' bill'. – Elizabeth Read Foster, *The Painful Labour of Mr Elsyng*.[1]

The nineteenth-century parliamentary agents who are our principal concern practised a profession shaped in the main by developments which belong largely to the second half of the eighteenth and the early nineteenth centuries. Their immediate predecessors sprang up as those developments took place. But if we ask about their remoter ancestors it is necessary to remember that much of what gave a distinctive professional content and status to parliamentary agency did not exist before the late eighteenth century. It is a question of asking through whose agency bills made progress. Counsel apart – for they had a defined role and status – our concern is with people performing imprecise but necessary activities rather than a defined professional role. Anyone instrumental in the furtherance or management of a private bill, or opposition to it, may be regarded as an agent for the party promoting or opposing it. The Member who presented or moved a bill was to that extent its agent. The solicitor who, going further than to draw a bill, 'solicited' and managed its progress through Parliament was thereby its agent or 'solicitor in parliament'. So was the officer or official of either House who by showing favour or in some other way helped along a bill.

Amid much that is obscure it seems reasonably clear that the assistance of someone 'indoors' was often desirable and possibly sometimes necessary. It is not surprising that by the early eighteenth century there are indications of individuals seeking parliamentary clerkships in order better to serve their clients as 'agents'.

Sir John Neale has given us a vivid picture of the activities of officers and servants of the Elizabethan House of Commons in relation to private bills.[2] Of the Speaker he tells us that his 'goodwill could make all the

---

1   *Trans. American Philosophical Society*, new series, 628.

2   J.E. Neale, *The Elizabethan House of Commons*, chapter 17.

difference to a bill's fate, that . . . unless the House intervened. . . it was he who decided the order in which bills were read'. Though the Speaker received a £5 fee for every private bill before first reading 'before he deliver it out of his hands', recognised fees were not all. At least from 1553 the City of London made him regular and increasing free gifts for favour shown towards the city's affairs. Such gifts did not always ensure the passage of a bill. In 1597 a measure promoted by the city failed despite the Speaker's considerable efforts for 'its furtherance', secured by a deputation and a £5 gift. The City does not appear to have been alone in making such payments to the Speaker. The Clerk of the House was also in receipt of payments to secure his favour and, we are told, in 1567 claimed such gifts as due to him. And the Serjeant at Arms, with his control over admissions to the House, was peculiarly well placed to assist or hinder parties to private bills. We are left in no doubt that this officer had his clients. As a Member put it in 1585: 'Here be the shoe-makers, crying and following, ready to pull their bill out of my hands. I pray you, Mr. Speaker, let the Serjeant call them in. He knows them; they be his clients'.[1] The post-Restoration Clerks of the House certainly appear to have included in their activities those pertaining to an agent. William Goldesbrough senior (Clerk, 1661-78) received in March 1672, thirty guineas 'for his many favours and respects to this City', and twenty guineas in 1678.[2] Paul Jodrell (Clerk 1683-1727) had 100 guineas from the City of London in 1694 for his pains and service in assisting to pass the City's Act to satisfy debts due to orphans, plus his bill of £50.[3] Jodrell was a practising solicitor when he became Clerk of the House and remained in practice. In 1699 he acted for the Earl of Meath in an action before the House of Lords. He was therefore a 'solicitor in parliament'; first, literally; second, in a sense analogous to that of a modern parliamentary agent who might act on behalf of suitors before the Lords; and third, as an agent for private bills. His will mentioned his 'parliamentary business'. The appointments made by Jodrell while Clerk of the House are of considerable interest in connection with the early history of parliamentary agency. We do not know exactly when he appointed Zachery Hamlyn as his personal clerk and the first effective, albeit unestablished, Clerk of the Journals. But Hamlyn was there by 1709 and still there in 1742.[4] It

---

1 *Ibid.* p. 328.

2 Repertories of the Court of Aldermen, City of London Record Office, 78, fol. 124; 82 fol. 171.

3 *Clerical Organisation,* p. 45. For accepting 1,000 guineas and 20 guineas respectively on the same occasion Speaker Trevor and the chairman of the committee on the bill were expelled.

4 *Ibid.* p. 42.

has been observed that Hamlyn was 'undoubtedly. . .a parliamentary agent, and very well placed to be one as unofficial clerk of the Journals, Jodrell's servant, and with one of Jodrell's sons in the Committee office and another at the Parliamentary bar'.[1] Hamlyn, we are told, advised Robert Harper − of whom more will be noticed presently − on his first bill in 1717, the promoters of the Don Navigation Bill, 1722, and the Weaver Navigation Bills of 1726 and 1727. In 1728 Hamlyn was instructed by the town clerk of Exeter to discuss with the city's Members a bill to suppress players. And it was to Hamlyn that George Legh, whom Miss Lambert calls the 'barrister-agent' for the Weaver Navigation Bill, 1727, turned to settle the petition, the Speaker's breviate, to attend Committees, to make proper blanks in the bill to the House of Commons, and to search for several papers relating to former Acts. For these services Legh paid Hamlyn £19.11s.4d.[2]

These details, taken with Legh's own activities, provide a glimpse of the probable state of affairs at the time and suggest the view that eighteenth-century parliamentary agency was largely a joint affair. Legh prepared the petition (which, as we have seen, Hamlyn settled) and the bill (settled by counsel). He secured copies of petitions against the bill, drew a counter-petition in its favour − which he got signed by the cheesemongers of London − made copies of the bill for committee use, and drafted more than one 'case' for distribution among Members. He briefed counsel − and appears to have lost the bill in the Lords as a result of presenting a petition containing allegations he could not prove.[3] This last unhappy episode apart, Legh, it seems, performed many of the functions appertaining to an agent, yet found it desirable or prudent to give certain matters to an 'indoor' official, Hamlyn. There is much to be said for the view that seeing bills, or at least the more important bills, through Parliament was often a joint venture most conveniently undertaken partly by a solicitor-agent and partly by an official of the House. It would follow naturally from the absence of a private bill office and it accords well with the tendency of some individuals interested in acting as agents to seek clerkships in the House. Moreover it offers a resolution of the vexed question, often raised later, whether parliamentary agency originated among clerks of the House or outsiders. That question is not answered satisfactorily by simply choosing either alternative, but ceases to be a problem if, as in Legh's case, it can be shown that both the solicitor for a bill and a clerk of the House

1   S. Lambert;   *Bills and Acts: Legislative Procedure in Eighteenth-Century England,* (Cambridge, 1971), p. 40.

2   *Ibid.* p. 165.

3   *Ibid.* pp. 159-66.

share a claim to be regarded as 'agents' for a bill. There is other evidence of this, but before turning to it and to other appointments made by Jodrell there is Legh's final account to be looked at, for that is revealing in another way. 'For my trouble', it reads, 'during the Continuance of this Affair, which was about 10 weeks, for my frequent Attendances on Lords and Members both at Westminster and their houses and otherwise concerned in ye Bill and also upon Council and my attendances at ye several Committees and other Occasions at both Houses of Parliament and writing Letters and other trouble. . . '.[1] We have here not only another glimpse of such activities already seen to have been performed by Legh, but also one — the canvassing of Members and Peers in Parliament and at their homes — which was inseparable from the system of open committees such as existed before nineteenth-century reforms in private bill procedure. It must have been one of the more laborious and least professional activities of pre-nineteenth-century agents. The professional agents of the 1830s and 40s, when the committee system was in question and undergoing radical change, disdained and disowned it, yet acknowledged its necessity by observing that there was a distinct class of men who performed the task.

Among Jodrell's appointments were those of the four clerks without doors, who from 1696 received Treasury allowances with some regularity for help with public business, and who acted as committee clerks, though not exclusively so.[2] At least two of these, James Courthope and George Cole, appear to have engaged in agency activities. Cole, we are told, was paid, along with 'Mr. Wilson, Solicitor in Parliament', 'the sum of £105 in 1719 by the churchwardens of St. Martin's-in-the-Fields for fees and soliciting about the bill for rebuilding the church.[3] The Corporation of London's records, 1711/12, show that the City Remembrancer 'gave Mr. Courthope the Clerk for his trouble in this affair £2.3.0' — this affair being a Bill to repeal part of a clause of an Act of James I relating to Bankrupts.[4] There is an additional interest in this and other payments made by the City Remembrancer for that official had as good a claim as any 'solicitor in Parliament' to be regarded as a parliamentary agent, as his many charges to the City for routine procedural purposes show.[5] For what 'trouble' Courthope was paid

1 *Ibid.* p. 164.

2 *Clerical Organisation*, pp. 53-4.

3 *Ibid.* p. 187.

4 *Ibid.* p. 316.

5 O.C. Williams reproduced a number of these. See *Clerical Organisation*, p. 313 and pp. 316-17. By the 1840s the City Remembrancer was clearly acting as a parliamentary agent both for the City and in private partnership for other clients.

£2.3s.0d. we cannot tell, but the sum does not represent the committee clerk's recognised fees for those form another item in the account. The Remembrancer's bill of 1718 'for business done in passing the Act for continuing an Act for settling the Assize of Bread, etc.' includes among many items 'Paid Clerks' fees on commitment'. Dr. Williams added '(i.e. Committee fees)', reasonably enough until one notices an earlier item 'gave Mr. Jodrell in full for fees', which leaves one wondering whether the payment first quoted was for recognised fees or for other assistance in getting the bill through. In either case, one has again the picture of a solicitor on the one hand and a clerk on the other performing services which entitle them both to be regarded as 'agents'. Other examples reinforce that picture. The solicitor for the Balliol College Act 1695, included in an account made up largely of his own charges, an item 'paid for ye Briatt [i.e. breviate] of ye Bill'; the solicitor for the Farington Estate Act, 1698, the item 'p. the Brief for the Speaker', and the bill for Lady North and Grey's Naturalisation Act, 1706, had 'for making the brief for the Speaker'.[1] This service, then, seems to have been one necessary part of the process of getting a bill through which, along with ingrossing, had been assumed by the clerks or their employees. It has already been noticed that George Legh turned to Hamlyn the unofficial clerk, in 1727, to perform this and other functions which at a later date were certainly part of the work of men who could be regarded as professional parliamentary agents.

Of Robert Harper we know rather more, thanks to the work of Miss Sheila Lambert.[2] Between his admission to Lincoln's Inn in 1717 and the end of his professional career fifty years later Harper drew or was concerned with several hundred bills. He promoted or helped to promote at least ten bills each year from 1732 to 1762. Of the 1,238 Private Acts which received the Royal Assent in those 31 years Miss Lambert calculates that 458 were drawn by Harper, including 56% of the Private Estate Acts — Harper's speciality. He had, too, an extensive practice in Inclosure Bills. His concern with local bills was less extensive, but during his career he drew about fifty such 'not confined to any particular type of bill or any particular locality or promoter'.[3] He appears to have taken an interest in bills other than his own and noted

The accounts provided by Williams suggest that he was doing so at the beginning of the eighteenth century.

1 Balliol College deed, B.22, 64 b.: Lancashire County Record Office, DDF. 1301; PRO MSS. North.b17, fols. 25 and v.

2 See Lambert, *Bills and Acts* chapter 1.

3 *Ibid.* p. 152.

the time and place of committee proceedings upon them. In the absence of an officially printed list he compiled his own list of standing orders.[1] And for estate bills he drew up his own 'Memorandums' of procedure with marginal comments and corrections.[2]

In view of his activities, Robert Harper thoroughly deserves the title of parliamentary agent so far as that title is applicable to anyone operating under the conditions of the period. Harper appears, in fact, to have been essentially a draftsman who became a parliamentary expert, undertaking the management in Parliament of both bills he had drafted and others. He did not, and the conditions suggest that he could not, act exclusively as agent for all the bills with which he was associated. We know, for example, that in 1762 and 1766 John Rosier and George White, both clerks in the House and agents, were responsible for the printing of bills with which Harper was concerned,[3] and the probability is that he often worked with or employed an indoor co-agent. In short, apart from the extent of his practice, Harper exemplifies the type of solicitor in parliament-cum-agent previously noticed, who often needed indoor collaborators.

There is no reason to doubt that Harper's practice as a parliamentary specialist developed naturally from his work as a conveyancer, which of course he continued to perform throughout his career. By the time of his death in 1772 there is evidence of a number of similar 'outdoor' practitioners, though not with practices on the same scale. The accounts of William Strahan, King's Printer, show that from 1768 to 1776 he undertook parliamentary work for several individuals and firms.[4] Among them we may note a Mr. Kiernan, whose nine bills between 1769 and 1771 include matters as various as the Shrewsbury Hospital and Lowth Road Bills; evidently he is no merely local man. A Henry Davidson, a Mr. Seton and a Mr. Langland each have accounts; the first and second for both parliamentary and other work, the third for non-parliamentary printing. Davidson, as solicitor for the Clyde Navigation, has accounts for much miscellaneous legal printing. From 1773 the three are in partnership as Messrs. Davidson, Seton and Langlands with a number of Scottish bills to their account each session. A Mr. Towne is debited with the cost of printing for the Wakefield Road Bill 1771. A Mr. Woodcock has one estate bill in 1771, but the following year the account

1   BL 357, b 1(4).

2   For the text and possible date of this and other memoranda of procedure see Lambert, *Bills and Acts*, pp. 87-9.

3   *Ibid*. p. 46.

4   BL add. MS. 48801.

of Messrs. Woodcock and Barnard begins with both parliamentary and non-parliamentary items. We do not know how long these survived as parliamentary specialists or agents. But John Spottiswoode, who has an account on his own, and one in partnership as Messrs. Gordon and Spottiswoode is a different matter. For over half a century later an agent giving evidence to the Lords' Select Committee on Fees and Charges. . .on Private Bills of 1827 said he gained his knowledge by serving some thirty years earlier in the office of John Spottiswoode 'who was himself a great parliamentary agent'.[1] The firm of Spottis-woode and Robertson was named to that committee as one of the firms of 'outdoor' agents in practice at the time and it continued throughout the nineteenth century.[2] The evidence of one printer's accounts cannot of course indicate how many lawyers were by the 1770s trying their hands at parliamentary work, but clearly some were, at a time when private business was growing rapidly and the management of private bills, especially the pre-parliamentary work in connection with them, was about to become much more sophisticated as a result of the development of standing orders.[3] As has been emphasised already they no doubt needed the collaboration of 'indoor' clerk-agents, and it is to them that we must now return.

When W.G. Rose joined the Committee Office in 1791 he found all the committee clerks acting as agents.[4] Doubtless this included some who merely occasionally assisted a promoter or opponent in the absence of the machinery of a private bill office. But, lesser figures apart, there was, from the middle of the eighteenth century, a growing band of clerks who were in some cases substantial practitioners. A few may reasonably be regarded as founders or inheritors of practices which survived until parliamentary agency by the clerks was prohibited in the 1830s. From them, in one or two instances, descended major firms of nineteenth-century professional parliamentary agents. The Clerks of the House and the Clerks Assistant do not appear to have engaged in parliamentary agency during the second half of the eighteenth and the early nineteenth centuries. But virtually every branch of the Clerk's department had its agents, except the Private Bill Office which was established only in 1810, its clerks being from the

---

1   HL (1827) 114. p. 96.

2   *Ibid.* p. 39.

3   The Commons standing orders relating to notices and consents began to develop from 1774. See *Hist.PBProc.*, I, 43-5.

4   According to his evidence given as Principal Committee Clerk over forty years later, HC (1833) 648, Qn. 470.

outset forbidden to practise as agents. The Committee Office, as Rose's evidence suggests, engages our attention, as must the Journal Office where as we have seen Zachery Hamlyn had already established something of a tradition even before the post of clerk of the Journals and Papers had official status. In the longer run the Fees Office, established in 1774, and the Office of the clerk to the Committee of Privileges and Elections are of greater interest.

Some of the more significant individuals held posts, concurrently or consecutively, in more than one branch, as may be seen in the chart below

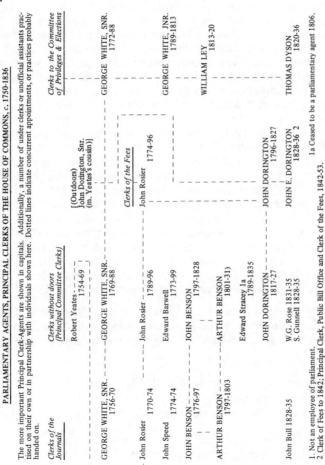

PARLIAMENTARY AGENTS, PRINCIPAL CLERKS OF THE HOUSE OF COMMONS, c. 1750-1836

The more important Principal Clerk-Agents are shown in capitals. Additionally, a number of under clerks or unofficial assistants practised on their own or in partnership with individuals shown here. Dotted lines indicate concurrent appointments, or practices probably handed on.

Clerks of the Journals
GEORGE WHITE, SNR. 1756-70
John Rosier 1770-74
John Speed 1774-74
JOHN BENSON 1776-97
ARTHUR BENSON 1797-1803
John Bull 1828-35

Clerks without doors (Principal Committee Clerks)
Robert Yeates 1754-69
GEORGE WHITE, SNR. 1769-88
John Rosier 1789-96
Edward Barwell 1773-99
JOHN BENSON 1797-1828
ARTHUR BENSON 1801-31)
Edward Stracey 1a 1789-1835
JOHN DORINGTON 1817-27
W.G. Rose 1831-35
S. Gunnell 1828-35

[(Outdoors)]
John Dorington, Snr. (m. Yeates's cousin)]

Clerks of the Fees
John Rosier 1774-96
JOHN DORINGTON 1796-1827
JOHN E. DORINGTON 1828-36 2

Clerks to the Committee of Privileges & Elections
GEORGE WHITE, SNR. 1772-88
GEORGE WHITE, JNR. 1789-1813
WILLIAM LEY 1813-20
THOMAS DYSON 1820-36

1. Not an employee of parliament.
2 Clerk of Fees to 1842; Principal Clerk, Public Bill Office and Clerk of the Fees, 1842-53.   1a Ceased to be a parliamentary agent 1806.

The many-sided Robert Yeates provides a starting point. Yeates became a clerk of ingrossment in 1749, was appointed a clerk without doors (i.e. a principal committee clerk) in 1754 and held that office until 1769. For the last ten years of that period he was also a principal clerk in the Treasury, having been appointed in July 1759 to 'do all the parliamentary business'.[1] The significance of that appointment is more conveniently looked at in connection with Yeates's successors; here it may be noticed that he has been described as, in effect, the first Parliamentary Counsel to the Treasury and that he had drawn Treasury allowances for drafting bills since 1752.[2] Was Yeates some kind of parliamentary agent before he became a clerk? It is not certain but seems likely, for in the year he became an ingrossing clerk 'Mr. Yates' was retained at ten guineas a year to watch the parliamentary interests of the Protestant Dissenting Deputies.[3] He certainly practised as an agent subsequently. The Weaver Navigation Bill of 1760, we learn, was to be redrawn for presentation by Mr. Yeates, 'solicitor in parliament'.[4] A substantial practice is suggested by the terms of the Letters Patent of 1767, granting Yeates a civil list annuity. This referred not only to his 'good and acceptable services. . .as one of our principal clerks of our Treasury' but also to his sacrifice in having, 'several years ago', voluntarily relinquished 'the Sollicitations of private bills and other affairs in our Houses of parliament. . .Sollicitations. . .attended with emoluments not only superior to the profits of his office in our Treasury but capable of being considerably increased'.[5] If Yeates gave up parliamentary agency for public work it is a reasonable surmise that he handed on his practice to John Rosier, who besides being in a number of senses his successor — though not his immediate official successor in the committee office — was his deputy, friend, and the executor of his will. Rosier's place in the scheme of things will be noticed below; it is convenient first to turn to Yeates's official successor as a principal committee clerk, George White senior.

White had been clerk of the Journals since 1756 and may have held a subordinate position earlier.[6] He had already established himself as a parliamentary agent. As early as 1762 he was indebted to Strahan the

1 *Clerical Organisation*, p. 165, quoting PRO T29/33, fol. 218.

2 Lambert, *Bills and Acts*, pp. 45 & 62.

3 B.L. Manning; *The Protestant Dissenting Deputies*, pp. 41-2, quoted Lambert, p. 45.

4 Lambert, p. 166.

5 PRO C66, 2714, no. 4, quoted Lambert, p. 46.

6 *Clerical Organisation*, p. 77.

printer in respect of no fewer than fourteen bills, so 1762 is unlikely to have been his first year as an agent.[1] Strahan printed for him for eleven bills in 1763, for twelve in 1764, and for fifteen in each of the following two years. Thereafter the numbers fell, but we must not assume that Strahan did all White's printing. Moreover, soon after being appointed a principal committee clerk he was heavily engaged in government business.[2] White, whose agency business in the early 1760s included both inclosure and local bills (among them the controversial Bridgewater Canal Bill) may well have been another who entered the service of the House of Commons because it would facilitate his work as an agent, but we have no proof. What is certain is that White and his elder son, George White junior, developed a substantial practice; they were probably the first partnership among the clerks to be referred to as a firm of parliamentary agents. The elder White was agent in 1766 for the Yorkshire Cloth Bill, one of Robert Harper's bills which Harper, presumably, only drafted.[3] Ten years later George White the younger, then an unofficial deputy committee clerk, is named in the Commons' Journal as the agent for a bill.[4] By 1783 they are George White & Son, agents for the Calico Printers and Manufacturers of Manchester.[5]

Though it means leaving Yeates and Rosier far behind for a while, it is worth looking further at the Whites and their successors. They offer the clearest and longest example of a continuous lineage leading to a major firm of nineteenth-century professional agents and thence to a prominent firm of present-day agents. In 1772 George White senior became Clerk to the Committee of Privileges & Elections — one of 'the great positions' as Speaker Abbot was to describe it early in the following century. Great or not, it had just acquired a new importance as a result of the passing of Grenville's Act reforming the method of dealing with disputed elections.[6] For a parliamentary agent it was a most attractive position not merely as one of authority; the work — and the

---

1 See Lambert, p. 48. Of Strahan's two ledgers in the British Library (Add. MSS 48800 & 48801) the first is no longer available for inspection and the details given here are from Miss Lambert's account; the second I have seen and referred to already.

2 See *Clerical Organisation*, pp. 143 & 181.

3 Lambert; p. 49.

4 35 CJ 636 (1776).

5 PRO T.1/592, quoted *Clerical Organisation*, p. 184. Williams there points out that from 1792 the Whites are frequently referred to in Treasury minutes as agents for private bills. He believed them to be 'the first among the clerks to build up a large professional business as parliamentary agents', but he does not appear to have appreciated how early the elder White was active as an agent.

6 10 Geo. III, c.16.

emoluments — were heavy only in years following general elections. The elder White was clerk of Elections until 1788, whereupon the post passed to his son and partner in parliamentary agency, George White junior. There can be little doubt that under the second George White the firm of White, parliamentary agents, became the largest in its day. As O.C. Williams has shown,[1] in 1803 White owed Luke Hansard over £2,149 for printing, a sum more than three times greater than that owed by any other parliamentary agent among Hansard's clients, and a list made by Speaker Abbot in 1812 showed White as agent for more than half the bills to be presented. In evidence to the select committee on Private Bill Fees of 1834, Richard Jones said White 'had been in the habit of carrying more private business than any four or five agents about the House'.[2] Jones provides the continuity between the younger White and his two successors as clerks to the Committee of Privileges and Elections. According to his evidence to the select committee just referred to he had managed White's parliamentary agency business from 1803 to 1813. When, in the latter year, William Ley succeeded George White junior as clerk of Elections he retained Richard Jones as unofficial assistant in connection with the business of the House and made him a partner in the continuing business of parliamentary agency, the firm being known as Ley & Jones. In 1820 Thomas Dyson became clerk of Elections and he, in turn, had Jones as a partner in parliamentary agency. Dyson was still clerk of Elections in 1835, when the clerks were faced with the choice between being agents and remaining clerks. Dyson, who by that time had quarrelled with Richard Jones and found another partner among the subordinate clerks, chose to leave the service of the House and to continue as a leading firm of parliamentary agents under the description of Dyson & Hall. Thus the modern firm of Dyson, Bell & Co., can claim a lineage stretching back well over 200 years.

It was suggested above that John Rosier may have taken over Robert Yeates's work as a parliamentary agent. Whether or not that was so, Rosier certainly acted as an agent from 1762 onwards, and once again we are faced with the possibility, but no proof, of an individual entering the service of the House partly at least to promote his business as an agent; in Rosier's case it was first as an unofficial assistant to Yeates in the Committee office. Strahan's ledgers suggest that Rosier did not practise on the scale of George White senior, but from 1762 on they show printing on Rosier's account in respect of two or three bills

1 *Clerical Organisation*, p. 183.
2 HC (1834) 540, Qn. 336.

annually for the rest of the 1760s, and a somewhat larger number in the early 1770s. In 1770 Rosier was appointed to the clerkship of the Journals, vacated by George White senior, and in 1774 he became the first holder of the newly-created principal clerkship of the Fees. Why a principal clerkship was established for this purpose is not clear, and the mystery is not lessened by the fact that no annual salary was attached to the position — though the clerk of the Fees was entitled to 10s. on every private bill fee he collected and to certain perquisites relating to stationery. But its establishment may have had much to do with finding for Yeates's successor as the clerk looking after Treasury interests in the House a position of standing with duties that were not too taxing. The three successive occupants of the office in turn enjoyed a Treasury salary — though paid to them by name and not as clerks of the House — until the office was reorganised in the 1830s; Rosier already had a Treasury salary when he became the first clerk of the Fees.

When Yeates died in 1769 the Treasury appointed 'Danby Pickering, Esq., to do the parliamentary business of this office performed by the late Mr. Yeates with a salary of £600 a year. . .' and 'John Rosier, Esq., to assist Mr. Pickering in the execution of the said business at a salary of £100. . .'[1] Pickering, a lawyer of some distinction, thus became Parliamentary Counsel to the Treasury, which Yeates had been in fact but not in form[2] But the Treasury had discovered — as had other departments and, be it noted, some promoters of private bills — that they needed the services of a clerk on the establishment of the House of Commons to manage their parliamentary business. John Rosier and his successor performed that task for the Treasury and eventually for other departments of state, acting as parliamentary agents for the government, not of course in the modern sense of that term but rather as the precursors of the Public Bill Office, into which the office of Clerk of the Fees was to be transformed in the nineteenth century. The Clerks of the Fees, it might be said, were only incidentally that. Some detail of Rosier's work for the Treasury, and that of other clerks for other departments, was provided by Dr. Williams:[3] general descriptions of the Clerk of the Fees' principal duties came only in the nineteenth century. In 1826 the Clerk of the House, John Henry Ley, in his evidence to the Select Committee on Committee Rooms, said the clerk of the Fees was 'the clerk of the House of Commons who,

---

1   PRO T.29/40, fols. 117-18, quoted *Clerical Organisation*, p. 169.
2   See Lambert, pp. 68-9.
3   *Clerical Organisation*, pp. 175-7 & 179-81.

on account of the convenience of the situation of his office, transacts the business of the government'.[1] In 1835, when the arrangements were under review, the then clerk of the Fees, John E. Dorington, told another select committee that his duties as 'Parliamentary agent to the Treasury', were 'to conduct the Treasury business in Parliament much as a Parliamentary agent conducts a private bill'.

Rosier's services to the Treasury evidently were valued. In 1770 his salary was doubled, for his 'extraordinary trouble and diligence'.[2] Further increases followed quickly. In addition to his duties of supervising the passage of Treasury bills, drafting them (or more probably the routine ones) and resolutions for Committee of Supply, Rosier was awarded a further £100 per annum in 1779 'in consideration of his attending to the private bills brought into the House of Commons and taking care that nothing passes therein which may be prejudicial to the interest of the Crown and the public'.[3] A later age no doubt would have regarded that responsibility of the clerks of the Fees as scarcely compatible with their being great parliamentary agents for private bills on their own account. Yet that is what Rosier's successors became. Eventually the Fees Office rivalled and overtook the office of the clerk of Elections in the volume of its private agency business.

John Dorington succeeded Rosier as clerk of the Fees, and to his Treasury business, in 1796, without, it would appear, having held any subordinate clerkship. He must have been well known to Rosier. His mother, Roberta, was Yeates's cousin, and both he and his father, also John, had been, like Rosier, beneficiaries under Yeates's will. The father, who is not known to have had any clerical post about the House, may have been a parliamentary agent; the son certainly was an agent before he became clerk of the Fees, according to statements made by him and others later. John Dorington told a Lords select committee in 1827 that he had been a parliamentary agent 'for more than forty-five years'.[4] And, in 1836, when the clerks composed their collective memorial relating to compensation for having to choose between their clerkships and agency, they pointed out that John Dorington had practised 'previous to 1780'.[5] Though few details are available, it is evident that by the early years of the nineteenth century Dorington

1   HC (1826) 403, pp. 25-7.
2   *Clerical Organisation*, p. 170.
3   *Clerical Organisation*, p. 170.
4   HL (1827) 114. p. 39.
5   HC (1836) 249, Appendix 11.

had a practice second only to that of White among the clerks. We have the statement by an 'outdoor' agent that on starting his own practice about 1805 he 'like all the other agents at that time. . .put it [his first bill] into the hands of Mr. Dorington'.[1] That suggests that his position as clerk of the Fees had given Dorington special standing or advantages as a parliamentary agent. When Speaker Abbot, in 1812, came to make his list of bills to be presented, already referred to and further discussed below, Dorington came next to George White in the number of bills for which he was responsible. In time Dorington took into partnership his son John E. Dorington, who succeeded his father as clerk of the Fees in 1828. In partnership with two subordinate clerks in the fees office and his brother John Dorington (not a clerk) John E. Dorington developed the firm of Doringtons & Jones until, by the time a choice had to be made bwtween clerkship and agency, it was, so far as these things can be measured in terms of bills handled, the largest firm of parliamentary agents. As will be seen in more detail in the next chapter, John E. Dorington and Arthur Jones, one of his 'indoor' partners, elected to remain in the service of the Commons. But continuity was maintained through the other 'indoor' partner, who went to make, in partnership with Dorington's brother, the firm of Dorington & Co. one of the leading firms of professional parliamentary agents. It was the ancestor of the present-day firm of Rees & Freres.

Certain other clerks of the House of Commons to appear as parliamentary agents in the period under review may be noticed more briefly, though none of them appears to have been important to the later history of parliamentary agency. John Speed, clerk of the Journals 1774-6 and Rosier's successor in that position, was noticed by Dr. Williams as the first clerk of whom he had been able to discover direct evidence of employment as a parliamentary agent.[2] But he cannot be so regarded. In fact, the evidence put forward by Dr. Williams was in respect of a bill sponsored by the Board of Works on behalf of the Commissioners for building Westminster Bridge in 1767 — that is several years before Speed became a Commons' clerk. It tends therefore to support the view that Speed was another who may have become a clerk because he was an agent. The minute unearthed by Dr. Williams is worth recalling, for it indicated what Speed did as an agent. 'The Commrs agree to pay John Speed £10. 10s. in full for his trouble in soliciting the bill thro' both Houses of Parlt; and more to him for revising the said bill, drawing a clause, and making a fair copy for the

---

1 HL (1827) 114, p. 91.
2 *Clerical organisation*, pp. 187-8.

House; drawing the Brief and a fair copy thereof, making out amendments and examining the Ingrossment, £5. 5s'.[1] The Bensons, John and Arthur, successively clerks of the Journals (1776-97 and 1797-1803) and Principal Committee clerks (1797-1828 and 1801-31), maintained in partnership a practice which extended over a long period and may have been substantial. As Dr. Williams discovered, their printing debt to Luke Hansard in 1803 was the largest among those of the parliamentary agents for whom Hansard printed after that of George White.[2] But in Speaker Abbot's 1812 list they were down for only two bills. With Arthur Benson's departure from the Journal Office the tradition of parliamentary agency established there by Zachary Hamlyn appears to have been interrupted, though John Bull, clerk of the Journals 1828-35, revived it in a small way.

There remains that other home of 'indoor' parliamentary agency, the four clerkships without doors or principal committee clerkships. These were sinecures during the greater part of the period now being considered. Apart from the Bensons, just noticed, others already discussed held principal Committee clerkships concurrently with other positions: John Rosier had been a Principal Committee clerk from 1789 to 1796 and so had John Dorington from 1817 to 1827 while clerks of the Fees. Edward Barwell, Principal Committee clerk 1773-99, may be noticed not because he appears to have had an extensive practice but as illustrative of the advantages a clerkship might have had at the time for agent and client. As Miss Lambert puts it, 'no outside agent could have done what Edward Barwell was able to do . . . in 1774: he promised to give the client warning when a petition in which he was interested was to be presented to the House; he was able not only to do this, but to give his client a copy of it before it was presented, so that he might prepare his opposition'.[3] Edward Stracey was twenty-one years old when, in 1789, he became an ingrossing clerk and one of the clerks without doors for life and, in Dr. Williams's words, he 'contentedly drew the salary of one sinecure, and the fees of both sinecures for forty-four years'.[4] After George White and the Bensons, Stracey figured third in Luke Hansard's accounts of 1803 with a debt of £483, suggesting activity as a parliamentary agent on a not inconsiderable scale. But his distinction — apart from that as a sinecurist — was to become in 1804 while still a parliamentary agent, Counsel to the Chairman of

1 PRO, Works 6/36, quoted *Clerical Organisation*, p. 188.
2 *Clerical Organisation*, p. 183.
3 Lambert. p. 50.
4 *Clerical Organisation*, p. 156.

Committees in the House of Lords at a time when the Lord Chairman's supervisory role over private bills and therefore over the activities of agents was developing rapidly. It was too much for the reforming Speaker Abbot, who complained not only to the Lord Chairman but eventually to the Prime Minister. Abbot had some cause to resent Stracey's appointment to a position in the House of Lords without his approval, but he appears to have been concerned principally with the advantages Stracey would obtain as an agent over his fellow clerks in the Commons and that Stracey would receive fees, in Abbot's own words, 'from the parties for settling their bills, which he was afterwards to approve, exercising, of course, not a very impartial judgement on such bills as were not previously submitted to him and paid for'. For two years Stracey held out, but in 1806 he undertook to give up his fees on private bills, though he continued as Counsel to the Lord Chairman and to enjoy his Commons' sinecures until 1833.

On 24 February 1812 Speaker Abbot summarised in his diary the state of affairs relating to private bills.[1] It ran as follows:—

24th.   Last day of private bills

1811							1812
368	Applications for Bills						315
302	Bills presented			163	)		
	To be presented —				)		
	White	40	)		)		
	Dorington	17	)		)		
	Benson	2	)		)		
	S.Gunnell	4	)		)		
	Goodiff	1	)	78	)		
	Jones	10	)		)		
	Rose	2	)		)	257	
	Bull	2	)		)		
					)		
					)		
	By strangers possibly			16	)		
						between	
66	Dropped					50 and 60	
	Bramwell	8					
	Ellis	6					

1   PRO 30/9/35.

All the named agents, except Bramwell and Ellis, were clerks of the House of Commons or their unofficial assistants. The pre-eminence of White and Dorington has already been noticed. This list, of course, is not a complete list of agents presenting bills that year, but of agents whose bills had still to be presented on the last day. It might be thought likely that it would be experienced clerks of the House rather than outdoor agents who would leave things that late, so it is probable that the possible 'strangers' or outdoor agents are under-represented here. It seems certain that a growing number of solicitors, and some who had no legal qualifications, were by this time handling bills, especially run of the mill inclosure and estate bills, and it would be surprising if there were not those among them who were attracted to specialising in this work. Messrs. Bramwell and Ellis, about whom Abbot appears to have had an afterthought, were distinguished from the 'strangers' listed earlier, only by being familiar to the Speaker, for they had by this time established themselves as regular 'outdoor' agents. George Bramwell had practised since the early 1790s in partnership with the deputy Serjeant at Arms, Clementson; as Dr. Williams discovered, they were the one outdoor or partially outdoor firm to have a three-figure debit with Luke Hansard the printer in 1803.[1] Charles Thomas Ellis, of the Inner Temple, was clearly in practice by the 1790s. His importance to us is as the writer of one of the earliest treatises for the use of solicitors undertaking parliamentary work. Both the appearance and the character of a number of treatises which appeared in the first thirty to forty years of the nineteenth century testify to the growing interest in parliamentary practice.

Ellis's first treatise, *The Sollicitor's Instructor in Parliament concerning Estate and Inclosure Bills,* published in 1799, was addressed to the solicitor's profession generally and not to a distinct class of agents.[2] He usually uses the word 'sollicitor', though occasionally employs 'agent', apparently interchangeably. In the advertisement he remarks: 'It being frequently necessary to apply to Parliament either to inclose Open Fields or to take off certain Restrictions from Estates or to give fresh Powers to the Tenants . . .' tis presumed that a compilation of this kind may be desirable to the Young Sollicitor, nor altogether useless to the Profession at large . . . '. It is, in form, a handbook for those unfamiliar with basic procedure, offering, as the title page states, 'The Standing Orders of both Houses of Parliament relative thereto (i.e. Estate & Inclosure Bills), with Plain Methodical Directions for Passing such Bills'.

---

1 *Clerical Organisation,* p. 185.

2 BL 518 k22(5).

It treats of the two types of bills separately and claims 'to state the Proceedings under their Proper Heads in the Order in which they occur in Practice'. Well over half its 133 pages are given over to Forms and Bills of Costs. In the *Sollicitor's Instructor* Ellis had set out to relate the 'immediately applicable' standing orders and practice to Estate and Inclosure Bills; three years later he applied the same method, to a much wider field in his *Practical Remarks & Precedents of Proceedings in Parliament* (1802).[1] He remarks in the preface to that work on 'the great spirit' of the age for improvement which had 'rendered applications to Parliament for private bills so frequently necessary', and that 'it is rather singular, the forms and methods of proceedings have not been collected for the use of the Gentlemen of the Law'. Once again he is addressing the legal profession generally, though it is clear that Ellis's solicitor is doing the work of a parliamentary agent. Ellis assists him mainly by an exposition of the standing orders, on the importance of which he lays great emphasis, by a systematic commentary on their particular application to various types of bill by subject matter, which takes up the greater part of the work, and by copious provision of forms, notably forms of petition.

Like others to be mentioned, these manuals are much more enlightening about formal procedures than about practice. They offer but brief glimpses of the solicitor-agent's parliamentary work; of these the most interesting are those relating to the difficulties of getting a committee on a bill and the importance — for we are still in the days of open committees — of having regard to its composition in the case of opposed business. The agent, clearly, must canvass in the first place for attendance. He is advised 'On the day fixed for the Committee (to) request a Member or two to attend it. There should be eight Members . . . but the number is not rigidly observed', especially where there is no opposition.[2] The agent must get 'as soon as the bill is committed, a list of members to whom it is committed . . . and application should be made by him to some or all of them as the particular circumstances of the case may require, requesting them to attend the committee'.[3] It is particularly important, Ellis observes, to 'produce the attendance of as many members as you can in every stage of the bill' when there is opposition.[4] In the Lords, obtaining the necessary committee of five is

---

1 BL 514 c5.

2 *The Sollicitor's Instructor*, pp. 20 & 42.

3 *Practical Remarks* &c. p. 44.

4 *The Sollicitor's Instructor*, p. 34. He repeats the advice in *Practical Remarks*, p. 39.

not easy, and the agent must, after the bill is committed, procure 'such Lords as he has influence with to attend'.[1] Ellis is, of course, writing before the composition of Commons private bill committees became a topic of reform on which, as we shall see, parliamentary agents had decided views, and these glimpses of the old state of affairs afford an indication of what must have been a considerable pre-occupation for an agent, especially if he was not on familiar terms with some Members. Ellis lays emphasis on the importance of consulting the Chairman of Committees in the House of Lords; which provides evidence that the Lord Chairman's role was well developed when Ellis wrote his earlier work in 1799. There we learn, in respect of an Estate Bill starting in the Lords, that 'It is advisable to wait upon the Chairman of the Private Committees in the House of Lords with the Bill a few days before you go into the committee, to know if he approves it'.[2] And the Lord Chairman's supervision of bills starting in the Commons is evidently also established by 1799, for writing of such a bill Ellis advises, 'As soon as the bill is printed either write to or attend the Chairman of the Private Committees in the House of Lords to know if he approves the Bill'.[3] But for all the importance he attaches to attending to the wishes of the Lord Chairman, Ellis is not able to specify or detail what that involves. This is true of other writers, some of whom are to be noticed presently. The principles upon which the Lord Chairman exercised his very wide powers of supervision were not reducible to a written code and so made readily available to the occasional practitioner before Parliament. Unwritten and flexible, they were accessible only to those who had frequent communication with the Lord Chairman and, from 1804, his Counsel. It was this developing aspect of 'practice' as opposed to 'procedure' which was to do much — perhaps most — to distinguish the regular and 'professional' parliamentary agent from the occasional practitioner who necessarily remained a 'stranger'.

It was not only solicitors aspiring to act as parliamentary agents who needed hand-books: evidently there was a demand from Members of both Houses of Parliament. It was for these that George Bramwell wrote his two small volumes.[4] Neither was intended for general

---

1 *The Sollicitor's Instructor*, pp. 14 & 53.

2 *Ibid.* p. 16.

3 *Ibid.* p. 34.

4 G. Bramwell, *Proceedings of the House of Commons on Passing Bills* (printed for private use, 1809), pp. 109. BL 514 f.24. Later editions (1816, 1823, 1837) were published under the title of *'The Manner of Proceeding &c.'* and *The Manner of Proceeding on Bills in the House of* Lords (1831). BL 708 h.31.

circulation: in the preface to the first Bramwell asks those who accept a copy 'not to allow it to be multiplied', and the second is described as 'Not Intended for Sale', but, as the Preface has it, produced 'in deference to a desire expressed by some Lords'. In the Preface to the 1809 work Bramwell describes his treatise as 'being the general result of experience and observation in the course of an extensive practice in soliciting Bills, during the period of twenty years' and in the work of 1831 he refers to 'a long and extensive practice in passing Bills as a parliamentary agent, now carried on by himself and partners', thus confirming the impression that he was practising by the 1790s, and that his firm survived, as will be noticed in a later chapter, into the important formative period of the 1820s. Both works wear an antique air, setting out in large print and schematically the basic forms of procedure, providing an elementary word-picture of what happens in each House to both public and private bills, though Bramwell is clearly interested most in instructing Members about the latter. A taste of his style may be gleaned from his chapter (E) on 'The First Reading of the Bill'. He schematises thus:–

(E1) How Prepared
(E2) When to be Presented
(E3) By Whom
(E4) How Presented

Under 'How Prepared' (Bramwell is of course discussing private bills) we get one of the few references to the agent or parliamentary agent, and this a confusing one. 'The draft of the bill is prepared by the agent of the parties who are suitors for the bill . . . in cases of difficulty or importance it is generally settled by counsel'. But he continues in the following paragraph: 'After the draft is prepared it is submitted to the perusal of the parliamentary agent to examine whether it be confirmable in its titles and provisions to the petition and order of leave, and to the orders and rules of the House'.[1] Presumably 'agent' in the first quotation is intended as a synonym for 'solicitor'. We learn further under 'By Whom' that 'All bills are presented by one of the Members ordered to prepare and bring in the same, or by a Member subsequently added to them . . .', and under 'How Presented' we are given a word-picture of the old style introduction of a private bill:-

> The member, intending to present the bill, seats himself at the bar of the House, with the written copy and two prints of the bill, the order of leave, and brief of the bill in his hand; and upon being called to by the Speaker, he answers 'a bill', upon which the Speaker without putting the question, desire him 'to bring it up'. The

[1] *Proceedings* &c., p. 37.

> member then carries up the bill (making three obeisances to the chair) and delivers it to the clerk at the table'[1]

Bramwell makes no reference to the work of the parliamentary agent in connection with this quaint ceremony. He does, however, indicate the agent's responsibility at a later stage: prior to third reading, we are told, it is the agent's responsibility, 'usually, . . . now' to examine the ingrossed bill for conformity with the House bill as amended in committee, a task formerly undertaken by the committee clerk and the clerk of the House.[2]

A Practical Treatise of Passing Private Bills through Both Houses of Parliament by John Halcomb, Barrister at Law, was published in 1836.[3] Halcomb, who does not appear to have been a parliamentary agent but may have been a parliamentary draftsman, claimed to give 'full directions for Members who have charge of Private Bills, and for Solicitors, &c'. Although Halcomb remarks in the dedication on the difficulty he had experienced when, for a short time, he was a Member of Parliament in acquainting himself with the nature of private business and calls his work 'a first publication of this nature', its 362 pages pursue the same plan as *The Sollicitor's Instructor* but on a considerably larger scale. Over 100 pages are devoted to the standing orders, to stereotyped forms of proof before committees of the House of Commons, and to tables of fees. We have in this work another indication of the need for a ready-made working manual that, hopefully, will provide for the lawyer unfamiliar with parliamentary work a safe guide to parliamentary agency. So conscious is Halcomb of this that he cautions the reader at one point 'to note carefully the distinction between committees on private bills and committees on private petitions . . . for, from the want of attention in this particular, mistakes are of frequent occurrence'.[4] The greater length of Halcomb's work compared with Ellis's speaks of course for the great development that standing orders had undergone in the period between the two works. The railway age had arrived by the time Halcomb published, and he devotes considerable attention to the preliminary steps before a petition is presented, and especially to notices, advertisements, deposits and the preparation of plans. Aware of the frequent changes in standing orders and the rapid development of practice, he promises on the

1 *Ibid.* pp. 37-8.

2 *Ibid.* p. 76.

3 BL 1129 e.

4 John Halcomb, *A Practical Treatise* &c., p. 52. Before the establishment of official Examiners in 1846 the committee on the petition was concerned with compliance with standing orders.

contents page 'at the end of every Session of Parliament a Supplement to this Volume, showing any change in the practice of either House of Parliament and all new standing orders that may be made . . .'. I have no evidence that he attempted to carry out this plan. On the preparation of a bill he is meticulous and didactic; it 'must be confined strictly to the matter prayed for by the Petition, great care and judgment being . . . requisite in the framing of the Preamble and clauses . . . to answer the Ends of the Parties . . . and . . . obviate such objections as are likely to arise . . . The Preamble must be so shaped as not to encumber the Promoters . . . with any proof that can possibly be dispensed with, nor expose them needlessly to opposition . . . nothing more (should) be stated than is strictly necessary and can be satisfactorily established by evidence. . . '. Halcomb proceeds to underline the importance of considering what clauses will or will not be allowed in the Upper House, where the 'strict but very salutary Superintendance and Examination of private bills 'is exercised' by the Noble Chairman of their Lordships' committees'.[1]

It would be tedious as well as superfluous to comment in any detail on further examples of this genre. Among them may be mentioned Anthony Hammond's *Treatise on the Practice and Proceedings of Parliament* (1825); *Practical Instructions on the Passing of Private Bills*, by a Parliamentary Agent (1827) and Benjamin Lumley's *Parliamentary Practice on Passing Private Bills* (1838). The first two I have not examined. Lumley's work carried further and in more modern (and peremptory) language the kind of exercise in reducing practice to stereotyped forms carried out by Ellis and Halcomb. It is perhaps of interest to notice that Lumley made more of the power of the Lord Chairman than did the writers previously referred to, advising that before second reading in the Commons every bill should be submitted to the Lord Chairman, who would give directions as to what alterations he required; no such alterations were to be departed from without the Lord Chairman's consent, and Lumley advised that should such alterations render the bill unsatisfactory to its promoters the prudent and economical course was to abandon it.[2] The general interest of these works is not in their detail but their character, which is so strong an indication that as the scope of private legislation expanded rapidly and

---

1   *Ibid.* pp. 67-8.

2   Lumley, *Parliamentary Practice,* pp. 109-110. Benjamin Lumley described himself in the work as a parliamentary agent, and appears to have practised in the late 1830s and early 1840s. But he became much better known for his theatrical pursuits and as an author of fanciful fiction. See *The Earl of Dudley, Mr. Lumley, & Her Majesty's Theatre (1863); Reminiscences of the Opera (1864) Serenia; or Recollections of a Past Existence* (1862) &c.

the work for professional — that is specialist — parliamentary agents, whether clerks of Parliament or outsiders, developed, a larger number of occasional practitioners, usually solicitors, sprang up. They needed ready guidance on the more formal aspects of procedure, which the works just discussed gave them, but they could not so readily be given insight and experience of the less tangible aspects of the profession, and more especially of the practice associated with the Chairman of Committees in the House of Lords. No doubt, such practitioners were a necessity especially at the height of legislation associated with railway promotion and municipal improvement. They remained for a considerable time a feature of and in some ways a problem for the profession.

As we leave these works we may notice first certain important changes in procedure which they incidentally reveal and secondly the brief and somewhat different treatise by T.M. Sherwood which ran through three editions between 1828 and 1834.[1] Ellis, and Bramwell in his early edition, had noted and accepted the practice whereby 'all who come have voices' in Commons private bill committees. Ellis had written, in his *Practical Remarks &c.* (P.45), 'The order "that all members who come to the committee have voices" is generally applied for and made, when a bill is opposed'. Sherwood, whose work has important critical elements absent from the others, commented disapprovingly on this practice in his earlier editions and was able to note in his third edition that the practice with its 'pernicious effects . . . happily has been entirely abandoned'.[2] This represented a useful step towards reform of the constitution of private bill committees which, as may be seen in a later chapter, professional agents strongly supported. Another matter emerging from a comparison of Ellis and Bramwell's early treatises with those of the later writers is the important change in procedure whereby Commons private bill committees gradually assumed consideration of the principle of a private bill, and suitors ceased to be heard at the Bar of the House on Second reading. 'At a (Commons) committee', Ellis had written, 'petitioners are by the rules of the House to be heard only against particular clauses and provisions in the bill, and will not be permitted to offer any reasons against the principle of the bill'.[3] That this was no longer so was recognised by Halcomb and Lumley, though somewhat tentatively, Lumley observing that 'petitions praying to be heard by counsel against the bill are now

1   Thomas Moulden Sherwood, *A Treatise on the Proceedings to be Adopted in Conducting Private Bills through the House of Commons.*

2   *Ibid.* (3rd. edn.), p. 34.

3   C.T. Ellis, *Practical Remarks,* p. 50.

usually referred to the committee on the bill'.[1] But the change and its apparent corollary — that committees are as much concerned with the preamble as with the clauses of a bill — was first expounded and defended by Sherwood in his 3rd. edition.[2] Of this important change Clifford observed:—

> As trading ventures grew in importance and number the unfitness of either House for inquiries so prolonged and elaborate became even more clear, and the increase of public business . . . made a complete delegation of these duties more necessary and inevitable. There was thus ready acquiescence in the gradual encroachment by committees on the power of the Houses over preambles. These encroachments seem to have begun early in the present [nineteenth] century. The change was made by no specific resolution in either House, and can be marked by no exact date. After 1820 there are few instances in which Counsel appeared before the whole House. Two orders, the last of their kind, that petitioners should be heard at the bar against private bills, were made by the Commons in 1824. Neither took effect.[3]

Until the early 1770s solicitors or agents managing bills on behalf of suitors had to cope with but a handful of standing orders governing the conduct of private business in each House, compliance with which cannot for the most part have presented very serious difficulty or demanded much expertise. From 1774 the situation changed. In that year came the first of the Commons orders dealing with notices, deposits, applications to owners, and proofs of consent, and the parallel orders requiring proof of compliance before committees on petitions. In 1774 they were introduced in respect of bills for inclosing, draining and improving lands and for making turnpikes; in the subsequent twenty years comparable orders were made in respect of river and canal bills, bills for bridges, for providing water supplies, and for paving, lighting and otherwise improving towns. In the first decade of the nineteenth century similar orders were made in respect of bills relating to county rates, gaols, churches, chapels and burial grounds (1810), railways, tunnels, piers, ports, and harbours (1810), and ferries and docks (1811). And the process continued. Thus over a period of sixty years or so, from a few scattered standing orders, there grew as Williams put it, 'an impressive code of orders, some of general application, and the remainder applying to bills for some sixteen different and specific purposes'.[4] The first printed edition of the Commons

---

1 Lumley, p. 116.

2 Sherwood, (3rd. edn.), pp. 49-51. The corollary was not, in fact, secure when Sherwood wrote; in 1843 the competence of a committee to amend the preamble of a bill was questioned. See *Hist.PBProc.* I, 99.

3 Clifford, II, 860-1.

4 *Hist.PBProc.* I, 41. The reader is referred of course to Dr.Williams's study of

standing orders as a whole was published in 1810; the edition of
1830, the fifth since 1810, contained 149 orders. With detailed
differences the Lords standing orders underwent a comparable
development. In consequence of these important developments, the
demands made on the parliamentary agent of the early nineteenth
century were much greater than those made on his predecessors. They
were also, such was the rapidity of development of the standing orders,
changing demands; in particular the more elaborate nature of the pre-
parliamentary work in connection with many bills meant that the
indoor clerk-agent, whatever his other advantages, may not have been
so well-placed as the outside practitioner to meet some of the demands
made upon him.

The proliferation and growing complexity of the standing orders,
the increase in private legislation, and the growth in the number of
outdoor agents lay behind the establishment, in 1810, of the Private
Bill Office. The growing pressure of public and private business had
led to irregularities in the Ingrossing Office.[1] There was need for
further regulatory standing orders which could hardly be effective
without supervisory machinery. In 1809 Speaker Abbot turned his
attention to these matters. He began, apparently, by thinking in
terms of making general and obligatory the employment of a clerk of
the House in connection with the solicitation of private bills, for he
told the solicitors that 'some one of the Clerks attending the House
should be employed by the Parties having business before the House as
a Parliamentary Agent or Solicitor; who may be ready to answer any
question and give any explanations which may be required in the
course of the business depending'.[2] Not surprisingly the outdoor agents
disliked this, and the Society of Gentleman Practisers eventually
received an assurance 'that the duty which is intended to be imposed on
the Clerks of the House is merely that which at present lies on no one
to perform . . . it will not exclude the usual Parliamentary Agents
from any part of their employment . . .'[3] Whatever he had originally
contemplated, Abbot disavowed any desire 'to create a *monopoly* of
Parliamentary Agency & Solicitorship in the Clerks of the House of
Commons', but observed that something must be done in face of
'the increasing multiplicity of Private Bills, coming not only from

the development of the Commons Standing Orders and particularly to *ibid.* I,
62-46, where Williams summarises the state of the standing orders in 1830.

1   See *Clerical Organisation,* pp. 231-4.

2   E.A. Freshfield (ed.), *The Records of the Society of Gentleman Practisers &c.,*
p. 214.

3   *Ibid.* p. 221.

respectable and known persons but from all corners of the United Kingdom'.[1] It would appear that a good deal of discussion may have taken place on what should be done for some months later, on 28 May 1810, Abbot noted in his manuscript diary, 'Hatsell, Ley and I settled finally the plans and resolutions for the Private Bill proceedings'.[2] The Speaker, the clerk of the House and his deputy must largely have done the work of the Select Committee 'to consider of providing more effectually for the Accuracy and Regularity of Proceedings on Private Bills', for there is no record of evidence having been given to that committee and it reported on the day Abbott made the above entry in his diary. The resolutions of this committee were adopted by the House and became the standing orders on which the Private Bill Office was based.[3]

In addition to its general importance in the development of private bill procedure the establishment of the Private Bill Office is a landmark in the history of parliamentary agency in at least two respects. First, several of the Resolutions and three schedules, subsequently made standing orders, mentioned or laid duties upon the parliamentary agent, giving him official standing if not a very precise status. Thus Resolution 1 went (in part) 'a Book to be called "The Private Bill Register" to be kept in a Room to be called "The Private Bill Office"; in which Book shall be entered by the Clerks to be appointed for the business of that Office (who shall not be employed or act as Agents in the management or conduct of any Bills in the House of Commons, nor be in partnership with any person so employed) the Name, Description, and Place of Residence of the Parliamentary Agent in Town, and of the Agent in the Country (if any) soliciting the Bill; and all Proceedings, from the Petition to the passing of the Bill ...'. Resolution 7 provided that 'notice of the day and hour on which the Committee on the Bill is appointed to sit, be given in writing three clear days beforehand by the Agent Soliciting the Bill to the Private Bill Office' and the eleventh Resolution placed a similar duty of written notice on the agent soliciting the Bill before any private bill was reported to the House. Secondly, 'outdoor' agents were no longer dependent for all sorts of practical reasons on the co-operation of 'indoor' clerk-agents, as I have already suggested they must often have been in the absence of a properly organised channel of contact. Alexander Mundell, an outdoor agent who had probably been in practice since the late 1790s told a Select

1   Abbot to Perceval, 4 January 1810, cited Lambert, p. 192.
2   PRO 30/9/34.
3   The Committee was HC (1810) 321. The resolutions are at CJ (1810) 421, and were made standing orders on 5 June 1810.

Committee in 1834 that he had nearly always needed to employ a clerk of the House before the Private Bill Office was established but had never employed one since.[1]

'It is not too much to say that, from the moment at which a Private Bill was drafted until it had passed through the six stages in both Houses, the dominating fact in its history was, in ordinary cases, the Power of the Lord Chairman of Committees', wrote F.H. Spencer, with reference mainly to municipal legislation in the early decades of the nineteenth century.[2] The extraordinary authority, ill-defined and seemingly largely self-assumed, of the successive Chairmen of Committees in the House of Lords forms, as much as any developing code of standing orders and other procedural innovations, the context in which parliamentary agents worked from the last years of the eighteenth century onwards. Nominally a sessional appointment, it was held for the greater part of the nineteenth century by two strong personalities, the 6th Earl of Shaftesbury and the 2nd Baron (1st Earl) Redesdale, who energetically developed and exploited the authority of the position.

The basic function of the Lord Chairman, that of chairing Committees of the whole House, has been traced back to the 1730s.[3] By the mid-eighteenth century his position in this respect was well-established.[4] Soon after, the beginnings of a special function in connection with private bills may be discerned: in 1765, we are told, nearly half the private bills were reported by two peers one of whom was Lord Sandys, the Lord Chairman.[5] By 1780 the Lord Chairman was being paid a salary of £1,500 a year. We know, from C.T. Ellis's observations in the *Sollicitors' Instructor* of 1799, that before the end of the century the Lord Chairman had assumed a supervisory role over private bills. Lord Walsingham, Chairman of Committees 1794-1814, was probably the first seriously to develop the function. The House doubtless was recognising what had already become established practice when, on 23 July 1800, it passed three resolutions, the first of which resolved 'at the commencement of every Session' to nominate a Chairman of Committees of this House, and the third 'That such Lord also take the Chair in all Committees of Private Bills, unless where it shall have been

1 HC (1834) 530. Qn. 530.

2 F.H. Spencer, *Municipal Origins,* London School of Economics, Studies in Economics and Political Science no. 22 (London, 1911), p. 111.

3 Lambert, *Bills & Acts,* p. 91.

4 See J.C. Sainty, *Officers of the House of Lords 1485-1971,* House of Lords Record Office Memorandum No. 45, and *The Origins of the Office of Chairman of Committees in the House of Lords,* HLRO Memorandum No. 52. p. 111.

5 *Spencer, p. 97.*

otherwise directed'.[1]   From 1804 Counsel was appointed to assist the Lord Chairman in his duties in respect of private bills, the first holder of that position being the Commons sinecurist and parliamentary agent, Edward Stracey, who received a salary of £750, doubled in 1808.

The Chairman of Committees thus became in effect a permanent paid official, with expert assistance. It seems likely that originally he was concerned with the form of bills rather than their substance. Certainly towards the end of Lord Walsingham's period as Lord Chairman a bill which he found in principle objectionable could nevertheless pass: in 1811 we find Walsingham's signature among those of a number of peers who, most unusually, entered a reasoned protest in the Journal against the principles involved in Pryce's Estate Bill, which passed and became law.[2]   But the transition from control of form to influence over substance is an easy, probably an inevitable one, Walsingham's formidable and energetic successors developed the authority of their office greatly. By the mid-1830s the Lord Chairman was the *de facto* committee in the Lords on an unopposed bill and had constituted himself the judge of public and private interests. As a leading parliamentary agent then put it, 'we all know in the House of Lords all unopposed bills go before one tribunal, namely Lord Shaftesbury; nobody else sits on them at all . . . he sees that the public are properly protected and private rights also'.[3]

The 6th Earl of Shaftesbury became Chairman of Committees in 1814 and continued until 1851. The official biographer of his more famous son has described him as 'completely absolute in his own department' and a man who 'expected and as a rule obtained implicit submission from all concerned'.[4]   Most of what has passed between successive Lord Chairmen and parliamentary agents is unrecorded and lost to history, but there is evidence enough to indicate Shaftesbury's stern and authoritative demeanour, and his influence over agents and the bills for which they were responsible. The anonymous Parliamentary Agent who in 1827 wrote *Practical Instructions on the Passing of Private Bills through Both Houses of Parliament,* noted that 'the

1   LJ xlii, 635-6.

2   LJ xlviii 364. The other signatories were Lord Chancellor Eldon, the Duke of Norfolk, and Lord Redesdale. For the issues raised by the bill see Clifford, I, 297-9.

3   Evidence of St. George Burke, Select Committee on Private Business, HC (1837-8) 679, Qn. 106.

4   E. Hodder, *Life and Works of the 7th Earl of Shaftesbury,* p. 355. Hodder goes on to say 'he carried these autocratic habits into his domestic life, where he was more feared than loved'.

sooner the Bill is presented the sooner will the Solicitor be enabled to
arrange the clauses with Lord Shaftesbury' . . . It is necessary to forward
to Lord Shaftesbury three days prior to the sitting of the committee on
the bill a printed copy with the blanks filled up, when His Lordship
adds to or expunges from it whatever he thinks proper'.[1] In the same
year, T.M. Sherwood, whom we shall see in the next chapter as the
founder of the leading firm of outdoor agents, told a Select Committee
(with Shaftesbury in the chair) that when a client approached him,
his first object was to select 'from a collection of Precedent Acts . . .
always preferring the most modern bills, as they have more recently
passed through that Ordeal to which they are subjected by the
Penetration of the Noble Lord who sits as Chairman of the Lords
Committees'.[2] Another witness, an attorney, having consulted his
parliamentary agents, found that 'they are very particular in introducing
any alteration, because they know the Noble Chairman will never trust
them again if they are not very particular in adopting the precise
language he has suggested'.[3] A decade later the agent St. George Burke,
asked if in point of fact 'the Counsel of Lord Shaftesbury controlled
the form of Bills in the House of Commons', said, 'Yes, and I never
presume to pass a Bill in committee until Lord Shaftesbury has seen
every clause'.[4] In 1833 John E. Dorington had described to a Select
Committee this aspect of the Lord Chairman's functions.[5] Lord
Shaftesbury and his Counsel examined a printed copy as soon as a bill
was presented to the Commons; Counsel indicated to agents what
clauses or amendments were required, which would be inserted in the
Lords if they were not inserted sooner; and the Lord Chairman was
consulted about and gave what amounted to directions concerning
other proposed amendments. To submit to the Lords a bill to which
the Lord Chairman objected, Dorington added, would be a pointless
expense. In 1837, a Commons committee clerk explained how the
Lord Chairman's role encouraged, or at least facilitated, the treatment
of the Commons committee stage on a private bill as little more than a
formality: — 'An unopposed bill is generally attended by only one
Member; the whole proceeding is almost formal, the agent having
previously submitted the bill to the Chairman of Committees in the
other House, and his Counsel, he generally tells the Member that

1   Cited Spencer, *Municipal Origins*, p. 107.

2   HL (1827) 114, p. 83.

3   *Ibid.* Evidence of F. Lane, p. 89.

4   HC (1837-8) 679, Qn. 110. Another agent described Shaftesbury's superintendance as a 'very nearly perfect security', *ibid.* Qn. 557.

5   HC (1833) 648, Qns. 2361-74.

everything is right, that he need not give himself the trouble of looking into the clauses; he need only sign the bill and put his initials to the clauses, and in the course of five minutes a bill of considerable length is disposed of in that way, though the House has entrusted it to a committee to look narrowly into the matter'.[1]

Soon after 1840 model bills were distributed to the parliamentary agents by the authority of the Lord Chairman. Of the notices circulated to agents in his name, it will suffice to quote one, peremptory in tone.

House of Lords

5 March 1844

The Earl of Shaftesbury perceives that many of the Bills which have been presented this Session do not contain the Stamp Office Clause which he last year sent to the different Parliamentary Agents, and that other Clauses (which were also sent), and Amendments to Clauses required by the Government have not been inserted; he desires the Parliamentary Agents to recollect, that the introduction of many of these Clauses by the House of Lords must be fatal to their Bills; and he desires they will also understand, that he holds them responsible to him for the observance of those directions which they have received from him on these points in the last Session'.[2]

The Notice continued with a recapitulation of the Clauses and Amendments alluded to.

By the time the redoubtable Shaftesbury retired in February 1851 the House of Commons had entrusted to the Chairman of Ways & Means, assisted by Counsel to the Speaker, the supervision of private bills on its behalf. But as Dr. Williams remarked, the House of Commons has never permitted the assumption by the Chairman of Ways and Means of 'a position so autocratic as that of which Lord Shaftesbury founded the tradition'.[3] It is to be noted that when Shaftesbury's retirement was announced the Duke of Richmond said in the Lords that attempts to influence Lord Shaftesbury in matters relating to private bills had invariably evoked from him 'I shall do no such thing'; the Duke continued 'He kept the attorneys and agents in very good order for when they once got a good dressing down from Lord Shaftesbury they never made any such attempts (sic) again'.[4] In contrast, a member of the House of Commons spoke about the same time of 'the very extraordinary and anomalous power which appeared

1   HC (1837-8) 679, Qn. 106. Cited *Hist.PBProc.*, I, 92.
2   HLRO, MS P.O 164.
3   *Hist.PBProc.* I, 103.
4   Parl. Deb. HL (1851) 114, cc 50-51.

to have been vested in Lord Shaftesbury', and of some clerk being sure to whisper, when a clause was proposed to a Commons committee, 'You had better not put that in, for Lord Shaftesbury will throw it out'.[1] Despite that Member's hope that no such power would be entrusted to Shaftesbury's successor, the second Lord Redesdale, who succeeded Shaftesbury and was Lord Chairman for thirty-five years, emulated his predecessor. Of Redesdale's manner and authority, and of his attitude to Parliamentary agents and to those who essayed to practise without being proficient, we shall have more than a glimpse in chapter 4 below, where the enquiry into parliamentary agency over which he presided is examined. One illustration of his dealings with agents will therefore suffice here. In the summer of 1854 the Society of Parliamentary Agents received notice of details to be set out 'concisely and clearly' on all bills to raise or regulate capital.[2] After some consideration the Society replied in December, ('with much respect') observing that 'the difficulties which attend a strict compliance with the requirements of this notice . . . are . . . so great as to be in some cases insurmountable . . . also there are grave objections to setting out on the face of a Bill the whole affairs of a company . . . such a statement might seriously affect the rights of parties not before Parliament'. The Society's President added that he saw no objection to giving such information in Committee. But the Lord Chairman was unmoved, promptly replying, 'I can understand some companies not liking to make such statements, but not any well-regulated company'; it was a matter of the public interest. Having asserted his point the Lord Chairman continued, 'I hope that the Society will never hesitate to make any representations to me which the general interests of their clients appear to require'.[3]

As we turn to take a closer look at those who practised parliamentary agency in the second and third decades of the nineteenth century it is fitting that the proceedings of a committee chaired by Lord Shaftesbury should provide our first source of information.

---

1 *Hist.PBProc.* I, 103.
2 Min SPA, August 1854.
3 *Ibid.* 14 & 17 December 1854.

3

THE AGENTS – I

'Supposing the Solicitor to be perfectly acquainted with the Parliamentary Practice, is it necessary for him to employ a Parliamentary Agent?'

'Certainly not; it is competent to the whole World to approach Parliament'. – Evidence of T.M. Sherwood, Parliamentary Agent, to the Lords' Committee upon Fees and Charges on Private Bills, 1827.[1]

As late as 1909 the Secretary of the Society of Parliamentary Agents emphasised that parliamentary agency was 'an open profession'.[2] The accounts here and in chapter 5 cannot embrace every occasional practitioner, but they attempt to chart the development of professional parliamentary agency from the second decade of the nineteenth century, and to notice those individuals and firms practising with some regularity and in some instances exclusively as parliamentary agents. Important practices had been established by the 1820s. The great expansion of private legislation in the next two decades attracted others, often firms of solicitors, to parliamentary agency, sometimes with inadequate knowledge of what was involved. The attraction was strongest in the mid-1840s. Officers and clerks of both Houses of Parliament were forbidden to practise as parliamentary agents from 1836. Later in the nineteenth century that event was regarded, mistakenly, as the starting point for professional parliamentary agency by outsiders, it being supposed that the clerks of the two Houses alone acted as agents until they were prohibited.

The House of Lords Select Committee on Fees and Charges upon Private Bills, of 1827, relied largely on parliamentary agents as witnesses. It received evidence on their number and identity, notably from John Dorington, Commons' clerk of the Fees, and E.G. Walmisley, clerk of the Journals, House of Lords. Dorington named as 'indoor' agents – i.e. officers of the Commons –

'Myself and my son in partnership, Arthur Benson and Mr. Rose (partners), Samuel Gunnell, William Gunnell, Thomas Dyson, G. Dyson, Richard Jones, David Jones, Charles White, and Mr. Bull – and as 'outdoor' agents – 'Messrs. Bramwell, Brown(e), Sherwood,

---

1 HL (1827) 114, p. 83.
2 Min SPA, 16 June 1909.

Ellis, Hayward, Sisson, Richardson, Mundell, Spottiswoode & Robertson, Moncrieff & Webster, and Chalmer.'[1]

Walmisley gave a similar list of 'outdoor' agents, though he described Moncrieff & Webster as 'Moncrieff, Webster & Co.', and added 'Mr. Connell'. Presumably Dorington omitted Connell accidentally, as he was Richardson's partner. Thinking of 'indoor' agents as officers of the Lords, Walmisley named two, 'myself and Mr. Parratt, the copying clerk'.[2] Several of the outdoor agents named gave evidence. Mr. Mackley Browne told the Committee that he had practised as an outdoor agent since 1813, after being employed by the indoor agents Benson and White. He was not a solicitor.[3] George Bramwell said he had practised 'since about 1790', originally having been in partnership with Clementson, former Deputy Serjeant-at-Arms; he was a solicitor but did not act in both capacities.[4] Thomas Moulden Sherwood testified that he had been an agent for seven years. Asked if he was 'a Solicitor or Attorney upon the roll of any Court', he said 'No'.[5] Although he was not a qualified lawyer John Richardson told the committee he had served an apprenticeship and expected to become a Writer to the Signet that year; he had been an agent for Scottish business for twenty-one years. Asked how he had obtained the necessary knowledge, Richardson said it was through contact with Dorington. 'The first session I came up I had a bill and, like all the other agents at that time, I put it into the hands of Mr. Dorington'.[6] Allowing for an element of exaggeration in the statement that 'all the other agents' did likewise, this suggests that the function of an outdoor agent may sometimes have been a very humble one. It also lends support to the view, already mentioned, that before the establishment of the Private Bill Office it was a great advantage if not a sheer necessity to have an indoor connection whether or not it took the form of a partnership, as does the evidence, noticed above, by Browne and Bramwell of their former indoor partnerships. In contrast, Alexander Mundell, who had practised for 'upwards of thirty years', told the committee he had gained his knowledge by serving for two years in the office of John Spottiswoode, 'who was himself a

---

1   HL (1827) 114. p. 39. For the Commons offices held by Dorington's indoor agents see *Clerical Organisation,* appendix X.

2   *Ibid.* p. 43.

3   *Ibid.* pp. 56 & 61.

4   *Ibid.* p. 63.

5   *Ibid.* p. 77. Subsequently Sherwood was called to the Bar, and was listed as Counsel and Parliamentary draftsman in the Law Lists 1834-9.

6   *Ibid.* p. 91.

great parliamentary agent'[1] It was seen in chapter 2 that Spottiswoode was practising by the early 1770s.

To one witness, Thomas Ebbs, the committee devoted more time than in some respects he appears to have deserved. Ebbs had been for three years managing clerk to T.M. Sherwood; he had probably been dismissed, and was unemployed at the time he gave evidence. He had a jaundiced attitude towards the profession (unless all parliamentary agents were rogues). Asked to specify 'improper' charges made by agents, he answered, 'I should say from the first item in the Bill to the last they are all exhorbitant'.[2] But Ebbs was the only witness to draw the committee's attention to the relative importance of the agents. Of the 'six or eight' indoor agents he said, 'two have the greater part of the business and of the 'six or so' outdoor agents 'maybe three get the chief or principal number of the Bills'.[3] Though his number of agents is smaller than the Dorington-Walmisley lists Ebbs's evidence on this important point was valid. E.G. Walmisley told the committee that he had practised agency 'since I have been Clerk of the Journals, which was from January 1819',[4] and John Dorington 'for more than forty-five years'. Dorington, when asked if there were more agents 'than there used to be', said 'not more in the House of Commons, but more of what are called outdoor agents', adding that outdoor agents charged more because they shared their profits with the instructing solicitor, a practice which, according to Walmisley, explained why outdoor agents were getting more of the business.[5]

The committee concluded that there were two indoor agents in the Lords, 'eight or nine' in the Commons, and a rather more numerous body of outdoor agents 'most of whom employ themselves in the business exclusively and are not . . . generally attached to any branch of the legal profession'.[6] The committee was prudent not to attempt to enumerate the outdoor agents more precisely; they were a quickly growing band. In 1829 T.M. Sherwood took a partner — Thorp — and,

1 *Ibid.* p.96.

2 *Ibid.* p. 27. But Ebbs had a narrow view of the scope of agency.

3 *Ibid.* p. 20.

4 *Ibid.* p. 44.

5 *Ibid.* pp. 39 & 41 and 46.

6 *Ibid.* Rept, pp. v-vi. 'Not generally' was justified only if it meant 'not all'. Ebbs had told the committee that (outdoor) agents were not generally solicitors or attornies; asked for names, he mentioned four who were and two who were not solicitors, but he said those who were not had the greater part of the agency business.

in 1832, another — George Pritt — who had been an agent since 1830.[1] T.M.'s sons, Thomas and Edward became agents and partners in 1834 and 1839, and the elder Sherwood retired from the agency in 1833, possibly with a view to practising at the parliamentary bar. He is named as counsel on at least three occasions in 1835 — for the promoters of the Chelsea Waterworks Bill, the Sheffield & Rotherham Railway Bill (his instructing agents being named as 'Sherwood & Thorpe'), and for petitioners against the Great Western Railway Bill .[2] The same source shows that another outdoor agent, St. George Burke, was active by 1835, being named as agent for the Great Western Railway Bill. Thereafter St. George Burke's name occurs frequently as agent, and in 1837 it is coupled with that of R.L. Venables, either as a partnership or as joint agents for another G.W.R. Bill;[3] in 1844 both became partners in the firm founded by T.M. Sherwood. The firm was usually known as Pritt & Co. from 1833 to 1844 (though occasionally referred to as Sherwood & Thorp), and from 1844 to 1847 as Burke, Pritt & Venables. Burke resigned his partnership in 1847 to practise at the parliamentary bar; from then until 1867 it was known as Pritt & Co. or Pritt, Venables & Co. Since 1867 it has been known as Sherwood & Co.

Moreover, although John Dorington had rightly placed 'myself and my son in partnership' at the head of his list of indoor firms in his evidence to the Lords Committee of 1827, the firm of 'Doringtons' almost immediately lost its purely indoor character. John Dorington died in 1827, and was succeeded as clerk of the Fees by his son John E. Dorington, who had been appointed additional parliamentary agent to the Treasury in December 1825.[4] For his private agency work John E. Dorington had as an outdoor partner his brother, John Dorington junior, who was never a clerk in Parliament. Of course John E. Dorington's principal partners remained his indoor partners, Arthur Jones and, to a lesser extent, G. Ellicombe. The prestige of his firm — and it was by a large margin the premier firm of agents in the early 1830s — rested on the Doringtons' long experience of promoting bills from 'inside' and their special status as Treasury agents, and O.C.

1 According to his evidence to the Select Committee on Private Business, 1840, 1st Rept — HC (1840) 56.

2 HLRO Books of Evidence (Private Bills) H.C. 1835 1st vol. As a barrister (by 1834) T.M. Sherwood could of course appear before private bill committees without being agent for a bill, but he seems to have taken the view that even as an agent his duties included 'advocating the Bill in Committee'. HL (1827) 112, pp. 77-8.

3 HLRO. Standing Orders Committee Book, HL (1837).

4 PRO, Treasury Minute Books T.29/252p.64.

Williams rightly classed 'Dorington & Jones' as an indoor firm in his analysis of the (incomplete) list of agents promoting bills in 1832.[1] Very reasonably, but as the future showed wrongly, J. E. Dorington informed the Select Committee on Officers' Compensation, 1836, that the profitability of his firm depended on his personal involvement.[2] Almost as soon as he submitted that statement Dorington may have realised that, with one partner 'outside' and the possibility of at least one of his indoor partners choosing to go 'out', his firm had every prospect, in the changing circumstances of the time, of flourishing without him, for he chose to remain an officer of the House and to relinquish parliamentary agency. If he did so he was right, for after the prohibition of the clerks came into effect the firm of J. Dorington & Co. remained for long a leading firm of parliamentary agents. Its establishment did indeed involve one of the partners in 'Dorington & Jones' (G. Ellicombe) giving up his clerkship to continue as an agent but its principal partner made no such choice. The conditions in which parliamentary agency was operating had been changing. More than a hint of those changes had been given to the Lords Committee of 1827. Profit-sharing was not the sole explanation of why more business was going to outdoor agents, as John Dorington senior and E.G. Walmisley had asserted, and before we leave that Committee too far behind it seems appropriate to interrupt this account of the agents and review what the 1827 committee had heard and concluded on profit-sharing and other matters.

Profit-sharing, functions and charges

In referring to profit-sharing, Dorington and Walmisley had touched upon a matter which was to vex the profession for a long time, as a question of professional ethics and one which involved the status and functions of a parliamentary agent, and the nature of his relations with his clients' solicitors. Indeed, it raised by implication the question of who were a parliamentary agent's clients, the promoters of (or petitioners against) a bill or their solicitors. If profit-sharing were defensible it could be only on the assumption that it was the solicitor for whom the agent was acting and profit-sharing was their own affair. Behind that assumption lay the further question of whether a parliamentary agent's functions and therefore his relationship with a local solicitor were analogous to those of a London solicitor who for convenience and economy did things which could be done only in

1   *Clerical Organisation*, p. 262.
2   HC (1836) 249, Appendix 12.

London as an agent for a solicitor in the country. This is, of course, a common legal practice with obvious advantages: the country solicitor is employing the London solicitor to do things he could do equally well himself at greater cost.

The indoor agents denied profit-sharing. 'I have constantly refused it, and I do not believe there is a single Officer of the House of Commons that would do it', Dorington told the committee.[1] Among the outdoor agents, Mackley Browne said he shared his profits with solicitors. He thought that 'from the nature of the term agent, it had originally sprung from the same source as all other agency in the Profession had . . . '. He thought it right that parliamentary agents should act as agents 'on the same Principle as all other Solicitors in London do'. He had found it a 'very disadvantageous' practice but conveived it to be 'perfectly honourable'. Although he had been told by Solicitors that other agents had approached them trying to get his business by offering to share profits, he could not name any, and said 'I believe I am the only one who acted upon the Principle of sharing the Profits with the Solicitor . . . I consider myself a Town Agent . . .'.[2] Mundell & Richardson were not questioned on this point. G. Bramwell said he had never shared profits but he knew profit-sharing 'obtained' in 'the practice of one or more of the present Agents'.[3] T.M. Sherwood also denied the practice, adding, 'I have refused many Bills which have been offered to me upon those Terms'.[4] However, Ebbs, his former clerk, alleged that Sherwood did share, giving the committee a detailed list of items on which part of the profit, in some instances three-quarters of it, went to the instructing solicitor.[5]

The committee did not take this matter very seriously, reporting that 'whether this practice be creditable or not in itself', it did not appear to be a matter of public concern if total charges could be checked.[6] But in the course of pursuing this and other questions relating

---

1   HL (1827) 114, p. 41.

2   *Ibid.*, p. 61. In other words Browne accepted the analogy of country and London solicitor – rather oddly because he was not a solicitor. In fact he had taken counsel's opinion (Sir Samuel Romilly) on both the propriety of acting as a parliamentary agent and profit-sharing, and been reassured on both points. He considered the only qualification needed by a parliamentary agent was 'a perfect knowledge of the Practice'.

3   *Ibid.* p. 67.

4   *Ibid.* p. 81.

5   *Ibid.* p. 21.

6   *Ibid.* p. vii.

to charges it called for the production of accounts of charges by the agents giving evidence, which, are revealing. First the accounts do not suggest that for comparable work the outdoor agents' charges were significantly greater than those of indoor agents. Walmisley, the indoor agent, and G. Bramwell submitted accounts for Estate bills; the former's charges being £226-17s.-0d., and the latter's £208-8s.-10d.[1] Dorington & Son put in an account for an unopposed improvement bill which came to £497-18s.-6d., and Mackley Browne one of £498-1s.-4d., for a similar unopposed bill. A turnpike bill (unopposed) handled by Doringtons cost £218-9s.-6d., and one submitted by Mackley Browne £250-10s.-0d. Two unopposed inclosure bills delivered to the committee by Walmisley and Bramwell involved charges of £259-7s.-9d. and £256-12s.-0d. respectively. Second, these accounts show something of much greater importance. With the exception of the estate bills, on which preliminary proceedings before judges were necessary, the indoor agents' accounts show that they concerned themselves with the parliamentary proceedings and not with what could often be extensive activity prior to those; the usual first item in their charges is 'perusing, settling and altering the Bill', (occasionally 'Drawing the Petition'). In contrast the outdoor agents were often involved in consulting with and advising their clients, preparing notices, considering engineers' reports, drawing the bill and petition and other matters, including consequential correspondence. Mundell & Richardson submitted long accounts of charges, showing activities of this kind over many months prior to the deposit of the petition or bill. The first item in Mackley Browne's account for the Glastonbury Canal Bill (Session 1826-7) is 'Correspondence in 1825, 1826 and 1827'.[2] In short, the functions of parliamentary agents, so far as the outdoor agents were concerned, were becoming both extra-parliamentary and much more important as counsellors and draftsmen than the word 'agent' may suggest. At the time when prohibition of agency by the clerks was being considered it was suggested that they enjoyed no particular advantages over outdoor agents. One might go further and say that some years before that, as these accounts show, the outdoor agents, provided they were competent, were becoming more useful to their clients, especially with complex and heavily-opposed bills, than their indoor counterparts. One witness testifying to the 1827 committee emphasised this: Mr. Steed Girdlestone, solicitor, of Wisbech, said he generally did not employ outdoor agents — 'Mr.

---

1 But it should be noted that Estate bills, unlike others, were taxed by the Masters in Chancery.

2 The accounts are reproduced as Appendix (D) to the Report.

Dorington has conducted our business' — but there were advantages with a bill of exceptional importance and complexity, 'because there is a great deal of business to be done out of the House . . . the Outdoor Agent has more time to give to it; the Indoor Agent has other duties to perform . . .'.[1]

What was becoming important in the late 1820s was to be more so in the next decade. Much more preparation and expertise were to be demanded of agents. Although the 1827 committee defined the role of agents as 'conducting Private Bills through Parliament'.[2] they recognised implicitly that the agent had or should have a wider function as well as a distinct expertise. 'There is' they observed 'one principal source of expense in these Proceedings, which often enhances its amount through every stage of a Private Bill . . . the imperfect form in which the original Bill is often prepared . . . if the Bill reaches the Parliamentary Agent (as often happens) at the very latest moment . . . the obvious consequence is . . . repeated attendances before Committees, amendments, new clauses, and re-commitments, which lead the Party into expenses necessarily indefinite, and probably very considerable'.[3] Bramwell had told the committee that it had 'not very frequently' happened to him, and sometimes the expenses were 'thus materially increased', but Sherwood had been much more emphatic. Bills were frequently sent up imperfectly drafted, and at the last moment, 'from the want of acquaintance with the nature of the Acts, and from disregard of my suggestions'. He had received, he thought, fifteen bills within the last fortnight for presentation of private bills, and it was utterly impossible to do justice to them.[4]

Fortunately the committee did not heed Ebbs on these matters, for he, at a time when the distinct need for a profession of agency was becoming manifest, showed his hostility to the agents (or his late employer) by suggesting that their functions (and therefore their charges) should be viewed as narrowly as possible. Correspondence and charges therefor were unnecessary for it was the duty of the solicitor to make himself acquainted with standing orders, and a charge for settling the bill undesirable for that was 'peculiarly within the province of the Solicitor', he could draw a bill as effectually as any

---

1 *Ibid.* p. 70.

2 *Ibid.* p. v.

3 *Ibid.* p. viii. There was a further recognition of the distinct character of parliamentary agency when the committee suggested consideration of 'whether to subject all persons desirous of acting as parliamentary agents to the previous approbation of the Clerk of the Parliaments' (p. vii).

4 *Ibid.* pp. 71 and 83.

agent, who would either do it carelessly or 'in such a way as to incur as many additional expenses . . . as possible . . .'.[1]

The committee found that some charges made by agents were for work 'which was not actually performed',[2] noted that other charges were held by some witnesses to be excessive, 'more especially as the Agent appears to be entitled by long usage . . . to a considerable solicitation fee . . .'.[3] and, observing that agents' charges are 'not regulated by any known or uniform standard', recommended legislation to give power to audit and tax charges of parliamentary agents, 'when required by the parties concerned'.[4] Taxation of costs in the Commons had been provided for in 1825,[5] and the committee thought the Act providing for that 'may, with proper variations and additions, serve as a suitable precedent'. This recommendation was acted upon.[6] It did not provide for 'the parties concerned', for like the earlier Act it could be invoked only by promoters and in respect of the promoters' costs. Moreover, the machinery for taxation long remained defective and inefficient, until the passing of the Costs Acts of 1847 and 1849, which conferred rights to taxation on opponents as well as promoters, and provided for the appointment of taxing officers in both Houses.[7]

The committee's recommendations on Fees are outside the scope of this work, and there was no reference in their report to those items of costs appearing in agents' accounts of charges under the heading of 'Gratuities'. These, Henry Ley told the Commons Select Committee on Fees, etc., of 1833, were paid by the parties to private bills to supplement the low salaries of assistant committee clerks, by usage not authority. As it would be 'inconvenient' if some agents paid more than others there was a scale agreed between the agents and the clerks

---

1 *Ibid.* p. 32.

2 *Ibid.* p. vi. The only example was a charge for copies not actually made.

3 *Ibid.* Rept p. vi. J. Dorington had told the Committee that this fee was for the following duties: 'To conduct the Bill through the various stages of the House; to communicate with the Members of Parliament; to procure their attendance on the Committee and on other proceedings; to attend the Committee, and prepare the Bill for the House'. Sherwood made it cover rather more, including 'attendances upon and . . . consultations with my Clients', *ibid.* pp. 39 and 77-8. Even Ebbs would allow this fee, which appears to have become standardised at 25 guineas, though some agents charged less, and all seem to have increased it in difficult cases. See Appendix (F) to the Report, which also includes the reduced charges Ebbs proposed to the committee for other duties.

4 *Ibid.* Rept p. vii.

5 6 Geo 4 c. 123.

6 7 & 8 Geo 4 c.64.

7 10 & 11 Vict c.69, and 12 & 13 Vict c. 78.

and approved by him. He had known them to be struck out on taxation, and known instances of agents refusing to pay them, but, he added, they began 'long before my time', and — a delightful piece of casuistry — 'being regulated, may be called gratuitous fees'.[1]

There was another vexed question about which there was perennial argument, and which, having been noticed, need not be pursued — that of 'printers' discounts' and the propriety or otherwise of agents receiving these without passing on the saving to their clients. Printing costs could be a considerable part of private bill promotion, and printers often allowed discounts to the agents as valuable and regular customers. T.M. Sherwood (whose printer was Hansard) defended the practice on exactly the grounds given above; it was solely a matter between the agent and the printer, and did not affect the client — 'a discount allowed by almost all tradesmen in England for prompt payment'. He stressed that a long time elapsed between making disbursements out of the agent's own pocket and payment by the client, but this, though strengthening the case for agents benefiting from discounts, was not in Sherwood's view the justification. On one exceptional occasion his clients had advanced a sum for disbursements; 'that was the Liverpool and Manchester Railway Bill, which was a Bill of very great importance, and the disbursements were known to be very great; but in that case I did not in fact receive above £600. 0s. 0d., and the charges amounted to nearly £1,500. 0s. 0d.' Asked 'upon what principle' he took a discount on the printer's bill in that case, Sherwood said 'I consider that is an account between the printer and the agent, as it is between . . . any other tradesman and a gentleman; the effect to the client is precisely the same. I presume that if the solicitor to the Liverpool and Manchester Railway Bill had himself employed Messrs. Hansard & Son, he would have had to pay the whole amount of the printer's account, Mr. Hansard not allowing him a discount, he not being a regular customer'.[2] The committee concluded that this did not seem an 'undue profit'.[3]

Several other sources indicate a growing number of outdoor agents active about the time the Commons forbade their clerks to practise agency. The first volume of the Books of Evidence for 1835 (the earliest extant), covering 25 railway and other bills for public works, names the agents for the promoters and opponents of 14 of them. The indoor firms of Dyson & Hall are named twice as promoters' agents

1   HC (1833) 648, p. 25.
2   HL (1827) 114, pp. 81-2.
3   *Ibid.* p. vi.

and Dorington & Jones once for opponents, while 17 outdoor firms are recorded as having made 22 appearances.[1] The Lords Committee Minute Books for the period 1837 to 1840 confirm this picture. The most informative are those for the Standing Orders Committees, much of whose business was concerned with railways. From the Standing Orders Committee Book for 1837 it is evident that some of the outdoor agents already named had considerable practices. J.R. Hayward, named as an agent by Dorington & Walmisley 1827, made twelve appearances before Lords Standing Orders Committees in 1837; the agent St. George Burke made eleven, in addition to one under the description 'Messrs. Burke & Venables'. Ten outdoor agents are recorded as appearing before Standing Orders Committees in that year, eleven in the sessions 1837-38 and 1840.[2] With three exceptions they are agents already named in this chapter. Two of the exceptions need not be named, having no other history as agents; the third, recorded as 'Mr. Bircham', in the Minute Book for 1837 is worth noticing as a member of a firm of solicitors one of whose partners was later to play a prominent part in the controversy over the proper qualifications for agents. The Lords Committee Books of proceedings on opposed bills rarely name agents, those on unopposed bills never do, but the Minutes of proceedings before Appeals Committees (which, rather illogically are bound in the same volumes as minutes on unopposed bills in HLRO) do so frequently. Generally, they name the same outdoor agents as the sources already referred to; the proceedings before Appeals Committees for 1839 and 1840, for example, show that such agents as Connell and Richardson had much business before these committees. Two points are worth noticing about these records: first, that where agents for inclosure bills are named they are often not the firms or individuals mentioned in this chapter, which bears out the view that solicitors in the Harper tradition often coped with these; secondly, the Minutes for the session 1837-8 include eight named agents who do not appear otherwise in the records on which this chapter is based.

A contemporary unofficial source[3] purports to give the 'principal'

1   An episode during the proceedings on one of these bills, the Glasgow Water Bill, suggests that John E. Dorington was accorded by some private bill committees a special status among parliamentary agents. Though the promotion and opposition to the bill was in the hands of experienced outdoor agents (Mr. Mundell, & Messrs. Richardson & Connell), Dorington was called in and examined along with Robert Chalmers (2nd. committee clerk) as to whether certain standing orders had been complied with. Dorington could hardly have been concerned with this in his official capacity of clerk of the Fees, though Chalmers might have been.

2   HLRO Committee Minute Books (Standing Orders Committees HL 1837-40).

3   *The Family & Parochial Almanack,* The Company of Stationers, (London,

68

parliamentary agents, naming eight indoor firms and ten outdoor firms,
as follows:

Indoor   — Dorington & Jones, (Fees Office)
Dyson & Hall (Election Office)
Gunnell & Son (Committee Clerks' Office)
George Gunnell (Ingrossing Office)
Jones & Walmisley (Election Office)
John Bull (Journal Office)
Wm. G. Rose (Recognizance Office)
G. White (Committee Office)

Outdoor   — J.H. Barrow, Bramwell & Tinner (possibly Fenner),
M. Brown, J. Florance, J.R. Hayward, H. Hundman,
Macdougall & Bainbridge, Richardson & Connell,
Sir W.R. Sydney, Sherwood & Sharp (Thorp?).

As we have already seen, several of the indoor agents included in this
list could by no stretch of the imagination be regarded as 'principal'
agents, only Dorington & Jones, Dyson & Hall, and Jones & Walmisley
having any considerable business by 1836. G. Ellicombe, who is not
included in this list, has at least as much claim to be there as the others.
The outdoor agents mentioned certainly included important firms, but
I have no other evidence of Messrs. Barrow, Florance & Sir W.R. Sydney.

Why are Scottish names so conspicuous in the lists so far encountered
or presently to be noticed? That young, ambitious Scottish lawyers
should seek to make their fortunes in London, and that some of them
should be attracted by parliamentary agency, seems an obvious yet
inadequate explanation. In any case the attraction of parliamentary
agency as a path to fortune could not have been all that great until the
later 1830s and early 1840s, whereas many of the people mentioned
were active as agents much earlier. The probable explanation is that
there had long been established in London a distinct body of Scottish
Law Agents, agents, that is, in the more general legal sense, offering
their services to other lawyers, no doubt primarily but not exclusively
to Scottish lawyers, as experts in Scottish law and London procedures.
Scottish lawyers would send them their parliamentary business, thus
they would become parliamentary agents as well as agents in the wider
sense, and other lawyers would then turn to them for parliamentary
work, for some must surely have realised that in that field experience
was a great qualification. Moreover, they must have stood out from the
generality of London attorneys as agents for they had their separate
entry in the annual law lists. Among the twenty-eight Scottish Law

1836), p. 35.

Agents listed in 1835 were several of the individuals and firms named in this chapter.[1]

Officers and clerks in Parliament barred
from parliamentary agency

The House of Commons forbade Members to act as agents for reward in 1830.[2] The exclusion of Officers and clerks of the two Houses from parliamentary agency was a product of the parliamentary spring-cleaning which followed the Reform Act of 1832. To be noticed are the Report of the Select Committee 'to take into consideration the Fees, Salaries and Emoluments received by the Officers and Public Servants of the House of Commons, &c.', 1833; the third report of the Select Committee on Printed Papers, 1835; and the report of the Select Committee on House of Commons' Officers Compensation, 1836.[3]

The 1833 committee elicited from the Private Bill Office a return of parliamentary agents who had petitioned for bills in the previous Session, viz.[4]

		Petitions deposited
Indoor —	(Commons)	
	J.E. Dorington & A. Jones	34
	R. Jones & J. Walmisley	26
	T. Dyson & R. Hall	18
	J. Bull	1
	W.G. Rose	3
	S. Gunnell	2
	G. Gunnell	3
	G. White	1
	G.B. Ellicombe	1
	(Lords)	
	E. Walmisley	11
	E. Parratt	5
		105

1 Clarkes New Law List, 1835. Parliamentary agents were not specified.

2 CJ (1830) 107.

3 HC (1833) 648: (1835) 606; (1836) 249. They will be referred to as the 1833 committee, &c.

4 HC (1833) 648, Appendix 15. I have added the indications: indoor, Commons & Lords, and outdoor; the number of petitions presented by each class;

Outdoor —	Sherwood & Thorp	21
	M. Brown(e)	18
	Bramwell, Son, & Fenner	9
	Hayward	15
	Spottiswoode & Robertson	6
	Richardson & Connell	10
	Moncrieff & Webster	4
	Mundell & Son	2
	Wallace, Solicitor, Belfast	1
		86
		191

It can be seen that, in terms of petitions deposited, a considerable part of parliamentary agency was in the hands of outdoor agents before agency by the clerks was ended. It is also clear that among the Commons' clerks only the first three partnerships had substantial business. Of these, only J.E. Dorington (clerk of the Fees), his partner, A. Jones (2nd. clerk in the Fees Office), and Thomas Dyson (clerk to the Committee of Privileges & Elections) were indubitably officers on the establishment of the House. The position of Richard Jones was anomalous; though Dyson's official, or at least his recognised, assistant he had no official salary or emoluments, other than an entitlement to a set of public reports and papers from the Vote Office, and depended for payment entirely upon Dyson.[1] His position was probably uncomfortable also. A parliamentary agent of long experience, he had recently quarrelled with Dyson, with whom he had been in partnership, and formed a partnership with J. Walmisley, whose inexperience was probably the explanation of an embarrassing episode which came to the attention of the 1833 Committee and will be noticed presently. J. Walmisley, and Dyson's new partner, R. Hall, were clearly unofficial and unestablished assistants, paid by Dyson for work in connection with Election Committees.

In their examination of John Henry Ley, the clerk of the House, the members of the 1833 Committee were concerned to know whether or not 'any inconvenience' followed from clerks attending to private business (Qns. 81, 83). They received no direct answer. Ley was loth

and some initials. The list is otherwise as in Appendix 15, which the late O.C. Williams purported to be quoting (*Clerical Organisation*, p. 262); after observing that 'the number of agents mentioned is smaller' (i.e. than in 1827), he, strangely and inexplicably, omitted seven firms.

[1] See *Clerical Organisation*, p. 243, and P. Marsden, *The Officers of the House of Commons*, p. 137.

to condemn the existing arrangements. He thought private business was 'more satisfactorily done by clerks on the establishment than by other persons', for 'the House ought to have persons responsible to the Speaker, to inform him if the parties should attempt irregular proceedings'. There may have been something to be said for·that view at a time when there existed no such responsibility for private bills as was later placed upon the Chairman of Ways & Means and the Counsel to the Speaker. Unfortunately, evidence given later to the committee did not help to support the assumption that indoor agents would necessarily be the guardians of propriety. Nor was Ley's case strengthened by his adding, 'I would rather, however, that the clerks acting as agents should confine themselves to giving instructions to the attornies upon the practice of Parliament than they should take any active part in contests and mix themselves up in them'. Ley admitted that they 'take part in conducting Bills throughout, whether contested or not'. Neither Ley nor the committee (so far as can be judged from its report) appears to have realised that he was making a case for the supervision of private bills rather than for indoor agency. Asked whether their getting involved in contests produced inconvenience, Ley, instead of directly answering, observed: 'There are only two offices in which the clerks are great parliamentary agents. Mr. Dyson for two or three years together has very little to do in respect of his official duty, and Mr. Dorington has not a great deal to do as Clerk of the Fees'. The first part of that observation is borne out by Appendix 15 (see above p. 69, n. 4). As to the second part, it must be remembered, as Ley recognised elsewhere in his evidence, that Dyson was liable to be heavily occupied with Election Committees in sessions following general elections, and Dorington had other and more onerous duties as Parliamentary Agent to the Treasury. Ley had a more equivocal attitude to the relatively small amount of private business held by the Committee Office clerks. He thought, on the one hand, that they were sufficiently occupied without private business and, on the other, that there was no harm in each of them having a few private bills so long as their official duties were not neglected (Qns. 214-16).

No evidence was given that clerks engaged in parliamentary agency were generally neglecting their official duties or, as agents, taking improper advantage of their positions. But one instance of the latter was brought to the 1833 committee's attention. The complaint of a Mr. Henry Archer against the firm of Jones & Walmisley pointed to what was, wrote O.C. Williams, 'the chief objection to private business being conducted by the clerks . . . that clerks, having an opportunity of examining all proceedings at the earliest moment, enjoyed exceptional facilities for vexatious opposition'. The firm's action, Dr. Williams continued, 'was to substitute, quite illegally, a document of their own for a paper deposited in the Private Bill office . . . a proceeding impossible to an outside agent'[1] In his earlier work O.C. Williams wrote quite differently of the same incident: 'In spite of one complaint of sharp practice, which . . . turned out to have been more a formal than a real misdemeanour, it was agreed by witnesses that clerks acting as agents enjoyed no advantages over outside firms'.[2] It is perhaps worth noticing briefly what happened. Archer, a party to the promotion of a railway bill, believed he had cause to question Walmisley's competence as his agent − so he told the Select Committee. Therefore he watched Walmisley with some care. Noticing that Walmisley had deposited a subscription list which he (Walmisley) had prepared in insufficient detail to comply with standing orders, Archer taxed him with his error, whereupon Walmisley hastily prepared another in the proper form and substituted it for the first. Walmisley admitted his offence, but complicated matters by trying to implicate Archer. It is clear, however, that Walmisley did not include in the second list anything that he was not in a position to have put into the first (Qns. 1219-67). He had, from inexperience or carelessness, failed to comply with standing orders and had taken a course, presumably not open to an outside agent − at least without suborning one of the clerks − to correct his mistake. Whatever lesson was to be drawn from the episode, it was one which hardly lent credence to Ley's picture of indoor agents as safeguards against irregularities.

The committee's conclusions on parliamentary agency must be seen in the context of the desire for economy in and rationalisation of the pay of the clerical establishment which had been one reason for its appointment. They were based, probably, as much on its members' sense of what was fitting in changing conditions as on the evidence. The committee was 'impressed with a sense of the inconvenience which may result from the employment of officers of the House in private parliamentary business', and strongly objected to it. Having perceived the nettle, the committee timidly tugged at a small leaf. 'Feeling . . . much disinclination to interfere with the interests of persons who having been permitted for many years to devote their attention to private business, now derive considerable income from this source', the committee recommended merely that the clerks in the Private Bill Office and the Committee Office 'be forthwith prohibited' and that every officer thereafter appointed and not already so engaged 'be prohibited from undertaking the solicitation of Private Bills . . . '

1   *Clerical Organisation,* p. 264.
2   *HistPBProc.* I, 53.

(report, pp. 9-10). The clerks in the Private Bill Office were already forbidden to practise, and the ban on the Committee clerks would have left the 'great' indoor agents untouched; little wonder no action followed.

The 1835 committee had added to its terms of reference an instruction to continue the inquiry into House of Commons' offices, to report what recommendations of the 1833 Committee had been adopted and what further regulations might be necessary. It re-opened the whole question of agency by the clerks. Though finding no grounds for complaint that the clerks had neglected their official duties it embraced, more firmly than its predecessor, the principle of prohibition. 'After next Session', it reported, 'no Officer or Clerk belonging to the establishment of the House should be allowed to transact any private business before the House for his emolument or advantage, directly or indirectly'. (Rept, p.17). Its recommendations for applying the principle made some distinctions, viz.:

(i) No officer or clerk appointed since the session 1833 to transact thenceforth any private business, or directly or indirectly participate in any benefit arising therefrom;

(ii) The Committee clerks, their assistants, and the Private Bill Office clerks to be prohibited forthwith;

(iii) Other officers and clerks on the establishment previous to 1833 to be required to cease practising by 1 January 1840, unless within twelve months of the date of the report any such officer or clerk declared his intention to surrender public office, in which case he should be entitled to such compensation as may be determined.

Both committees gave attention to the functions and emoluments of the two principal indoor agents, Dorington and Dyson. Dorington himself impressed upon the 1833 Committee the nature and importance of his activities — not the functions suggested by his title of clerk of the Fees, but those which he and his predecessors had long carried out on behalf of the Treasury, and from which he derived the greater part of his official emoluments. 'The duties of the Parliamentary Agent to the Treasury', he related, 'are to conduct the Treasury business in Parliament much as a Parliamentary agent conducts a Private Bill. I am in perpetual communication with the Treasury, Board of Trade, and with the Solicitors of the Boards of Stamps, Excise, Assessed Taxes, &c., both on the business relating to their departments before Parliament, as well as any Bills which may affect them' (Qn. 395). He went on to explain (Qns. 396-411) that he prepared the resolutions of Supply and

Ways & Means, and other resolutions which on perusal of a bill he deemed necessary preparatory to its introduction; that he had to be entrusted with knowledge of the government's intentions especially in connection with new measures of taxation; and that he had a duty to ensure that 'the forms of the House' were observed in connection with all public business and to facilitate that business. He saw to it that amendments were introduced into public bills, as required, at the proper stage, that the bills were ingrossed correctly and sent to the Lords. He added, 'I also draw most of the Finance Bills, and various clauses for different Bills in progress'. It was for the performance and personal superintendance of this work, for taking 'care that all the proceedings during the whole time are correct', and 'for carrying on correspondence with the Public Boards and drawing the attention of the Treasury to the different Bills in the House which I think they ought to see', that he received his Treasury salary of £1,100 and £35 in lieu of stationery. For managing the passage of the Militia and Mutiny Acts he received £42 from the War Office, and for passing the Marine Mutiny Act £26.5s.0d. from the Admiralty.[1] Asked if such an office was necessary for public business, Dorington thought 'they could not get on without it', a view with which the committee seems to have concurred.

The combination of 'the management of Revenue and other Public Bills and the function of Clerk of the Fees' impressed the 1833 committee as an economical arrangement which ought to continue; they proposed to render it even more economical by instituting a parliamentary salary of £1,000, and no receipts from fees, for 'the Clerk of the Public Bill & Fee Office' (Report, p. 6). Parsimony apart, the new description was in recognition both of the character and importance of the office. The 1835 committee also supported this long-standing arrangement, but proposed that the business, and the clerk's emoluments should be under two heads. 'To conduct the business of the Treasury, Revenue Bills, Bills of every public department, and all public Bills before Parliament, English and Irish, brought in by individuals . . .' the holder of the office should receive an annual salary of £1,000, 'and no payment should be made by any other public office or department for the public service'. Second, for collecting all fees, not merely private bill Fees, payable to the House, and performing the duty of 'Paymaster of all salaries and charges on the House establishment' he should be allowed above the beforementioned

1 Thus the major (and only fixed) part of the emoluments of the clerk of the Fees was not a parliamentary salary. As clerk of the Fees he received 10s for every private bill and enacting clause; in that way he had £290 in 1829 (*ibid.* Qn. 84-92).

salary a percentage of £1.10s.0d. on the sums collected and received. The committee had noted that Dorington's emoluments (but not, of course, his income as a private parliamentary agent) had averaged £1,381 for the years 1833-4 (report pp. 4-7). As considerable cuts in salaries and emoluments were a general feature of both committee's recommendations, it was doubtless considered that Dorington was being treated with comparative generosity. It seems reasonable to assume that the terms, and the emphasis laid on the importance of his office, were meant as an inducement to Dorington to stay and relinquish his private practice.

It was otherwise with Dyson. He received but £100 *per annum* in fixed salary from the Treasury. Most of his highly variable official income was derived from fees on Election Committee proceedings, 'paid by the individuals litigating'; he had received in this way £1,759. 8s. 3d. in 1831, 'because there was a new Parliament', and, in 1832, £29. 25s. 0d.[1] The 1835 committee calculated that Dyson had, on average, £1,126 annually from this source. Neither committee attached importance to the office he held; the 1835 committee would have recommended its abolition, but accepted Ley's view that it should continue, proposing to consolidate with it the office of clerk of the Recognisances, and to add the duties of settling allowances for witnesses before Election Committees and of clerk to the Taxers of Private Bills. For all this the committee proposed a fixed salary of £600 per annum. Perhaps the committee expected – or hoped – that Dyson would jib; it noted that, 'Mr. Dyson is also employed largely as an Agent for Private Business, before the House, which engages the chief part of his time' (report p.8).

The 1836 committee was charged with considering what compensation should be granted to officers and clerks of the House 'for the loss of Salary, Fees and Emoluments which they will suffer in consequence of the changes recommended by the Select Committee of last Session being carried into effect'. It is to be noticed that the recommendations of the 1835 committee envisaged compensation for loss of public office but not for relinquishing private agency business. That this was a grievance may be seen from 'the Memorial of Several of the Officers and Clerks of the House of Commons engaged in

---

1 Ley's evidence to the 1833 Committee, Qn. 25. According to a return made by Dyson for the 1836 Committee the lean year in which he had only £29.16s. 0d. was 1829; his figure for 1832 was no less than £2,568. 5s.11d, a more likely figure in the political circumstances. In any case, as Dyson had to pay his unofficial clerks from his own pocket, somethng else was clearly needed when election business was slack.

Soliciting Private Bills', placed before the committee.[1] They submitted 'that when, from no blame imputable to them, the public service is conceived to require an important change, it is hardly consistent with any principle of equity that they should be made the sufferers. The mode of compensation directed by the committee of last session will compel many of the clerks to quit the service of the House, who would be most happy to remain if in lieu of receiving compensation for loss of office, they could obtain it for their private business'. It was of no avail, though Dorington, it may be thought, was treated exceptionally.

From J.E. Dorington, T. Dyson, and G.B. Ellicombe the committee had separate submissions.[2] Dorington showed his emoluments for the period 1828-35. Constant, apart from variations in the sums received annually from private bill fees, they averaged £1,412 per annum. He added, preferring the third person, 'his private business has produced him annually rather more than that sum, and is now considerably increasing . . . . The Committee may, perhaps, imagine, that he can dispose of his business; he can assure them this is not the case . . . perfectly certain and profitable during the time he continues personally engaged in it, it is not a property which can be disposed of except on indifferent terms'. Dorington calculated that if given 'full compensation' − which meant if he retired on pension − he would receive £1,053 per annum.[3] But he would 'be happy to remain in the service of the House' for three-fourths of that sum. This bold approach, or perhaps the importance with which this committee, like the earlier committees, viewed his office, stood him in good stead. Noting that 'Mr. Dorington has made his election to decline after the present Session all business as a solicitor of Private Bills, and to give his undivided attention to the duties of this House', and 'taking into consideration the long and valuable services of Mr. Dorington and the important duties he will have to perform', the committee recommended he be allowed an annual salary of £1,900, 'as Chief Clerk of the Public Bill and Fee Office, in consideration of his performing the several duties recommended by the Report of the Select Committee of last Session . . . in lieu of all other salary, fees, perquisites, and emoluments

1   HC (1836) 249, Appendix 11. It began, not without a touch of bathos, 'The Clerks of the House have enjoyed the privilege of soliciting Private Bills from time immemorial. Mr. Dorington's father practised previous to 1780, and his son has carried on the business since his death, a period of more than 56 years'. Mr. Dorington was, of course, John E. Dorington.

2   *Ibid.* Appendices 12, 15, and 14.

3   Under the provisions of 3 Geo. 4, c.113.

whatsoever' (report, p.6). Though not, perhaps, equalling the three-fourths of his 'full compensation', there was clearly a compensatory element in this award, which no other officer remaining in the service of the House was to receive.

John E. Dorington, who had already served for 36 years in 1836, remained in the service of the House of Commons until 1853, and continued to have an important connection with private bills. The Select Committee on Standing Orders Revision of 1843 asked the parliamentary agent, St. George Burke, 'do you give notice to the different Departments when a Bill is going into Committee?' and was told, 'Yes, Mr. Dorington does it; he is the agent for those public offices' . . . We supply him with . . . copies of the Bill for him to send round'.[1] Dorington gave the same committee details of this activity, and of his function of transmitting to parliamentary agents clauses or amendments desired by Government Departments.[2] Even after the development of the supervisory functions of the Chairman of Ways & Means, Dorington remained the intermediary. Thus the Chairman of Ways & Means told a select committee in 1851 that in communicating with the Government he went through Mr. Dorington, 'who seems to be the general overlooker of these points for the government offices', and when Departments communicated with him 'Mr. Dorington is generally the intervening person'.[3]

To the select committee of 1836 Thomas Dyson made no plea, contenting himself with an account of his emoluments for the years 1829 and 1831-5, those for 1830 having been lost in the fire at Westminster. The committee appears to have been no more anxious than its predecessors to retain Dyson. Indeed, it reported that his decision to resign office afforded an opportunity for consolidating the duties of the clerk of Elections with those of the committee clerk's office, and recommended for Dyson an annuity of £800, in consideration of his 28 years' service. G.B. Ellicombe had no record of long service to support his claim for compensation. Having elected to go, he was awarded £488, being two years' average salary since his appointment in 1830. He went expressing a grievance which shows that the attractions of indoor agency had operated that recently. 'I beg to state', he wrote, 'that I served the full period of my articles with a Solicitor in London, and relinquished my profession upon the expectation of holding a permanent situation at the House, with full liberty to conduct

1 HC (1843) 550, Qn. 450.
2 *Ibid.* Qns. 593-622.
3 HC (1851) 35, Qn. 206.

Private business as my predecessors had done. I am, however, most unwillingly compelled to surrender my situation at the House of Commons . . . and this without any blame being attached to my conduct . . .'.

Important as the prohibition of agency by the clerks was in principle, its effects have sometimes been exaggerated. J.E. Dorington, as we have seen, chose to remain indoors; so did his leading indoor partner and subordinate in the Fees Office, Arthur Jones. Thus ended their connection with the firm of J. Dorington & Co. – or at least any overt connection, for one is left wondering what private agreements they may have had with Ellicombe as to who should stay and who should go. Indoors, G.B. Ellicombe had practised both independently and in partnership with Dorington and Jones; outside he was a partner in the firm of J. Dorington & Co., which continued to flourish. There is, of course, no evidence of any arrangement among them. When Thomas Dyson went he took with him his unofficial assistant and partner in agency, R. Hall, who having no official emoluments had no compensation. They became, as Dyson & Hall, an outstanding firm of professional parliamentary agents. Richard Jones and John Walmisley also went – with no compensation having no official income – to form a firm of some importance but hardly a leading one.[1] Of the remaining five Commons' clerks mentioned in Appendix 15 to the Report of the 1833 Committee as having private business, John Bull, clerk of the Journals, had died in 1835, and the four committee clerks, W.G. Rose, S. Gunnell, G. Gunnell, and G. White, remained indoors and gave up their small private businesses. Of the two Lords' clerks mentioned, E. Parratt remained indoors and E. Walmisley went, to form with another member of the Parratt family the firm of Parratt & Walmisley, again no leading firm.

It hardly amounted to an upheaval, and was certainly no adequate basis for the impression given by Clifford, or the official myth which developed later in the nineteenth century, that the prohibition of the clerks was the origin of professional parliamentary agency. It was a

---

1 Subsequently, Jones & Walmisley claimed compensation, jointly and individually, for losses caused by the fire at Westminster. For 'a great variety of different Acts of Parliament . . . put by . . . for facilitating their business as Parliamentary Agents' they claimed jointly £50. John Walmisley claimed £81.15s.10d. for 'various items', and Richard Jones £260. for 'one set of Private Acts . . . 200 volumes . . . invaluable in his business as a Parliamentary Agent . . . (and) other books'. Jones believed there was 'now but one set of Private Acts in existence, the property of Mr. Bramwell of the Temple, who, on being asked to sell the same, asked 1,000 1. or guineas'. – Select Committee on the . . . Fire in the Houses of Parliament, HC (1837-8) 8, Appendix pp. 18, 19.

slender enough foundation for O.C. Williams's statement that 'several of the Clerks chose . . . the alternative [of leaving the House], thus founding some of the leading firms of Parliamentary agents . . .'.[1] In fact a number of important wholly outdoor firms already existed, and of the many firms active in the late 1830s and the 1840s, three — that founded by T.M. Sherwood; Dorington & Co.; and Dyson & Hall — were by far the leading firms. The first had no indoor connections, and only the third was the result of a straightforward choice between clerkship and agency.

The first Speaker's Rules for
parliamentary agents

The 1835 Committee had urged that parliamentary agents 'should be in some degree answerable to the Speaker and the Clerk of the House for correct conduct and for their observance of the Rules and Orders of the House' (report, p.17). Clearly the committee was concerned particularly about arrears of fees said to exist at times, and suggested that no agent should be allowed to proceed on any matter until fees due on any previous proceeding he had conducted had been paid. There was no wish to place any restriction on the number of agents. On 16 August 1836 the House was moved by Joseph Hume to take notice of this recommendation, and resolved that 'Mr. Speaker be requested to prepare and publish such regulations as he may think best calculated to accomplish the object of the Committee'.[2] In pursuance of this resolution the first Speaker's Rules were announced to the House in March 1837, and ordered to be printed.[3] They are reproduced in Appendix H below. It is to be noticed that they provided no positive control over entry to the profession; that, as may be seen from chapter six below, was to be long in coming.

The Commons' Supplements to Votes & Proceedings between 1836 and 1847 include much material relating to private bills. Their bulk is accounted for mainly by the reports from private bill committees on railway bills, who were required as a result of the recommendations of the Select Committee on Railway Bills of 1836 to report on some twenty financial, technical and other points before any railway bill was

1 *Hist.PBProc.* I, 53.
2 CJ (1836) 81.
3 CJ (1837) 13, HC (1837) 88.

allowed to proceed.[1] From 1841 these reports begin to name the parliamentary agents for and against the bills, at first only occasionally; those for 1841 name twelve agents, four of whom were former indoor agents; those for 1842 identify fifteen. The reports for 1845 and 1846 evidently were compiled with more uniformity, many though not all including the agents' names. Their greater regularity of form was probably a consequence of the important experiment of small, impartial private bill committees which pressure of business forced the Commons to make in 1844 and to repeat more extensively in 1845. A reform introduced by the Lords with marked success in 1837 hitherto had been resisted stoutly by the Commons, in favour of the old principle of committees of indefinite size and local representation. The experiment was recommended in the second report of the Select Committee on Railway Bills of 1844, and successfully moved by Gladstone, as chairman of the committee, on 4 March 1844.[2]

The table which follows is compiled from the reports of railway bill committees for 1846. Clearly it is not a complete list of agents engaged in the promotion of and opposition to railway bills, as can be seen from the number of petitions involved. The identification of agents in the reports is a growing habit, not an invariable feature. Nevertheless it may be treated as a reasonably representative list, so far as a list confined to a single year can be. It offers an interesting comparison with Appendix A, which includes a substantially complete list of agents active in promoting bills during the period 1847-9, and compiled on a basis only possible from 1847 onwards. The present table shows the large number of oppositions some agents were involved in. Multiple oppositions were of course, a feature of many railway bills. For instance, included in the oppositions conducted by Burke, Pritt & Co. (Sherwoods), are 27 against the London & Oxford Railway Bill. The reports on which it is based reveal one interesting if occasional feature, which would not be found in agency later — instances of firms acting for both promoters and opponents of a bill. Burke, Pritt & Co., for example, were agents for the promoters of the Blackburn, Chorley and Liverpool Railway Bills, and for two railway companies petitioning against it, and Dyson & Co. acted on behalf of three petitioners against

1   HC (1836) 511. For the twenty points, which as O.C. Williams remarked, placed upon private bill committees the kind of responsibilities later required to be exercised by government departments, and a summary of other recommendations of this committee, see *HistPBProc.*, I, 62-3.

2   HC (1844) 79, and Parl. Deb. HC (1844) 78, cc. 516 ff. See for the proposals of the Committee, *Hist.PBProc.*, I, 85, and Clifford I, 841-2. For the views of parliamentary agents on the important question of the constitution of private bill committees see below, pp. 93-100.

the St. Helens Canal and Railway Bill as well as being the promoters' agents.

Parliamentary Agents named in Report of Private Bills Committees on Railways (Commons) 1846.

Firm	Promotions	Oppositions	Remarks
1 Bircham & Co	–	17	Primarily solicitors, active in agency later
2 Browne & Son	–	3	Pre-1827 outdoor firm
3 (Bulmer & Co.	1	9	Local business (Leeds area). Durnford a prominent name in agency later
(Bulmer & Durnford	2		
4 Burke, Pritt & Co. (Sherwoods)	56	136	Pre-1827 outdoor firm
5 Cameron & Bain	1	–	
6 Deans, Dunlop & Co.	11	37	Scottish business
7 Dorington & Co.	13	68	
8 Drew & Co.	–	4	
9 Dyson & Hall	5	50	
10 Grahame & Weems	6	14	Scottish business
11 Jones & Walmisley	2	13	
12 Mr. Lang	9	7	Mainly Scottish business
13 Law Anton & Turnbull	–	12	
14 Parkes & Co.	6	43	
15 Richardson, Connell & Loch	8	41	Scottish business. Pre-1827 outdoor firm
16 Spottiswoode & Robertson	–	1	"
17 Webster & Co.	2	12	"
18 Other firms promoting a single bill or engaged in oppositions only	1	53	(Conducted by 23 firms)

4

MATTERS OF PROCEDURE
1836-1868

In the thirty years or so from 1836 select committees of the House of Commons relating to private business averaged at least one a year, and committees on standing orders revision were almost equally numerous. Parliamentary agents had much influential evidence to give on the problems of private bill procedure during the period of its most rapid development. Sometimes they gave it as individuals, but increasingly on behalf of the association, then formed, which developed into the Society of Parliamentary Agents and whose early history is referred to in chapter five. At its start the association appears to have been a club rather than a professional body. Its earliest minute to refer to business records that 'a general opinion was expressed that all standing orders are a nuisance, and that the Select Committee of '42 are noodles'. No doubt time has purged any contempt. Soon, in more serious vein, the association was resolving to draw up and circulate at its own expense a statement, 'in consequence of Mr. Speaker having decided that it was incompetent for Committees to alter the Preamble of Bills'.[1] The statement, if drafted, has not survived, but the subject was one of several to be looked at here on which parliamentary agents had their say — and in having it helped to shape procedure.

Proof of compliance with standing orders

That 'standing orders were a nuisance' could seriously be held in at least one respect: in face of the volume and character of railway legislation from the mid 1830s the old arrangements for proving compliance with standing orders were becoming excessively costly and burdensome, especially as they afforded many opportunities for vexatious opposition. The leading parliamentary agents deplored the kind of opposition thus facilitated, though lesser practitioners, more concerned with conducting oppositions, may not have done.

The old practice of the House of Commons relating to proof of compliance was based on a standing order of 1734, which, was in turn based on a resolution of 1716.[2] It was loosely worded, requiring that

1 Min SPA, Dec. 1842, January 1843.
2 CJ (1714-18) 496 and (1732-37) 396. For the detailed history of this and associated standing orders see *Hist.PBProc.*, II, 102-4.

no bill for repairing any highway, or for other works to be carried on by tolls or duties levied on the subject be brought in until the petition had been referred to a committee which was to examine 'the Matter thereof' and report the same to the House. Thus originated the Committees on Petitions, as indeterminate and often as large as any eighteenth-century private bill committee. In 1774, when the first standing orders requiring the giving of notices and the making of deposits were made, these committees were given the duty of reporting whether standing orders had been complied with. In practice, the main function of committees on petitions became that of reporting on compliance with standing orders, without any discretionary power, and, as Dr. William's observed, 'canvassing prevailed, and all ingenuity was exercised by opponents in tripping up promoters on standing order points'.[1] It is not so certain, however, that the wider function of reporting 'on the Matter thereof' had become entirely obsolete, as Dr. Williams thought, before the orders just referred to were superseded in 1836. T.M. Sherwood, writing in 1834, noted that 'the duty of the Committee on the Petition is to exact from the Petitioners for the Bill *prima facie* evidence of compliance with Standing Orders, and such a substantiation of a *prima facie* case of expediency as may justify the introduction of the Bill'.[2] Though he went on to emphasise that the powers of the committee were 'limited to the execution of this duty' and that they could not 'admit the arguments or the evidence of parties inimical to the prayer of the Petition', he also drew attention to the way in which the intention of the standing orders governing the committee on a petition was 'not infrequently evaded, by an expedient which does not seem quite defensible. A Member hostile to the Bill is supplied by the adverse parties with such questions as they would put were they permitted to oppose; and availing himself of the right . . . as a Member of the Committee to ask any questions and to call for any evidence . . . raises an opposition . . . which it is the object of the Standing Order . . . to prevent'.[3]

It was a sometime partner in the firm founded by Sherwood, St. George Burke, who, among the agents practising in the promotion of railway bills in the later 1830s, was foremost in condemning as unworthy and vexatious much of the opposition on standing orders and deploring the opportunities afforded to it by current practice.[4] By the time he

1 *HistPBProc.*, I, 68.

2 T.M. Sherwood: *Treatise, etc. on Private Bills,* 3rd.edn (1834), p.7.

3 *Ibid.* p. 8.

4 For example before the Select Committee on Standing Orders, HC (1837) 489, Qn.201. It must, of course, be noted that procedural arrangements were not

first did so steps had been taken towards reforming this aspect of procedure. The ad hoc committees had been replaced by a sessional Select Committee on Petitions of 42 members, with power to divide into sub-committees; standing orders had provided for the petitioners complaining of non-compliance to be heard by themselves, agents, and witnesses; and committees on bills had been forbidden to entertain questions of compliance with the standing orders directed to be proved before the committee on petitions. These changes had been supported by parliamentary agents and were welcomed. But the habit of exploiting standing order points to fight bills was well-established. With the spate of railway bills in 1844 and 1845 the prolixities of proving and disproving compliance brought serious congestion which palliatives like reducing the quorum for the committee on petitions could do little to allay. Before a Select Committee on Standing Orders Revision in 1845 Burke gave lengthy evidence[1] He referred to an 'unworthy system' of opposition. He favoured the appointment of a single officer of the House, so long as he was one in whom the parties might have confidence, to inquire into proof of compliance. By a majority, that committee rejected the proposal, but reform was urgent and the matter was considered again in 1846 both by a select committee of the House of Lords, concerned principally with the extravagant expenses connected with obtaining Acts of Parliament, and a Commons committee on private bills, chaired by Joseph Hume, with wider terms of reference.[2] Both concluded, in the words of the former committee's report, that proofs of compliance should be taken 'before some proper authority of both Houses of Parliament, whose report might be received as evidence of the facts by the Standing Orders Committee'.[3]

These recommendations led to the appointment, by both Houses in 1846, of official Examiners to take proofs of compliance of petitions for private bills. From 1855 the Houses shared common Examiners and in 1858 their powers in respect to both Houses were assimilated. Doubtless it was pressure of business that did most to bring about this important change. And it was not only parliamentary agents who had influenced the committees just referred to. The head of the Railway

the only cause of difficulty in connection with compliance; the requirements of standing orders imposed great problems especially on promoters of railway bills. Burke told this committee that it was impossible to meet accurately every minute requirement.

1 HC (1845) 570, Qns. 90-249.

2 Lords Committee on Railways, ordered by the House of Commons to be printed HC (1846) 489: Commons committee HC (1846) 556.

3 HC (1846) 489, Rept. p. iv.

Department at the Board of Trade had given his opinion to the Lords' committee that complying and proving compliance with standing orders was the portion of the parliamentary system that worked 'worse than any other'; it was 'expensive and uncertain', frequently defeated the objects for which it was intended, and often led to the rejection of good measures on technical grounds.[1] But the evidence of agents, and particularly of St. George Burke, was prominent. Burke told the Commons committee that proofs of compliance 'incur enormous expense'. Though he was not prepared to commit himself as to the most expensive example, he mentioned 'the South Eastern Railway Bill' for which the number of witnesses in respect of standing orders was over 400 and the cost, he believed, over £10,000.[2] The appointment of Examiners could not by itself have sufficed to end that kind of thing, but the great extension in 1847 of power to admit proof by affidavit effected much improvement. Burke had deplored above all the lack of discretion in the system of proof before the Committee on Petitions which had led to 'that wretched system of standing orders opposition which takes place now'. He had spoken of having warned his own clients not to persist with frivolous objections based on minor errors of fact, but in vain, for they felt obliged to seize every chance to throw a bill out – the committee had no discretion and had to report non-compliance.[3]

The abolition of the committee on petitions, the establishment of Examiners, the extension of proof by affidavit, and certain associated reforms, it has been said, nearly halved the time taken on proofs of compliance.[4] In November 1846, the Speaker issued regulations for the deposit of petitions in the Private Bill Office and for determining the order in which they would be heard by the Examiners. A register was to be kept 'with blank lines numbered consecutively from 1 to 500'. Petitions were to set down for hearing in the order in which they were deposited, or on any blank line which the parliamentary agent chose. If two or more agents appeared simultaneously at the Private Bill office their names were to be put 'in a ballot glass', to decide in what order they should be allowed to select numbers on the register. At the end of the period allowed for the deposit of petitions the parliamentary agents were to be allowed 'to exchange by agreement the numbers originally assigned to their Petitions', or re-assign them to positions still blank

---

1   HC (1846) 489, Qn. 1034, cited *HistPBProc.*, I, 73.
2   HC (1846) 556, Qn. 954.
3   *Ibid.*, Qns. 983-990.
4   *Hist.PBProc.*, I, 75.

in the register. Finally a 'General List of Petitions' was to be made out by the Private Bill Office, 'according to the order in which they shall have been finally entered in the register', published for the convenience of agents and parties, and the petitions were to be heard by the Examiners in that order.[1]

The following year a Select Committee of the House of Commons on Private Bills, again chaired by Joseph Hume, questioned five prominent parliamentary agents about the new system. They all expressed unqualified satisfaction at a great improvement, and the committee itself described the new system of examiners as a success.[2] In 1863 Thomas Coates, who was about to become President of the Society of Parliamentary Agents, looked back on the old system and assessed the new. Proving compliance with standing orders, he said, was, 'in former days . . . a subject of great abuse . . . before the present system was established it was a regular part of the system that a Bill should be opposed upon the standing orders. . . . It was hoped by accumulating a number of slight matters the opponents might defeat the Bill'. Of the reformed system he went on: 'There must be an inquiry as to the fulfilment of standing orders, and I do not believe it can be done more efficiently and economically than it is now . . . futile objections are dealt with lightly and dismissed, and . . . important objections have all the attention given to them which they ought to have'.[3]

The functions of Private Bill Committes

It was noticed in chapter two that, gradually, in the first three decades of the nineteenth century the hearing of suitors against private bills at the bar of the House declined and, implicitly, the role of private bill committees was enlarged. When C.T. Ellis published his *Practical Remarks* in 1802 he was sure that the place to oppose the principle of a private bill was before the whole House on second reading; in those circumstances, he wrote, an order is made for the parties to be heard by their counsel at the time appointed for seconding reading.[4] George Bramwell, in 1809, noted that counsel 'may' be heard on second reading.[5] As late as 1825, another writer maintained that opposing petitioners could be heard in committee only against particular clauses, 'since the

1 The text is reproduced in *Hist.PBProc.*, II, 105-6.

2 HC (1847) 705, Rept. pp. iii and iv); Mins, of Evidence Qns. 509, 584, 585, 604-6, 811, 813, 818.

3 HC (1863) 385. Qns. 1481, 1482.

4 *Practical Remarks*, p. 39. Similar procedure applied in the Lords, *ibid.* p. 33.

5 *Proceedings, etc.*, p. 44.

principle of the Bill must be opposed at the bar of the House'.[1] In fact
the last orders for petitioners so to be heard — and they did not take
effect — were made the previous year. By the 1830s, parliamentary
agents and others writing or giving evidence on practice were aware of a
change though uncertain about its completeness. To a select comittee
of 1833 John E. Dorington said the quantity of business 'renders it
nearly impracticable to discuss the merits of a private bill on second
reading'; he thought it 'almost useless' to present a petition and raise a
question at that stage 'though that is certainly the proper stage for an
opposition on the whole of the Bill'.[2] In 1836 John Halcomb thought
it unfair to promoters for a bill to be thrown out on second reading,
remarking, significantly, that it was before they had an opportunity to
put their case.[3] Two years later, Benjamin Lumley told his readers,
'petitions praying to be heard by counsel against the Bill are now usually
referred to the committee on the Bill'.[4] But it was the important
parliamentary agent, T.M. Sherwood, in the third (1834) edition of his
Treatise on the Proceedings on Private Bills, etc., who provided the
fullest exposition of current practice — or rather of what he considered
practice ought to be, for he found himself arguing at one point against
'the doctrine laid down by Committees'.

Opposition to a private bill on second reading, though 'by no means
uncommon' was, Sherwood considered, not 'consistent with fairness or
propriety', unless the bill was obnoxious to the public interest. The
latter, he observed, was usually 'the professed ground', but 'opponents
substitute their own interest for that of the public'. He believed such
opposition ought not to take place on second reading, where 'the merits
or the demerits of a Private Bill cannot, with certainty, be known. . . .
It is in the Committee only that the merits or demerits . . . can be
proved; for it is there only that evidence is received . . .'.[5] Sherwood
was quite clear that the House no longer received evidence on second
reading. He appears to have been concerned, rather, with opposition
conducted through the assertions and representations of Members. His
view of the matter led him to consider the powers and duties of a
committee on a private bill, which he believed had never been 'clearly

---

1 Anthony Hammond; *Treatise on the Practice and Proceedings of Parliament,*
cited *Hist.PBProc.,* I, 57.

2 HC (1883) 648, Qns. 2127, 2136. Dr. Williams, who also cites this evidence,
rather surprisingly considered that it showed the change 'fully established' *Hist.
PBProc.,* I, 57.

3 *A Practical Treatise,* p. 92.

4 *Parliamentary Practice,* p. 116.

5 Sherwood; *Treatise on the Proceedings,* pp. 37-8.

defined or expressly stated'. He offered the following definition:

> The *object* of the reference to a Committee on a Private Bill may be thus generally defined, – the ascertaining the opinion of the Committee, whether the measure proposed be a necessary measure, and whether it be the most eligible mode of providing for that necessity. The powers and duties of the Committee are confined to the receiving proof in favour of, and in opposition to, the principle and provisions of the Bill; the making such amendments and alterations in the Bill as they may deem expedient; and the reporting such Bill to the House'.[1]

Though Sherwood wrote in terms of the limits to the powers and duties of committees, the importance of this passage lay in the way it maintained that private bill committees were concerned as much with the principles and expediency of a measure as with its provisions, with the preamble as with the clauses. It was before the committee that the preamble must be proved and could be challenged. And the committee was fully competent to amend the preamble not limited to settling the clauses. Sherwood found this 'the practice which of late years has invariably prevailed', yet it was here that he also found himself at variance with 'the doctrine laid down by Committees'. That doctrine he summarised thus: 'An opposition to the principle must be raised on the second reading and may not be urged in the Committee'. It was, he held, founded on a false, or at least an inexpedient and inequitable, analogy, between public and private bills. In respect to a public bill and especially to the practice of committees of the whole House, it was undoubtedly true. But the case of a private bill, 'where so much must depend on locality and circumstance, where it is impossible to arrive at any just conclusion without the examination of evidence, and where evidence is not received on second reading . . . ' – is quite different. Sherwood found 'the modern practice of permitting the opponents to impugn the principle in Committee . . . at once just and expedient'. He pointed out that committees had 'of late years' changed their custom of requiring opponents to prove their case before promoters were called upon to substantiate their preamble. It was now the practice for promoters to prove their preamble in the first instance. The older practice had been based on the ground that the principle of a bill was recognised by the House on second reading; the new one afforded 'one of the most conclusive arguments that the principle of the Bill may be questioned in the Committee'.

Evidently there was a gulf between theory and practice. When, within a few years, it became difficult to negotiate, parliamentary

---

1   *Ibid.* p. 46.

agents gave forthright and influential evidence, helping to establish an important modern principle of private bill practice.

In 1843 the committee on the Gorbals Police Bill, a bill with many objects, struck out of the preamble a part which they held had not been established by the evidence. The parliamentary agent for the promoters explained subsequently that either the committee sent or one of the clerks went to the Speaker, who 'said the proceeding was bad' and sent the bill back to the committee to restore the words. The committee sat again upon the whole bill and, understanding that they could not alter the preamble in any one point, threw it out altogether. The agent then obtained a re-committal and the bill passed with the preamble in the form desired by the original committee.[1] As a result of this unsatisfactory proceeding the Select Committee on standing orders revision of 1843 was asked to consider 'to what extent and under what restrictions Committees on Private Bills may alter the Preamble of Private Bills'.[2] Its Chairman, Lord Granville Somerset, was a staunch champion of local representation on private bill committees; its members included T. Greene, Chairman of Ways & Means. Among the witnesses were four parliamentary agents — A. Grahame, agent for the promoters of the Gorbals Police Bill; John Richardson, who had been agent for the opposition which eventually but not initially put in an appearance, J.R. Hayward, and that favourite of witnesses before select committees on private bill procedure, J. St. George Burke.

Grahame revealed that the provision thrown out at the committee's first hearing 'did interfere with other public bodies, but with consent'; there had been no petition against it and therefore no cross-examination; the committee, which had been 'numerously attended', had divided after hearing 'such evidence as the parties thought fit to establish their case'; and, having altered the preamble by striking out the provision referred to, the committee had indicated that they were still open to receive proof of its necessity. This strange invitation to the promoters to stage a kind of appeal before it against its own decision suggests a state of great procedural uncertainty. Richardson said it had stimulated his clients to appear and give evidence.[3]

The four parliamentary agents drew on their experience to tell the select committee what they conceived the usual practice to be. Grahame,

---

1 HC (1843) 550, Qns. 2, 3, 26-28. It is not clear whether the promoters or the second committee removed the offending matter. The agent contradicted himself on this point.

2 HC (1843) 550.

3 *Ibid.* Qns. 1-88, 89-180, 352-424, 201-316.

in his nine sessions as an agent, had found it 'decidedly' the practice of committees to alter preambles in the way that had been done in the Gorbals Police Bill; he had never known it resisted before, although he mentioned that his partner, Connell, had had a similar experience that session with another Scottish bill. If there had been formerly a rule that committees could not alter preambles, it should be changed. Looking back over his 'five and thirty years' as an agent, Richardson had a 'vague recollection' that when he started 'there was an opinion' that committees could not alter preambles, but added 'I am sure that for 15 or 20 years past committees have been accustomed to alter preambles constantly'. Hayward, who had then been 'connected with parliamentary business for 22 years', had 'never heard a doubt suggested till the present Session: when I have been asked "What is the practice of Parliament?", my answer has been, "You may alter a bill in Committee from the 'whereas' in the first page to the last word at the end of the Bill"'. He went, in detail, into some of the circumstances in which the preambles to ten of his bills had been altered in committee during the session of 1842. And St. George Burke, though maintaining that alteration of preambles was not 'a very common practice' as they were generally prepared 'in such manner that parties are enabled to prove them', had no hesitation in saying that the place to alter them was in committee. He cited an example from the current Session, a South Eastern Railway Bill, in which 'extensive alteration' to the preamble was necessary and had been made as a result of opposition on certain clauses. More strikingly and illustrative perhaps of inconsistency in practice, he instanced the Taff Vale Railway Bill of 1840, the preamble of which had recited an increase in tolls to which there had been opposition. The point had been discussed on second reading, divided upon, and carried by a majority of one; yet the committee on the bill (which had also divided) had struck out the toll provision.

Grahame confirmed that, as a practical agent, he would decidedly prefer that preambles should be altered in committee. He thought the extent of alterations could safely be left to the discretion of committees — subject, presumably, to the limitation to be noticed presently. For Richardson the practice was 'quite expedient and necessary. . . indispensible . . . if the object is to pass a consistent and efficient bill'; without the power measures excellent in general outline could be lost. But all four agents were insistent that there was, and should be, no power for a committee to amend a preamble in such a way as to extend the scope of a bill. St. George Burke, had never known this to have been done. Grahame, who could recollect an instance where matter was added 'within the notices' but only by leave of the House and upon an instruction to the committee, would not have committees allowed to add powers. That was 'quite unnecessary: under the present standing orders it is generally out of their power'. The doctrine, as supported by all the parliamentary agents, was (to adapt evidence given at various points by St. George Burke) that a preamble cannot be amended 'by putting (in) new matter which would involve any alteration of the standing orders' — by which he clearly meant any change in the applicability of standing orders. 'You certainly should not extend beyond your notices . . . but as to any alteration by striking out a portion or rendering it more clear as regards the wording . . . you can do that'.

Influential as it was ultimately, this view of practice was not liked by the chairman of the select committee. Lord Granville Somerset repeatedly referred to the injustice he conceived might be done if committees entertained any restrictions or cutting down of the original provisions of bills. He had in mind principally railway bills, and considered injustice would be done if a committee required or permitted the promoters to proceed with a smaller scheme than their bill had originally provided for. The parliamentary agents stoutly resisted this approach. The chairman's persistence led two of them, St. George Burke and J.R. Hayward, to question at length the necessity for preambles. Although, declared Burke, he favoured, in the public interest, a preamble 'which fairly stated the principal objects of a Bill', a preamble was not an essential part of a bill; if the power to alter preambles were completely prevented he would advise his clients to 'make the preamble as meagre as possible'. Hayward, whose practice had been 'to cut down preambles as much as possible', knew of public but not private bills without preambles; he was unaware of anything in standing orders requiring private bills to have them and if any restrictive rule were imposed preventing committees altering preambles it 'would oblige me and my friend Mr. Burke' to frame a preamble which said nothing. The persistent Chairman asked if 'practically speaking' it would be possible 'to lay down any rule enforcing such a preamble as would give full knowledge of the objects of the Bill?' That, said Hayward, would be 'practically impossible and quite useless if it were practicable'.

The respective purposes of second reading and committee stages on a private bill were not neglected. The agent, A. Grahame, contended that the objection to alteration of preambles in committee rested on the supposed rule that on second reading the House not only assents to the principle but adopts it as contained in the preamble. He believed that with both public and private bills the House assented to the principle on second reading, but did not adopt the words of the preamble. The preamble of a public bill, he continued, can be adapted to changes made in the committee stage and, by analogy, the preamble of a private bill was adaptable in committee. Encouraged by the Chairman of Ways & Means, he went further and assented to the view that a private bill second reading was *pro forma* and in reality the House sent the question of the principle of a bill to be decided by the committee. And this was the view put forward by St. George Burke, about to become a partner in the firm founded by T.M. Sherwood. Sherwood's treatise had not been mentioned in the proceedings. But perhaps its echo may be heard in the following stately exchange between Burke and the chairman of the committee:

> Qn.215 (St. George Burke): 'I hold this great distinction between public and private Bills, that on second reading of a private Bill (I may be wrong in my idea) the House do not affirm the principle of the Bill, but, on the contrary, they in no manner do so; they send it to the Committee to inquire whether the allegations are correct'.

> Qn.216 (Chairman): 'You would compare it to the finding of a Grand Jury, saying in effect that the general objects of the Bill are of a nature to be entertained by the House, but as to the particular points, to leave them to be ascertained by the tribunal to whom they refer the Bill' — 'Your Lordship puts it exactly according to my impression'.

Clearly Burke was destined for the parliamentary bar, where he had later a long and successful career.

The influence the parliamentary agents had on the findings of the committee cannot be measured precisely, but the findings and recommendations followed the agents' evidence, and the recommendations stabilised committee procedure on amendment of preambles in its modern form. The committee found that alteration of preambles by committee on private bills 'has been practised for many years' and that the alterations 'have not been of such a nature as to cause an extension of the objects of the Bill . . . as sanctioned . . . on second reading'. They recommended that 'this practice continue' under the limitations that 'nothing in any degree inconsistent with the notices given in compliance with the standing orders should be introduced . . . every alteration so made should be specially noticed in the report' and 'the ground of making it' should be stated.[1] The first limitation was, of course, of basic importance, the others, possibly, a concession to the chairman's misgivings.

The evidence reviewed above included an exchange on the virtues of private bill committees 'as they are now constituted'. They were, Grahame allowed, 'a great deal better than formerly'; but they could

---

1   HC (1843) 550, Rept. p. iii.

be improved. 'The more they approximate to a judicial tribunal the better'. Few things were more important to the nature of private bill procedure than the composition and character of committees on bills. To this matter and to the views of parliamentary agents, it is now necessary to turn.

Committees on Private Bills

In July 1837 the House of Lords adopted additional standing orders by which all opposed private bills were to be referred to committees of five disinterested peers, chosen by a committee of selection. Sitting hours were laid down and continuity of sitting from day to day provided for. The selected members were required to attend throughout the proceedings and other peers prohibited from taking any part in them. No peer was to serve on a committee on a bill in which he had any interest. At a stroke, as the result of a process not, to my knowledge, documented but which we may surmise reflected the wishes of Lord Shaftesbury, the Lords put behind themselves open committees, with the attendant possibilities of canvassing, packing and other forms of manipulation, and established for themselves the modern system of small impartial private bill committees. So rapid a radical change was not for the elected House. Before 1826 Commons private bill committees were theoretically unlimited in size, being composed of such Members as the Member in charge of a bill chose to name in the House and the locally interested Members serving for the county or counties affected by a bill, and there was no means of requiring committee Members to attend throughout the proceedings. Moreover, that they were 'large and floating bodies . . . from 60 to 70 up to 200 . . .' was not all; as C.T. Ellis pointed out at the beginning of the century, 'The order "that all Members who come to the Committee have voices" is generally applied for and made when a bill is opposed'.[1]
Thus Members who were not of the committee could be whipped in or otherwise persuaded to vote if it divided, without having taken any other part in its proceedings.

Private bill committees so constituted were hardly judicial in character or in practice, nor was the position of their chairmen impartial. In practice the chairman was usually the Member in charge of the bill, often, it has been said, being 'the advocate, or at least the friendly assistant and counsellor of the promoters', with a position resembling 'that of the chairman of a municipal committee endeavour-

---

1 F.H. Spencer; *Municipal Origins,* pp. 54-5 and C.T. Ellis: *Practical Remarks,* p. 45.

ing "to get a project through" '.[1] The timorous attempts at reform of private bill committees in 1825-6, produced a reduction in the theoretical maximum size of opposed bill committees to 120, but local representation, based on revised county lists of Members, was carefully preserved and no means were found for compelling attendance at committee proceedings. On the other hand the practice that 'all who come have voices' was discountenanced and appears to have declined subsequently: T.M. Sherwood, who in the earlier editions of his treatise wrote of 'the pernicious effects' of this practice, noted in his third (1834) edition that it 'happily, has been entirely abandoned'.[2] The manipulation of attendances at large committees obviously remained a preoccupation of parliamentary agents or at least some kind of agent of the parties. It was done not only to obtain favourable results in a division, but occasionally to prolong or even abort proceedings by getting a committee to adjourn *sine die* or vote its chairman out of the chair. Sherwood described these practices as 'most objectionable and dangerous . . . expedients . . . irregular and unparliamentary'.

Between 1837 and 1843 at least five Commons select committees considered or had their attention drawn to the constitution of committees on opposed bills. The detailed improvements relating to committees made in this period, including the establishment in 1840 of the Committees of Selection, revised, smaller, county lists, and better regulation of attendance at committees, form the background to the remark by the agent A. Graham, already cited, that committees were 'a great deal better than formerly'. But reform on the lines adopted by the House of Lords was strongly resisted on the grounds both that it was expedient to have locally interested Members to provide local knowledge and that Members had a right and duty to represent their constituents' interests in committees as well as in the House.[3] The Select Committee on Private Business of 1838 took evidence from four parliamentary agents, a solicitor with a parliamentary practice, and John E. Dorington who, of course, had by that time ceased to be a private parliamentary agent. In 1840 a similar committee heard three of those agents again together with one who had not appeared before the earlier committee.[4] Though from others there was 'conflicting

1 Spencer; *Municipal Origins,* p. 53. Spencer quotes the remark of a committee clerk to a select committee in 1825, who said he had never found the arguments of counsel or the evidence to have shaken a chairman's opinion.

2 Sherwood; p. 34 footnote.

3 The second argument had the powerful support of Sir Robert Peel, See *Hist PBProc.,* I, 81.

4 HC (1837-8) 679 and (1840) 56. The evidence now to be cited is from HC (1837-8) 679. Qns. 1-81, 89-190 (J. St. G. Burke); Qns. 191-317 (J.R. Hay-

evidence, these witnesses unanimously advocated small committees, judicial in character, and without local representation.

It will suffice, in the main, to look at their evidence to the 1838 committee, which was given a full explanation of the new Lords' system by witnesses from that House and had before it a resolution drafted by two of its members urging the adoption by the Commons of a similar committee system. All the agents condemned large committees; they were complained of by parties to private bills, their members did not hear all the evidence; the system 'diluted responsibility' (Hayward). St. G. Burke said they were 'a source of the greatest inconvenience to the solicitors in charge of the bill . . . in constant alarm . . . lest they be tripped up . . . when they have not a majority of friends in the room'. Irregular attendance by members, said Richardson, made necessary the repetition of evidence and argument. Richardson spoke most emphatically against locally interested Members on committees. 'The evil of local bias in the Members of the committee more than counterbalances the good of local knowledge'. He thought private bill committees 'so numerous as to be in a great degree irresponsible', and the means by which their meetings were brought about such as tended 'very much to destroy the confidence of the country in their decisions'. Both Richardson and J.R. Hayward commended the new Lords' committees as a very great improvement. The former summarised what he saw as the effect of having similarly constituted committees in the Commons, in the following terms:—

> the lesser number of the committee; its continuous sittings; the judicial character with which it would be clothed; its responsibility; and the respect it would attain in the eyes of the public, would make it a far better tribunal than the Committee . . . as at present constituted.

But it was canvassing, an activity inseparable from large irregularly attended committees, that most exercised the agents, or at least these leading agents who were witnesses. They spoke of it with a mixture of disdain and embarrassment, and with an occasional hint of the corruption that might sometimes be involved. It was a practice, said J.R. Hayward, 'that in both Houses has been carried on in committees on private bills to a disgraceful extent' (and, he added, on second and third readings). He 'apprehended' there was no canvassing of the new Lords committees, just as the establishment of a fixed Committee on Petitions had ended canvassing in that connection. Canvassing for private bill committees had increased in recent years; he was frequently asked if a canvass should be employed, and persons had been named to

ward: Qns. 501-582 (J. Richardson).

him who were prepared to go round to Members' houses requesting support for a measure 'and rather more than that'. J. Richardson observed that before the Lords adopted their new system canvassing prevailed there, but 'not to the same extent, or with the same indecency'. J. St. G. Burke, who was the first to give evidence, manifested the agents' unease. Collecting members for a division, regardless of whether they had heard the evidence, was the course adopted, but he hastened to say 'with regard to myself and some other agents, that we do not practise canvassing; there are persons who do it, and the solicitors generally are obliged to do it . . . it is certainly the custom that parties are always employed when a division is expected in taking a whip for the occasion'. Perhaps the most eloquent passage on this subject occurred at the end of J.R. Hayward's evidence and is here reproduced with a little abreviation. Hayward was being questioned for the most part by Joseph Hume.

306   Can you state in what way in committees on railroads or other strongly contested bills, the attendance of Members is secured on the Committees? — It is secured by application to the individual Members who form the Committee, through the medium of persons who are or pretend to be acquainted with them.

307   . . . I have been frequently spoken to in this way, 'Now you are the agent for this bill; you must see what you can do in getting us Members to attend'. My answer uniformly is 'I have nothing to do with that whatever; I am professionally concerned to carry your bill through as far as regards the bill itself; but with applications to Members I have nothing to do whatever; I consider it is not the business of a Parliamentary agent to employ himself in that way'.

308   With whom does it rest . . .? — In the case of a railway or other contested bill there is usually a deputation sent up to town; the deputation and the solicitor employ what means either can make use of, or think proper, to interest members in their behalf.

309   Can you state any of those means? — I would rather not state anything that is not within my positive knowledge . . . I have entirely abstained from entering into that question and I cannot give the Committee any particulars.

310   (Another member) I do not ask whether the means have been successful; have you known it proposed by the solicitor or deputation to use such means as offering shares to Members to induce attendance? — I have heard of such a thing, certainly.

311   From the deputation? — I have heard that spoken of.

312   By persons promoting the bill? — I cannot recollect by whom; I have heard that mentioned.

313   (Chairman) You do not know it of your own personal knowledge? — No.

314   (J. Hume) Have you any doubt that such means have been resorted to as offering shares to Members to interest them in passing measures of that kind? — I have heard it said from quarters

on which I place reliance, but I dislike believing it.

315 (Another member) You are not asked whether it is accepted but whether it is considered by the promoters as one means of inducing Members to attend? – I believe so . . . the people who canvass pretend to have influence with Members; whether they have or not, it is not for me to say; a person introduced himself to me one day, whose name I did not know, and he held a list of Members in his hand; he had crosses against the names of several whom he professed to be able to influence; he said it might be useful to me in some of the bills in which I was engaged if his services were retained.

316 Was there any sum mentioned by him to be paid for his services? – There was not; I cut the matter rather short by ringing the bell and having him shown out.

317 Was he a professional man? No; I do not believe there is a professional man who would do such a thing.

John E. Dorington, who should have known, told this committee that the persons going round canvassing 'call themselves Parliamentary agents, but I believe their principal business is that of canvassing members'.[1]   And one Charles Parker, a solicitor, complained to the Committee of a system which obliged solicitors to canvass – an activity hardly within their province as professional men.[2] John Richardson, who said many bills were carried by canvass, contributed the following intriguing passage:

511 In Scotch Bills there is generally a deputation sent up who are engaged in canvassing; I do not engage in it myself. At one time there was an individual of considerable literary distinction who, I know, was employed by those who came up from Scotland, in canvassing for several bills which I conducted. He had a carriage at his command, and went about during the day canvassing.

Finally, so far as the evidence to the committee of 1838 is concerned, we may notice the strong support of the agents' views given by Robert Chalmers, committee clerk; canvassing, he believed, was the greatest evil of the existing system and 'fixed committees, with compulsory attendance of named Members' would certainly get rid of it.[3]

It cannot be pretended that the arguments the agents put forward in 1838 had much immediate impact, though in the longer run their influence was probably considerable. The 1838 committee did not recommend the adoption by the Commons of committees comparable with those in the Lords. The following year a Select Committee on Private Business[4] divided upon and defeated a motion for the exclusion

1 *Ibid*. Qn. 600.
2 *Ibid*. Qn. 390.
3 *Ibid*. Qns. 448-9.
4 HC (1839) 51.

of local representation, and in 1840 another committee, after hearing the parliamentary agents again, found a change inexpedient. Force of circumstances — the torrent of railway bills — virtually compelled the House, under the guise of limited experiment, to adopt small committees, excluding local representation, for certain railway bills in 1844 and for all railway bills the following year. The select committee of 1847, to enquire into the private business of the House, recommended in its second report that all private bill committees should be constituted as committees on railway bills.[1] In the evidence accompanying its third report, the parliamentary agent, G. Pritt, urged the application of the committee system 'now adopted on railway bills' to all classes of bill; it had given satisfaction far beyond the old system. The great object, he said, would be to avoid canvassing and he did not think it had been the habit of parties to attempt to canvass Members of the new-style railway bills. But an agent less prominent in the profession than those usually called upon to give evidence favoured the retention of local representation for local bills, but railway bills he remarked, interestingly, were a different matter for they 'have assumed so much of a public character'.[2] Later in 1847 the House instructed the committee on standing orders revision to make provision for the constitution of all private bill committees to be 'assimilated as nearly as may be' to that of committees on railway bills but followed with a further instruction to make continued provision for local representation. As a result opposed private bill committees, other than upon railway or divorced bills, consisted, from 1847, of a chairman and four members not locally interested, and one member but not more than four members representing local interests. In 1850 the locally interested Members were deprived of their voting power; in 1855 local representation was abolished.

Parliamentary agents appear to have attached less importance to radical change in committees on unopposed bills, and to have shown less agreement among themselves. With unopposed bills the danger was that of the whole proceedings in committee being almost formal, and of bills containing undesirable provisions passing the Commons committee stage, as the Committee on Public and Private Business of 1837 put it, 'almost as a matter of course'.[3] Agents were evidently satisfied with — or awed by — the strict supervision of unopposed business by the Chairman of Committees in the House of Lords, who,

---

1 HC (1847) 235, p. 4.
2 HC (1847) 705, Qns. 647-50.
3 HC (1837) 517, cited *HistPBProc.*, I, 91.

observed St. George Burke in 1838, 'sees that the public are properly protected and private rights also . . . I believe you will find that every person has reason to be satisfied with the manner in which business is done in Lord Shaftesbury's office; the bills are very narrowly sifted there'. This agent went on to talk of the possibility of some kind of standing committee of the Commons on unopposed bills, but disliked the idea of counsel attached to such a committee, for fear of disagreement with the Lord Chairman's Counsel.[1] J.R. Hayward wanted a quorum of three on unopposed committees, would have limited attendance on them provided attendance could be enforced, and saw 'no objection' to a standing committee on unopposed bills in the Commons. He expressed satisfaction with the way unopposed bills were dealt with in the Lords, and said he had given no thought to the idea of appointing a salaried Chairman to supervise unopposed bills in the Commons.[2] John Richardson saw no reason to alter existing arrangements on unopposed bills; Lord Shaftesbury's superintendance was 'very nearly a perfect security'; a similar arrangement in the Commons could not but be beneficial 'if the duty were equally well performed'.[3] Two years later, when another committee considered this matter, there was a marked difference of opinion between agents giving evidence on the composition of unopposed committees. J.R. Hayward, while somewhat equivocal on the general question of their composition, strongly resisted the suggestion of a member of the select committee that local representation was desirable to represent the interests of those too poor to put in a formal opposition; the only way to oppose was by petition.[4] In contrast, G. Pritt advocated unopposed committees constituted solely of local members to ensure that the poor would-be objector could reach things through his M.P.[5] On this occasion, Burke suggested that local members should be on unopposed committees, without taking part 'for the exclusive benefit of any particular parties', and, therefore, without voting rights, a suggestion which, as we have seen, was later

1   HC (1837-8) 679, Qns. 106, 109.

2   *Ibid.* Qns. 255, 257, 259, 263-5.

3   *Ibid.* Qns. 549, 557-64. There is a passage at the beginning of Richardson's evidence to this committee which shows there still remained some difficulty about the terms 'parliamentary agent' and 'parliamentary solicitor' –
   501   You are a Parliamentary Agent? – I am
   502   Your practice is chiefly in Scotch Bills? – Yes, chiefly in Scotch Bills and appeals in the House of Lords; I am a Parliamentary solicitor.
Five years later Richardson told another Committee (HC (1843) 550, Qn 180) that the practice of Scotch agents and English agents . . . is different . . . The Scotch agents combine the duties of agents and solicitors together'.

4   HC (1840) 56, Qn. 19.

5   *Ibid.* Qns. 265, 277.

adopted for a while in respect of committees on opposed business.

Meanwhile a Committee of Selection, consisting of the chairmen of the Standing Orders Committee, the Committee on Petitions and its three sub-committees, had been established. During its first session, 1839, it experienced difficulty in manning unopposed private bill committees, frequently having to place upon them some of its own members, a problem which was considered by the Select Committee on Private Business of 1840. From this committee came the proposals which set the House of Commons on the road to establishing machinery for the supervision of private bills paralleling that in the Lords. The Chairman of the Committee of Supply was to chair all committees on unopposed bills (other than divorce bills) and to subject all bills to his 'uniform scrutinising examination'. For this duty he was to have a salary and the assistance of the recently appointed Counsel to the Speaker.[1] By the early 1850s the system of supervision in the Commons by the Chairman of Ways & Means was substantially established and the related duties had become the chief function of Counsel to the Speaker. In 1858 the holder of the latter office described his functions:

> It is my duty, under the Chairman of Ways and Means, to examine all private bills . . . Generally as soon as a private bill has been read a second time, I take it up and read it and make my notes upon it. I then see the agent for the bill, go through the bill with him clause by clause and point out to him what alterations and corrections I consider the bill requires. The bill is then submitted to me previously to its going into committee and I see that my requisitions have been complied with; any amendments which are proposed to be made in the bill are afterwards submitted to me. In fact, I watch the bill in its course until it passes the House of Commons.[2]

Not all later Chairmen of Ways & Means were to relish the powers and responsibilities given to them in respect of private legislation.

Private legislation in question

Even in its heyday private legislation was rarely without its critics. Some wished to uproot it in favour of extra-parliamentary procedure, others cast around for ways of alleviating the pressure of private business on parliamentary time. Parliamentary agents resolutely resisted proposals to remove private business from Parliament. As early as 1837 Lord Brougham observed that the most effectual remedy for any evils in process of private legislation 'would be to transfer elsewhere the

1   HC (1840) 463, p. iv.
2   HC (1857-8) 99, Qn. 186.

powers exercised by Committees of this House in reference to private bills'.[1] But the radical voice was heard more frequently in the Commons. In the mid-1840s, that tireless committee chairman, Joseph Hume, conducted his campaign against the private bill system as one which sacrificed the public interests. It was not railways, that great subject of private legislation, he had principally in mind, but the growing volume of local legislation. Behind Hume stood the Commissioners on Health of Towns and the reformer — and enemy of the municipal corporations — Edwin Chadwick. The select committees on private bills of 1846 and 47, over which Hume presided were the arena in which parliamentary agents first encountered proposals for radical change.

Before the committee of 1846[2] a good deal of evidence about the shortcomings of private legislation was produced. Edwin Chadwick found in the results of private legislation for the draining and cleansing of towns 'varieties of grievous defects from incompleteness . . . want of science or combination of means for the attainment of the requisite ends'. He alleged that works were not always carried out in the way Parliament intended, and, supporting what was clearly one of Hume's principal aims, wanted local inquiries into schemes conducted by 'competent and impartial officers'.[3] Lyon Playfair, then a Commissioner on the Health of Towns, gave his view that great loss had been sustained to the community by the unco-ordinated workings of the private bill system in Water and Improvement bills.[4] And a civil engineer, James Butler Williams, gave evidence, striking for its day, in favour of comprehensive water and sewerage authorities, responsible for compulsory, universal supplies and under the supervision of a department of the central government. He preferred a system of local to parliamentary inquiries.[5] Hume succeeded in obtaining from the then Chairman of Ways & Means the opinion that a good deal might be done on the spot in ascertaining compliance with standing orders, though the Chairman did not think that would save any expenses. He was 'decidedly' of the opinion that public interests should be protected by some responsible department before any private bill was introduced.[6]

The Scottish parliamentary agent, Archibald Grahame, dismissed

1   Parl. Deb. (HL) 1837), c. 1808.
2   HC (1846) 556.
3   *Ibid*. Qns. 251, 312.
4   *Ibid*. Qn. 401.
5   *Ibid*. Qns. 842-83.
6   *Ibid*. Qns. 367, 383.

local inquiry as practically impossible; expense, he said, 'might be greatly increased' by any such attempt. The decision, he declared, must remain to Parliament, 'not only in form but practically and substantially'. He was certain that departmental inquiry would not satisfy the public or save cost. Though he conceded that Improvement bills 'were often prepared hurriedly and contained ill-considered and unnecessary matter', he did not think more reference to departments would be beneficial; departments already looked into bills and made statements which Parliament accepted too readily; 'we find it a great inconvenience'. For the benefit of Chadwick and others who thought as he did, Grahame remarked that 'there are generally corporations and magistrates and associations who are willing to protect the public interests and do in fact protect them'. As a counter to the pressure for local and departmental inquiry he offered as his 'most important suggestion . . . the extension to the limit that is possible of the system of general Acts . . . to all classes of bills'.[1] By general Acts Grahame appears to have meant Clauses Consolidation Acts, a number of which had been enacted in 1845. As a consequence of a recommendation of this committee further Consolidation Acts were to be passed in 1847.[2]

To that recommendation of Hume's 1846 committee the Parliamentary agents were not opposed, and they — or at least the leading agents concerned with the promotion of railway bills — supported other recommendations which led to the establishment of the Examiners of Petitions and some reform of the requirements for proof of compliance with standing orders, matters which have been referred to in an earlier section of this chapter. The committee's most radical recommendation was that when 'only ordinary powers were sought' public General Acts should provide for them, 'under the authority and supervision of one of the public boards or departments', without application to Parliament.[3] This far-reaching proposal apart, the emphasis was on local inquiry. Private bills where necessary, should be referred to the appropriate department, whose inspectors should enquire 'on the spot . . . both as to compliance with standing orders and upon the merits of the measure'.[4] The committee recorded its agreement with the Commissioners on the Health of Towns, that no authority should be granted to construct works 'without previous local examination by competent and responsible public officers'.[5] The outcome was that two

1 *Ibid.* Qns. 893-944.
2 For the Clauses Consolidation Acts see above, p. 6.
3 HC (1846) 556, Rept, p. iv.
4 *Ibid.* Rept, p. v.
5 *Ibid.,* Rept, p. iii.

departments, the Admiralty and the Commissioners of Woods and Forests, were given certain powers to conduct local inquiries.[1] The great weakness of the Preliminary Inquiries Act, was that it added to rather than replaced a stage through which some private bills had to pass. Intended to save expense, parliamentary time, and to provide Parliament with more reliable information, it was unlikely to do any of these things if suitors and agents, and above all Parliament itself failed to attach importance to the local inquiry. Hume's committee in 1847 was left in no doubt by parliamentary agents that, on the whole, the agents were hostile to the innovation and regarded it as unsatisfactory.[2] The prominent agent G. Pritt said that 'as at present conducted' they were not desirable, and that what went on before them was conversation rather than evidence, upon which no reliance could be placed. A judicial inquiry, he held, could not save expense, unless Parliament was prepared to hand over its legislative functions; 'I think', he added, 'there will be repetition of the same evidence and the same proceedings before the House of Commons'.[3] Other agents, notably the former indoor agent G. Ellicombe, and the one solicitor questioned, spoke of the unwillingness of parties to accept the local inquiry and the consequent duplication of proceedings. An agent whose business was mainly Irish, was alone in holding that the preliminary inquiries had been a 'great improvement', though he, too, believed they would lead to 'very serious' expense and would not diminish opposition or shorten proceedings before parliamentary committees.[4] In 1850, a Select Committee on Local Acts (Preliminary Inquiries) heard no parliamentary agents before concluding that the inquiries had been on the whole unsuccessful. It appeared, they reported, 'that . . . the parliamentary investigation has generally proceeded as if no local inquiry had been held'.[5] The next year preliminary inquiries were abolished. The memory of them lived on, not least in the minds of parliamentary agents, as proof that no external tribunal

---

1 The Preliminary Inquiries Act, 9 and 10 Vict. c. 106.

2 The 1847 Committee issued three reports HC (1847) 116, 235, and 705, the last of which contains all the evidence. It ranged widely over questions of private legislation, including costs, and charges, problems of compliance with standing orders, and the functions of the Chairman of Ways & Means. In the course of doing so it examined no fewer than seven parliamentary agents and a solicitor with private bill practice. Like the 1846 committee, it recommended a general Enabling Act and urged that no further local bills should be allowed until the sense of Parliament had been taken.

3 HC (1847) 705, Qn. 722.

4 *Ibid.* Qns. 873, 867, 961, 2019.

5 HC (1850) 582, Rept., pp. iv and v.

could replace satisfactorily committees of Parliament for the purposes of private legislation.

Soon there was new pressure for marked changes in the conduct of private business and proposals for extra-parliamentary tribunals to deal with it. In 1858, the Society of Parliamentary Agents found it desirable to convene a special meeting to consider the proposals being aired 'for shortening proceedings and lessening expenses in the passing of Private Bills, with the view to offering such suggestions as would facilitate those objects'.[1] Ideas to which it was opposed included: A Commission instead of parliamentary committees; a separate committee or commission to take evidence; and joint Committees of both Houses to replace separate committee hearings. On the other hand the Society had a number of suggestions for improvement, among them longer hours for committee proceedings, a revision of House fees in both Houses 'so as to make them proportionate to the expenses attendant upon the private business', and some distinct committee to decide questions of *locus standi*. In practical terms for the parliamentary agents the last suggestion was probably the most important, for the business of committees on bills was prolonged and confused by issues of the *locus standi* of petitioners, and the decisions made by the committees manifested little uniformity of practice. The parliamentary agent, George Pritt, was presumably acting as the Society's chosen witness when he advocated before the Lords' Committee on Proceedings on Private Bills of 1858, 'some tribunal (a standing Committee probably might be the best) by whom the questions of *locus standi* should be decided . . . at a reasonable time before the Committee proceedings and after presentation of petitions. . . ' as a practicable means of saving expense, economising on committee time, and diminishing opposition.[2]

Though this foreshadowed a plan eventually realised by the House of Commons, the Lords Committee of 1858 just referred to and the Commons Select Committee of 1863[3] were both pre-occupied by those very notions to which the Society of Parliamentary Agents were opposed — the possibility of some external tribunal to replace private bill committees, of a joint committee of both Houses instead of the double committee hearing, or some combination of these ideas. Dissatisfaction with private legislation and the clamour for change came now not from the radical fringe in the Commons but from officers and Members

---

1 Min SPA, 19 June 1858.
2 HC (1857-8) 450, Qns. 651-2.
3 HC (1863) 385.

closely concerned with or involved in private business. Before the committee of 1858, for example, T. Erskine May, still at this time an examiner of private bills, developed his ideas for joint private bill committees and a permanent appeal committee. Upon invitation he extended his ideas to embrace a proposal for an extra-parliamentary judicial tribunal, preferably presided over by an eminent member of the parliamentary bar, with the two Houses concerning themselves only with principles after the tribunal had dealt with details. May's views were based on the belief that Parliament had practically, though not theoretically, surrendered its decisions on private bills to committees, and that it was now desirable to get rid of those committees and, above all, of the double inquiry. Though he would have conceded an absolute right to appeal from any external tribunal to a court composed of members of the two Houses, he asserted his belief that under his proposals a double inquiry would be 'an exceptional matter instead of a rule as at present'.[1] May repeated his views to the 1863 Committee, emphasising the 'great evil' of the double inquiry, 'a main ground of the immense costliness', and deploring the 'discrepancy of principle applied by committees' on private bills.[2] Before the earlier committee, the then Chairman of the Committee of Selection and Standing Orders Committee, Colonel J. Wilson Patten, though not ready to accept May's ideas, observed: 'I see so many objections to the present system . . . that I would listen to anything which I thought feasible'; he wished particularly to get rid of the 'double trial'.[3] And in 1863 the Chairman of Ways & Means, establishing a tradition among holders of his office which will be evident in the later debate, expressed his dislike of the system of private legislation on several grounds. 'It does not', he asserted, 'give satisfaction', and it had 'radical vices' of delay, costliness and 'the inferior competency of the tribunal', for which he knew no remedy. He wanted more business conducted by government departments under general legislation and condemned the two-fold inquiry before Lords and Commons.[4]

Before both committees, but particularly that of 1863, parliamentary agents resisted such views. In 1858, the agent G. Pritt seized upon the unwillingness of those who advocated an external tribunal to surrender appeal to parliament, remarking that if the preliminary tribunal was to be 'conclusive in its decision and . . . binding on Parliament' it depended on the constitution of the tribunal whether expense would be saved, but if appeal to Parliament were allowed it would in his opinion nearly always be made and so cause additional cost.[1]   The principal agent witness before the select committee of 1863 was Thomas Coates of the firm of Dyson & Co., and President of the Society of Parliamentary Agents 1864-8. His extensive evidence covered in detail questions of costs and expenses involved in passing opposed private bills, including House fees, solicitors', agents' and counsels' costs, as well as a vigorous defence of the system of private legislation.[2]   His support of the system substantially as it existed was given with great conviction. Admitting that 'of course, I am warped by my professional interest', he maintained 'there is no tribunal so satisfactory as a tribunal formed of two committees of the two Houses'. The system of two hearings he believed to be fully justified by 'the importance of the matters which are involved' and the frequency of 'some change in the frame of the bill' as it goes before the committee, and he offered the select committee instances of the value of a second hearing. The chief procedural effect of the abolition of a second House committee − and an effect to deprecated − would be, he believed, the discussion of and opposition to bills on the floor of the House. His evidence included a strong defence of parliamentary control over special powers. Upon this he remarked, 'If the general law gives power to any department of the executive to grant that which is a privilege ... I look upon it as a great evil . . . . The only fit tribunal to grant that is Parliament'.   Nevertheless he pointed out that the power to make provisional orders had considerably lessened the number of private bills − and reduced the emoluments of parliamentary agents. As one who had started practice as an agent two years before the passing of the first Clauses Consolidation Acts in 1845, he saw those measures as having greatly cheapened things. He did not think 'further to reduce into general laws the subjects dealt with by private bills' would have much effect on expense and would have disadvantages, for Consolidation Acts he found were inflexible devices. But he contributed a suggestion which looked forward to modern practice − the development of model clauses 'to which all agents should be required to adhere', modifiable in the light of experience by the House authorties.

Two other parliamentary agents spoke strongly in support of the existing system, though one of them believed that a single parliamentary tribunal, 'one conjoint committee' might give satisfaction, provided 'it would be competent to either House to recommit the Bill'.[3]   The

1   HC (1857-8) 450, Qn. 674.
2   Coates answered 400 questions, HC (1863) 385, Qns. 1458-1858.
3   *Ibid.* Qns. 2210-488, 3150-323.

former agent St. George Burke, by this time well established at the parliamentary bar, contributed his defence of the double hearing, observing that 'the great bulk of the railway companies' would prefer the element of appeal despite the additional expense. He had, too, a scheme of improvement to suggest. Promoters should be required before the committee stage to lodge a statement of their case in such a form that they would be compelled to reveal 'every subject matter with which it would be necessary for the committee to be acquainted' and so prevent concealment of important matters. Optimistically, Burke thought that such abbreviated pleadings, and counter-pleadings, could be satisfactorily confined each to a single sheet of paper.[1]

The long report of the select committee of 1863, doing perhaps less than justice to the evidence of the parliamentary agents, observed that 'there is general concurrence of opinion among the witnesses examined . . . that the present system on which the Private Business is conducted is not satisfactory, chiefly on the ground of the length and costliness of the proceedings in contested cases; but there is a great diversity of opinion amongst them as to the changes that are required'. But the committee noted that on one point all witnesses were agreed. 'The ultimate decision upon opposed undertakings now requiring the sanction of special Acts ought still to rest with the Legislature'.[2] In such a climate of opinion the committee could only conclude that no court of inquiry could be so satisfactory to the public as committees of Parliament. But there was one possible innovation which had been before the committee and which its report did not completely rule out. As we have seen a parliamentary agent had suggested to the Lords Committee of 1858 a distinct tribunal for issues of *locus standi*. To the 1863 committee Colonel Wilson Patten, the Chairman of the Committee of Selection and Standing Orders Committee, had suggested that there were other classes of facts, notably engineering and financial facts, especially relating to railways, which could well be investigated and reported upon by a tribunal 'out of the House', thereby saving Members and private bill committees a great deal of time. So far as concerned a tribunal 'out of the House', the 1863 committee turned down the proposal.[3] But Wilson Patten persisted with his plan for some kind of preliminary inquiry into engineering and other facts, held consultations with parliamentary agents and members of the parliamentary bar, and in July 1964 successfully moved the House to instruct

1 *Ibid.* Qns. 1217-22.
2 *Ibid.* Rept. p. iii.
3 HC (1863) 385, Qns. 3139-49; Rept. p. x.

the Select Committee on Standing Orders Revision 'to consider the expediency of constituting Referees under the authority of this House for the more speedy and economical decision of certain questions of fact commonly arising in the proceedings upon private bills'[1] In consequence the Court of Referees was set up in the following year.

The parliamentary agents, said the President of their society, 'felt it their duty to do whatever they could towards facilitating the experiment'[2] But they were sceptical. On the general question of a factual inquiry the agent, G. Pritt, judiciously observed; 'I think the time of the committee (on a bill) would necessarily be saved if mere questions of fact were inquired into outside, and that the facts, the result of those inquiries, were reported to the committee for their direction, without inferences being drawn. I think that if they have before them inferences drawn from the facts the inferences must either be conclusive or they must be open to appeal, and if open to appeal then I think you would have the expense of two inquiries instead of one'[3] But he also remarked bluntly that 'the difficulty is to know precisely what is a fact'[4] Towards the end of the session of 1865, the first in which the Court of Referees functioned, a select committee was appointed to look into its working[5] The parliamentary agents remained sceptical, emphasising, in the words of one of them that 'it is quite a mistake to suppose that the Referees have only been deciding on matters of fact; they have received evidence and given their opinion on that evidence'[6] The select committee proposed that the system should continue, with a distinct court for the determination of *locus standi* issues, and two other courts for factual inquiry. More significantly, it recommended that the two courts should in certain circumstances consider the whole of a bill referred to them and that 'in all cases, with the consent of the parties, the Referees may hear evidence and report upon the whole bill to the House'[7]

Thus, the House of Commons, in a confused way — and starting from a somewhat artificial device to separate fact from opinion,

1   HC (1864) 510-1, Rept. p. iii.

2   HC (1864) 501-1, Qn. 59.

3   *Ibid.* Qn. 236.

4   *Ibid.* Qns. 111, 218.

5   HC (1865) 393.

6   *Ibid.* Qn. 831.

7   *Ibid.* Rept. p. v. According to evidence given by Erskine May to a later committee, two bills were dealt with wholly by the Referees in 1866 and nine in 1867, with the consent of the parties (*HistPBProc.* I, 156).

inference and policy — seemed to be moving, and to some extent did move, in the direction of a tribunal relatively fixed in composition and not necessarily composed wholly of Members of the House, to replace private bill committees. The tendency continued for the next two years. Suddenly it was virtually all swept away. In February 1868, the Chairman of Ways & Means, J.G. Dodson, tried to get the House to authorise the Committee of Selection to refer any bill the committee saw fit to the Court of Referees, to be dealt with an reported as by a private bill committee. The paradoxical outcome of this move was the abolition of the Courts of Referees (other than the Court for *locus standi* issues) and the repeal of the relevant standing orders.[1] What part the parliamentary agents may have played in this reversal of policy it is impossible to say. But the agents had maintained their belief in a distinct and fixed tribunal solely for determining *locus standi* issues and for that purpose only the Court of Referees remained and continues as part of Commons' procedure to-day.

---

1 See *HistPBProc.*, I, 157-9, where O.C. Williams describes in detail the 'curious turn of events' whereby 'a strongly supported proposal to increase the jurisdiction of Courts of Referees was transformed into a reversal of the policy upon which the proposal was based'.

5

THE AGENTS – II

From 1847, when Examiners were appointed to undertake the examination of petitions for proof of compliance with standing orders, it is possible to trace private bills and the parliamentary agents handling their promotion at virtually the earliest stage of the parliamentary process. The petitions themselves have not survived, except from 1857 and incompletely, but the Examiners' Lists have, as published by the firm of Vacher.[1] From these lists may be derived a picture of petitions to Parliament for private bills, and the agents depositing them, between 1847 and 1939. For the period from 1890 the House Registers of Agents and Appearances have survived to provide a check. The Examiners' lists as published by Vacher, do not always include petitions for bills orginating in the House of Lords before 1858. However this is no serious omission for, excepting certain emergency arrangements in 1846 and 1849, the only bills which could be started in the Lords before 1858 were bills not involving a toll or charge – in practice personal and estate bills. They were not numerous. After 1858, when the Commons waived its privileges on money clauses, bills were allocated to the two Houses irrespective of subject matter by agreement between the authorities of the two Houses, and the Examiners' lists are virtually comprehensive.

In the five Sessions 1847 to 1851, 1,262 petitions for private bills were deposited by 66 firms of agents. Of these firms 21 were responsible for the deposit of only one petition each in the five years, so certainly need not be regarded as professional agents; 26 promoted between 2 and 10 petitions, 16 firms between 11 and 20, and only 9 were responsible for more than 20 petitions each in the five-year period. So even in the immediate aftermath of the railway mania, parliamentary agency was a full-time professional occupation for only a small body of people.[2]

The most striking features are the dominant position of three firms and, more predictably, the extent to which the business of these firms – and some of the smaller ones – depended on railway bills. Pritt & Co., the firm founded by T.M. Sherwood, was in terms of petitions

1   For a note on Vacher's 'Private Bills' see Appendix F.

2   There was a temporary decline in the number of private bill petitions during this period: the figures are:– 1847 – 490; 1847-8 – 235; 1849 – 147; 1850 – 174; 1851 – 216.

deposited by far the largest, with 354 petitions (268 for railways), followed by Dyson & Co. with 194 petitions (109 for railways) and Dorington & Co. with 190 petitions (86 for railways). No other firm promoted as many as 50 petitions in the five-year period. The next largest was the Scottish firm of Grahame, Weems & Grahame with 43 petitions (30 for railways), followed closely by G. & T.W. Webster with 40 petitions (25 railway). This too was originally a Scottish firm, which, more rapidly than the other Scottish firms, acquired English business.

The railway business of the three very large firms fluctuated widely in this period, reflecting of course the reaction from the railway mania of the mid-1840s, the slackest year being 1850 for Pritt & Co. (25 petitions compared with 144 in 1847) and Dyson & Co. (5 compared with 62 in 1847) and 1851 for Dorington & Co. (8 compared with 43 in 1847). These three firms in some degree found their clients in different areas of the country. Dorington & Co, most noticeably, were agents for promoters of railway bills in the area to the west of London (especially around Windsor), in South Wales and in the south-west of the country, the London & South Western Railway Co., being eventually one of their most important clients. Much of Dyson & Co's business was concerned with the promotion of railways in the London area, south-east and eastern England, and even more in the north-east of the country[1] As one would expect, the larger the firm the more exceptions there were to regional orientation or association with particular companies or groups of companies, but even the business of Pritt & Co., showed this characteristic; they were heavily involved with railway projects in the Midlands, and north-west England, though their most important single client was the Great Western Railway. None of these firms enjoyed the exclusive patronage of their major clients. For this there appears to be a number of reasons: first, it may safely be assumed that the volume of railway business was such that major promoters had sometimes to go to other than their preferred agent; second, amalgamations of railways led to changes in the agents employed, and to joint agency, though this is more evident in the later 1850s than in the period now under review;[2] third, changes in partnerships and amalgamations of firms of agents had their effects.

---

1   C.J. Parkes who joined Dyson & Co., as a partner in the late 1840s eventually became Chairman of the Gt. Eastern Railway Co., and could have been influential in bringing Dyson & Co. business from this quarter.

2   For example in 1855 Dysons were joint agents with Pritt & Co., for one railway bill and with Doringtons for another. These were five such instances of joint agency for railway bills in 1860, and seven in 1865.

Railway business may have been the foundation on which the three major firms, and with one or two exceptions, the smaller firms, were built, but in the longer run success in obtaining business in bills for municipal improvement, paving, water, sanitary and lighting schemes was at least as important. Though railway bills (669) were the most numerous category in the five-year period, numbers are not everything. There are small schemes and large ones, schemes exciting little or no opposition, and others bitterly contested. Numbers provide only a crude measure, which we have had to rely upon in writing of the agents' railway business because of the impracticability of recording the details, and attempting to assess the relative importance of each bill. While this is relevant to every type of bill, it is relevant in the highest degree to railway bills. Scrutiny of the titles and brief details of railway bills, shows that, notwithstanding the great and often hotly-contested schemes, bills were often for small purposes — the construction of a branch line, a single junction or station. Indeed, we may have here a clue to how the agents and Parliament coped with the flood of railway promotion; that is by using, when circumstances allowed, the device of a separate bill simple in terms and local in scope. In this way one of the problems of railway legislation — that major schemes were by their nature not local in character, affected a multitude of interests and did not fit comfortably into a system for local and personal legislation — may have been mitigated. Changes in committee procedure and the development of standing orders specially applicable to railway bills, could not by themselves have sufficed: in fact the need to prove compliance with standing orders sometimes aggravated the problem.[1] With 'improvement' bills (using this term in the widest sense) we can do rather better, showing not only that the three big firms had a very large share of this business — 125 of 255 petitions — but also that they obtained much of the business from the larger municipal corporations,

---

1 For the impact of railway legislation on procedure and see O.C. Williams, *HistPBProc.*, I, 61 ff., and above, pp. 5-7. One sympathises with St. George Burke, parliamentary agent, who on 19 April 1837, had to tell the Lords Standing Order Committee considering the petition for the Great Western Railway Deviation (Trowbridge) Bill, that there had been 'a hitch' in complying with standing orders. Proofs relating to plans, etc., were put in by several parish clerks, but the parish clerk of Woolston 'having been found with some difficulty in a public house in a state of intoxication and incapable of receiving the documents; they had been deposited with Captain Butler, a gentleman belonging to that parish . . .'. Captain Butler proved that in consequence of the clerk's state 'he had been for some time in the habit of desiring any documents relating to the Parish to be brought to him'. The committee, finding that standing orders had been complied with except that 'the requisite documents have not been deposited with the clerk of the Parish of Woolston in Berkshire', recommended that standing orders be dispensed with 'under the circumstances'. — HLRO. Lords Standing Order Committee Book 1837, p. 65.

improvement commissioners, lighting and water undertakings, both municipal and commercial. Pritt & Co., who led in this field as in railway legislation, with 47 'improvement' petitions, had among their clients Liverpool and Birkenhead, Manchester, Salford, Leeds, Bradford, Warrington, Reading, Norwich, and Sheffield; Dyson & Co. (43 petitions) had Leicester, Nottingham, many of the authorities and companies in the London area, Bristol, Sunderland, and Bolton; and Dorington and Co. (35 petitions) had much London area business, as well as Swansea, Brighton, Southampton, and Londonderry. The large firms did not, however, have a complete monopoly of business from the major municipalities; Birmingham's business, for example, went to Fearon & Clabon, a firm which though never large in terms of the number of bills handled, retained its independent existence into the twentieth century, without having much railway business as its original basis.

The Scottish firm of Grahame, Weems, & Grahame was (the 'big three' apart) the largest firm in terms of petitions handled during this period and the clearest example of a firm dependent on one or two clients. All its railway business was on behalf of the Caledonian Railway and most (indeed all, for the year 1847) of its other business was provided by Glasgow local authorities. It survived as a distinct firm into the 1930s, with certain changes of name,[1] but from the 1880s the greater part of its business was in the conduct of oppositions. Among other Scottish firms, Richardson, Connell & Loch, and G. & T.W. Webster may be noticed as 'old' firms, having been named to the Lords Committee of 1827. As Richardson told that committee that he had been an agent for twenty-one years it is not surprising that his name disappears after 1855, but his firm continued until about 1890, as Loch & Maclaurin and, later, Loch & Goodhart. Under this last title the firm registered as parliamentary agents in 1890 and conducted some Scottish business, but it did not register subsequently.[2] The following suggests that its agency work may have been occasional and 'tied': 'Mr. Lock (sic) who was somehow connected with the Duke of Sutherland's estates as a factor or otherwise, was an agent with a quite intermittent practice'.[3] Spottiswoode & Robertson was also mentioned to the 1827 committee. The evidence then given suggested that it dated at least from the 1790s, but, as was shown in chapter two, the

---

1 Changes in the titles of firms are not recorded, except where amalgamation or a complete change of partnerships makes continuity unrecognisable. Some of the modifications will be apparent from a study of the appendices.

3 HLRO, Register of Agents & Appearances, etc.

4 J.H. Balfour Brown, *Forty Years at the Bar* (1916), p. 236.

firm may have existed in the early 1770s. It was probably the oldest outdoor firm of which we happen to have a record to have a continuous existence to the end of the nineteenth century. It survived as an independent firm until 1900.

Among other firms active in the period 1847 to 1851 we may notice Jones & Walmisley the firm founded by the two former unofficial Commons' clerks, and Walmisley & Son (the same firm after Jones's retirement). Agency — and House clerkships — were in the Walmisley blood; by 1865 three firms of Walmisley — Walmisley & Son, John Walmisley, and Edward Walmisley were practising agency in a small way. The first is the firm already referred to, the second probably an offshoot of it. The third, Edward Walmisley, is the successor of Parratt & Walmisley, who on the face of it are the two Lords clerks who had been indoor agents. In fact, things were not so simple. The Walmisley of Parratt & Walmisley is indeed the E.G. Walmisley who told the 1827 committee that the two indoor agents to the Lords were himself and 'Mr. Parratt, the copying clerk'. E.G. Walmisley, slightly anticipating the Lords' decision to follow the Commons and stop their clerks being parliamentary agents, gave up the clerkship of Journals in 1835, and 'Mr. Parratt the copying clerk', Edward Parratt, succeeded him in that office. So the Parratt of the outdoor firm of Parratt & Walmisley, for whom we have no initial, must have been another member of the family[1] The firm, carried on by Edward Walmisley, remained active as agents at least until 1890.[2] Law, Anton, Holmes & Turnbull, a substantial firm in the late 1840s, originally depended almost wholly on railway promotions in north-east England and Scotland, soon declined at least in the number of promotions it handled, but stayed in existence, with amalgamations, until 1905. Its history had one unique feature, its business becoming, by 1875, largely and, by 1890, exclusively, Irish. The general trend was otherwise; most of the Irish agents of the 1840s

---

1 The Walmisleys and the Parratts had several family connections, in the Lords, viz.:

Edward Parratt ('Mr. Parratt the copying clerk') — Copying clerk 1822-35; clerk of Journals 1835-53.

Edward Meredith Parratt — clerk c. 1830-54; clerk of Judicial Office 1854-74, chief clerk 1874-86.

Robert Walmisley — clerk of Ingrossments 1822-35; chief clerk 1835-40.

Henry Walmisley — clerk 1822-66; clerk of public bills 1866-70.

William Elyard Walmisley — clerk 1823-35; clerk of Ingrossments 1835-49; clerk 1849-53; clerk of Public Bills 1853-66, clerk of Journals 1866-73.

For these and other members of the Parratt/Walmisley clerical dynasties (but not those who held Commons clerkships) see J.C. Sainty, *Officers of the House of Lords 1485 to 1971*, HLRO Office Memorandum No. 45.

2 HLRO. Register of Agents, etc. 1890.

to survive did so by acquiring English business. Two other firms active at that time and of future importance were Cameron & Martin, which exists today as Martin & Co., and R.H. Wyatt which developed a sizeable agency business by the mid-1850s and remained in being until the 1930s.

Appendix A below summarises the activities of parliamentary agents in connection with the promotion of as distinct from the opposition to private bills in the five years 1847 to 1851, when more firms undertook this work than at any other time. The first three sessions of that period, i.e. 1847, 1847-8, and 1849, were by far its busiest part, and Appendix A includes an analysis of the practices of the 47 firms of agents who handled promotions in those sessions. It may be assumed that most of the firms included in this appendix had at least as much business conducting oppositions, for, while not every private bill is opposed, some bills, particularly railway bills, excited multiple oppositions. The total of petitions against must have considerably exceeded the number of petitions for private bills.

The picture has one very unsatisfactory feature: the number of firms attracted to parliamentary agency whose parliamentary business was insufficient to give them the experience likely to lead to competence. As we have seen, the House of Commons had forbidden its members and its clerks from acting as agents and it had authorised the Speaker to make rules governing the conduct of parliamentary agency, but it had not laid down any qualification for agents. The search for such a qualification and an appropriate test of competence was to prove extraordinarily elusive. The Speaker's rules did something to protect the interests of the House but, unless 'misconduct' was construed very widely, little to protect promoters and opponents of private bills from incompetent practitioners. Between the assumed competence of the former clerks of the House based on experience but no legal qualifications and the assumed right of solicitors without parliamentary experience to act as agents there was ample scope for unsatisfactory agency. The situation was further complicated by the fact that there were men with legal qualifications, notably in the firms with no former inside connections, who were primarily agents and whose competence could be relied upon, and yet others, notably in the old-established firms, who, though without either legal qualifications or inside experience, were clearly able practitioners. This state of affairs was to trouble the profession for many years, but was never thoroughly examined until the appointment of the Joint Select Committee on Parliamentary Agency in 1876, and then the problem was not resolved.[1]

1 For a detailed study of this committee see below, pp. 140-149.

Formation of the Society of Parliamentary Agents

In these circumstances it is not surprising that some of those who regarded parliamentary agency as their principal profession formed an association whose earliest records date from February 1840 and which, from 1846, was called the Society of Parliamentary Agents. In a note written in the Society's minute book over sixty years later its Secretary wrote:

> The exact position and objects of the Society have been frequently the subject of inquiry by candidates for membership and by strangers. . . . The Society does not claim to represent the whole body of Parliamentary Agents on the roll and cannot do so while parliamentary agency is an open profession, but the Society endeavours to control the actions of its own members. It may be defined as 'A Social institution designed to maintain the profession of a Parliamentary Agent by the high standards of honourable conduct in its individual members and by concerted action in protecting the general interests of suitors and agents and in facilitating the progress of business in accordance with the rules, orders and practice of Parliament'.[1]

Fittingly for a 'Social institution' the earliest minute of the Society reads 'Dined at Grillons Hotel, 10 Feb. 1840'.[2] There are records of many such convivial occasions. But the Society (or Association as we should call it until 1845) had serious purposes, concerned as it was with both developments in private bill procedure and the standards of the profession. The Society's early minutes do not reflect the extent to which its members were concerned with the problem of professional competence, but, writing at the time of the events preceding the Joint Select Committee on Parliamentary agency 1876, one of the most distinguished agents, Thomas Coates observed:

> More than thirty years ago the matter was brought before the late Lord Shaftesbury (Chairman of Committees, House of Lords) by parliamentary agents: he considered it carefully but without any result. It has been discussed by the Society of Parliamentary Agents over and over again . . . We have always felt that so long as thousands of solicitors claim the right to practice as parliamentary agents, and we have never desired to interfere with that claim, it was idle to put any restriction upon admission to our profession.[3]

Who exactly were the Association's founders one can only deduce. A minute dated 10 February 1846 records 24 members, two of whom

---

1 B. Wicks, Secretary, Society of Parliamentary Agents, Min SPA 16 June 1909.

2 Min SPA, 10 February 1840.

3 Thomas Coates, A *letter to the President of the Incorporated Law Society about Parliamentary Agents,* Wm. Clowes & Son, (London, 1874). Coates, himself a solicitor, was a partner in Dyson & Co. from 1843 to 1883; and was elected a member of the Association of Parliamentary Agents in 1844.

had been elected in 1842, five in 1844 and one in 1845, from which it may be assumed there were at the outset, seventeen members, probably Messrs. Burke, Connell, Ellicombe, Grahame, Hall, Hayward, Macdougall, Parkes (Joseph), Pritt, Richardson, Robertson, Sherwood (T. & J.), Spottiswoode, Webster (G. & J.W.), and Weems. In the same minute the names of Robertson and Spottiswoode are underlined as 'original members', which may indicate that the proposal to form an Association came from them.[1]

The first rules of the Association were directed not at creating a 'closed shop', as was suggested from time to time later, but at ensuring that its membership was confined to genuine parliamentary agents, the basic rule being 'that no person shall be proposed as a member of the Society who shall not have *bona fide* practised as parliamentary agent two years at least previously, and have conducted bills through Parliament in that capacity', but this was not to apply to any existing or future partner in any existing firm, any member of which belonged to the society. This proviso and the rule that election was to be by ballot with at least ten members voting and 'three black balls shall exclude' did of course give the existing members strict control over membership, but there is no evidence to suggest that it was used in an arbitrarily exclusive spirit.[2] The rule which distinguished members of the Society from many others practising agency was that relating to the vexed question of financial relations between agents and instructing solicitors. As we have seen, the growth of outdoor agency in the period before 1827 was attributed by the Lords' indoor agent E.G. Walmisley to the readiness of such agents to share their profits with solicitors. Undoubtedly some did, and the Society of Parliamentary Agents drew a hard line between them and its own members by resolving early in 1847 'that it is contrary to the principle(s) of the Society that there should be any delegation of the duties of the Parliamentary Agent to the local solicitor or any participation in the profits proper to the Agent between the local solicitor and the Agent'.[3] The Society's minutes suggest that there was considerable discussion of this matter, and that in the month following the resolution just quoted, at least one member was asked to resign.[4]

---

1 This minute is one of several, not to be found in the minute books of the Society but on loose papers preserved with them.

2 Min SPA February 1844.

3 *Ibid.* 20 February 1847.

4 *Ibid.* 3 March 1847. The minute is not explicit on the reason for the resignation(s) but the implication seems to be there, and it is not clear whether one member or three were asked to go.

These rules were as far as it was practicable to go, though in June 1852 it was moved unsuccessfully that membership sould be confined to those whose profession was 'exclusively or mainly' parliamentary agency.[1] By 1853 the Society had 28 members.

During the 1850s the number of private bills (including personal and estate bills introduced in the Lords and, after 1858, other bills allocated to that House) averaged 273 annually, and only in 1853 and 1854 exceeded 300. But the first half of the 1860s saw a rapid increase — reaching its peak in 1866 with 648 bills, followed by a sharp decline, the average for the five years 1867-71 being 229.[2] Forty-seven firms of parliamentary agents coped with the 605 bills of 1865. Among them the big three, Pritt & Co. (Sherwood & Co. from 1867) with 103 bills, Dyson & Co. with 113, and Dorington & Co. with 69, retained their outstanding positions. The biggest single cause of the spate of legislation in the first half of the 1860s was the combined increase in railway promotions and amalgamations, and railway bills remained the principal business of these firms and the basis on which new ones to be noticed presently flourished for a while. But the leading position which Dyson & Co. took in 1865 owed much to increasing local authority business (just half their 113 bills were for railways). Among other agents already practising by 1851, Durnford & Co., Grahames & Co., Holmes & Co. and Wyatt & Co. had apparently healthy practices, but, as their business in the intervening period had shown, dangerously dependent on railway promotion. The firm of Martin & Co., though almost wholly dependent on railway bills in the mid-1860s had grown more steadily. It was associated especially with the development of railways in the Chester-Shrewsbury and North Wales area, and handled the parliamentary business of the Highland Railway.

There were new names, some disappearing or declining to insignificance as rapidly as the subsequent fall in the volume of railway business, but two of whom deserve more notice. The firm of Simson & Wakeford (first promotion 1860) developed a considerable business not noticeably dependent on railway legislation and in 1888 amalgamated

1 *Ibid.* 19 June, 1852. A century later, the Society informed the Joint Committee on Private Bill Procedure, 1954-6, that it was a voluntary association 'founded . . . by those officials of the House who after the Inquiry of 1836, resigned . . . to devote themselves exclusively to practice as Parliamentary Agents'. (1st Memorandum of the SPA, para. 1. HL (1955) 14, 58-1, Mins. of Evidence, p. 92).

2 These figures are based on returns made by Order of the House of Commons by the Private Bill Office on 10 August 1866 and 28 February 1872.

with Martin & Co., but the most significant new name was that of W. & W.M. Bell (first promotion about 1860), a firm of solicitors which was responsible for 28 bills (all but four of them railway bills) in 1865, and which remained important until its amalgamation with Dyson & Co., in 1919, to form the existing firm of Dyson, Bell & Co.

Appendix B below shows the 38 firms promoting bills in 1875, a year when the profession of parliamentary agency was much discussed. Apart from the decline in the number of firms and the evidence that there were still 'occasional' agents, usually solicitors, who were prepared to undertake the promotion of the odd bill, the most noticeable feature of this list is the disappearance of the name 'Dorington & Co.', and the most important − the appearance of Sharpe & Co. The historic name of Dorington appeared for the last time in 1874, the firm continuing under the name of J.C. Rees, its senior partner, from 1875 to 1886, after which it assumed its present title of Rees & Freres. The abandonment of a name to which so much prestige attached might today be regarded as at least unwise, but under its new names the firm remained one of the three major firms of agents until the turn of the century. Between 1905 and 1910 its business in the promotion of bills appears to have suffered a rapid decline, but it is one of the 'original' firms of agents that has continued to exist to the end of the period covered by this book, though not wholly independently.[1]

In contrast, Sharpe & Co. was a firm whose great importance lay in the future. Sharpe, Field & Jackson & Co., was established as a firm of solicitors in 1826, and as parliamentary agents must be classed among the 'occasionals': its only recorded activities were as agents to the opponents of two railway bills in 1846, and the promoters of three personal bills before the Lords in 1851-2.[2] In the 1860s Sharpe & Co. was joined by Andrew Goring Pritchard, who was the first member of the firm to develop its business of agency in a serious way. The firm acted for the promoters of six local authority bills (under the name of Sharpe, Parkers, & Jackson) in 1867, and thereafter had a growing business both with bills and applications for provisional orders. Close association with local authorities was the foundation of this firm's growing importance. A.G. Pritchard and his son (Sir) Harry Goring Pritchard became successively secretaries of the Association of Muni-

---

1 The later history of Rees & Freres provides an example of the process of amalgamations and absorptions characteristic of parliamentary agency in the twentieth century, and is recounted in some detail below.

2 The 'memory' of the present firm of Sharpe, Pritchard & Co., has it that Mr. Sharpe and Mr. Field fell out, and for a considerable time conducted their partner-by notes to each other, without being on speaking terms.

cipal Corporations. By 1900, Sharpe & Co., was a major firm, and with the growing relative importance of local authority legislation, its history one of steady expansion. The title of Sharpe, Pritchard & Co., was assumed in 1911, and from 1919, when those of its partners who were parliamentary agents became members of the Society of Parliamentary Agents, it has been one of the three major firms. Another new name to be noted in the list for 1875 is S.H. Lewin. Primarily a solicitor, Lewin began to undertake the promotion of bills in 1869, most of his early business being for local authorities in the Lancashire area. With subsequent amalgamations the firm of Lewin & Co., was one of considerable importance by the early twentieth century, and eventually became associated with Rees & Freres.

Between 1875 and the end of the nineteenth century petitions exceeded 300 annually only in 1882 and fell below 200 in only five years, but the relative importance of railway bills declined in favour of local authority bills. And the scope for provisional orders as an alternative to private bills rapidly increased. The earliest statutes conferring order-making powers likely to have made much impact on the work of parliamentary agents are the Piers & Harbours Acts, 1861 and 1862, and the Railway Construction Facilities and Railway Companies Powers Acts of 1864. In 1870 the scope for proceeding by provisional order was enlarged notably by the Gas & Water Facilities Act and the Tramways Act, but a more important enlargement came with the passing of the Public Health Act of 1875. The number of private Acts passed in 1883 was 237 (including 53 Provisional Order Confirmation Acts), while provisional orders totalled 241, including 67 made under the Public Health Act, 69 under the Electric Lighting Act, 1882, 17 under the Gas & Water Facilities Acts, and 23 under the Tramways Acts.[1]

The provisional order 'system' affected parliamentary agents by depriving them of business in relatively unimportant matters and providing them with new business in the conduct of the more important order applications. There was also business to be had in connection with provisional order confirmation bills, for such bills were from second reading onwards subject to private bill procedure and it was open to determined opponents of particular orders to petition against them and set in motion the whole business of an opposed committee stage.[2] None of the late nineteenth-century parliamentary agents has left a comment

---

1   Clifford, II, 709.

2   Possibly some of the firms of agents first appearing in the late 1860s and onward were solicitors who, having looked after order applications, went on to conduct bills.

on the system of provisional orders, but Clifford may well have had contemporary agents in mind when he wrote in his critical and detailed account of its development that 'many persons who are conversant with its practical working . . . object to its centralizing influence and other shortcomings'.[1]

There can be no doubt about the parliamentary agents' strong dislike of another development during this period — the passing of the Private Legislation Procedure (Scotland) Act, 1899. The long campaign for radical reform of private bill procedure, of which this Act was the sole legislative outcome, is examined in chapter seven. The measure deprived Scottish promoters of direct access to Parliament, though it did so in pursuit of a degree of devolution in private legislation apparently much desired in Scotland. No other statute passed during the period covered by this book deprived suitors of access to Parliament in the course of providing alternative procedures.

1890–1938

The number of private bills promoted did not decrease significantly in the last decade of the nineteenth century, the decline in railway bills being offset by the growth of local authority general bills and gas and electricity bills, increasingly promoted by local authorities, though there was a temporary dip in the mid-1890s. In 1890 32 firms of agents undertook the promotion of 244 bills, and in 1895 34 promoted 170. Appendix C shows the 33 firms handling the promotion of 269 Bills in 1900. The most outstanding feature of this list is the growing importance of two firms — Baker, Lees & Co. and Sharpe & Co. — both particularly concerned with local authority legislation. The firm of Baker, Lees & Co., which first handled the promotion of bills in 1895 under the title of Baker, Lees & Postlethwaite, had a special association with the urban district councils from whom it derived most of its business. In or about 1905 a separation appears to have taken place, and for a time the firm of Baker & Co., seems to have had the greater part of the business, being responsible for nine promotions in 1905 and twenty in 1910. In the longer run however, Lees & Co. became the more important firm, as may be seen from appendices D and E: from appendix E it will be noticed that towards the end of the period covered by this book, Lees & Co., ranked fourth among the firms of agents, and could be regarded as the leading firm acting on behalf of urban district councils. It retained an independent existence until the second world

1   Clifford, II, 676.

war, and was thereafter incorporated in Dyson, Bell & Co. Some reference has already been made to Sharp & Co., and it will be seen from appendic C and subsequent appendices that this firm, with its special relationship with the county boroughs and municipal corporations, took the leading place in the promotion of bills on behalf of many of these authorities.

Of others appearing in appendix C mention must be made of A. Beveridge, who by 1900 had been a parliamentary agent for nearly thirty years, practising for a time in partnership with his brother, and specialising in Scottish business. He was a vigorous opponent of schemes to replace private bill legislation by local procedures, expressing himself cogently on that subject in a pamphlet in 1888.[1] By the passing of the Private Legislation (Scotland) Act, 1899, his business was considerably affected though 'not diminished' according to the evidence he gave to a select committee on a bill to provide a similar procedure for Wales.[2] He became a (highly critical) authority on the Scottish Act and was the one parliamentary agent to give evidence on its working to the select committee on the abortive Welsh bill. He formed a partnership with Grieg & Co., an old if not prominent name in parliamentary agency, in 1911, and after the first world war his firm was conducted in association with that of Martin & Co.

Apart from the Scottish agents, and a small number of Irish agents who almost all in time acquired some English business, patterns of specialisation by subject matter or area were not very pronounced for the greater part of the period covered by this chapter. Towards the end of the nineteenth century certain special characteristics, if not a pattern, become more noticeable. The strong connection between the rising firms of Sharpe & Co., and Lees & Co., and local authority legislation has already been noted. With the contraction of railway legislation, a growing proportion of railway business came into the hands of one of the great firms, Sherwood & Co., which in 1900 handled 19 of the 63 bills promoted; this trend was to go much further later. Among the smaller firms, Tarhoudins & Hitchcock specialised in tramway bills, and, while the larger firms generally had a proportionate share of the business of conducting oppositions, some of the old established firms were losing their importance in promoting bills and depending more on opposition business. This is most noticeable in the case of the old firm

---

1 A. Beveridge, *Private Bill Legislation*, Vacher & Sons (London, 1888). The substance of this pamphlet first appeared as letters in the 'Scotsman'.

2 Select Committee on Private Legislation (Wales) Bill 1904. HC (1904243) p. 154.

of Grahames & Co.: in 1890 it was responsible for the promotion of five bills and the conduct of sixteen oppositions; in 1900 the figures were seven and forty, an indication of the changes in private bill legislation that were to produce a contraction of the profession[1] The 'open' nature of profession is shown by the number of firms who registered their partners as agents but made but a single appearance on petition or no appearances.

	1890	1900
Individuals or firms registering but making only one appearance on petitions	10	90
Individuals or firms registering but not making any appearance	6	25[2]

In 1894 the 'open' nature of the profession and foreboding about the future of private bill legislation gave the secretary of the Society of Parliamentary Agents some concern. In a somewhat proprietorial tone he noted: 'outsiders have the best of it this year — that is to say the Society generally possesses two-thirds of the business, but for September 1894, of 166 Bills deposited the Society own [!] 93 and outsiders 73'[3] But 1894 was an exceptionally thin year for private bills, and in a happier frame of mind he was able to record in 1897 (when 247 Bills were promoted), that 'the Session has been a prosperous one for most of the Society . . . ' though the passage through the Lords of 'Lord Balfour's Bill' — a forerunner of the Private Legislation Procedure (Scotland) Act — was 'inimical to their interests'.[4]

If the concern expressed in 1894 was somewhat premature, developments in the opening years of the new century soon provided strong indications that the volume of private bill business was likely to decline and with that would come a contraction in the profession. Parliamentary agents evidently felt a considerable sense of insecurity. The Private Legislation Procedure (Scotland) Act, 1890 was regarded as a serious blow to the future of private bill legislation, and therefore to the profession, and a special meeting of the Society was called in January 1901 to consider its working and 'the evident intention of the authorities to send all possible business to Edinburgh for decision'.[5]

1 HLRO Parliamentary Agents (Appearance Registers).

2 *Ibid.*

3 Min SPA, 1894. He also expressed concern at the state of the parliamentary bar, listing 39 names for 'twenty years ago' and 19 'now'. And it was not merely a matter of numbers for he added sourly 'comparisons are odious'.

4 *Ibid.* 1897.

5 Min SPA, January 1901.

The subsequent attempt to devise a similar procedure for Wales was seen as a further threat.[1] The vexed question of profit-sharing between agents and solicitors was raised in circumstances 'calculated to cast discredit upon the whole body of Parliamentary Agents'.[2]

The outcome was the prohibition by the authorities of both Houses of fee-sharing. Thus the Society of Parliamentary Agents' old rule was adopted, its Secretary recording: 'If it had been passed in 1877 (that is, following the recommendation of the Joint Select Committee on Parliamentary Agency) much injury would have been prevented'.[3] More seriously private legislation became a political football, the Irish nationalist Party using the obstruction of private bills with some success as a device for harassing the government and delaying public business. Some twelve bills were blocked during the middle of the 1905 session, and the Secretary of the Society of Parliamentary Agents recorded fears that 'if Private Bills are to be used for obstructing government business both front benches will insist on their removal'.[4]

The number of private bills showed a gradual decline between 1901 (with 235) and 1905 (with 182). Although there was a slight increase in 1906 (to 193), the period of Liberal government, with its vigorous programme of public legislation, brought a more marked decline, the highest annual total being 135 in 1909 and the lowest 111 in 1912. The first world war had a dramatic impact with only 28 bills in 1916. 'Indeed', wrote one member of the parliamentary bar in that year, 'it would seem from the dearth of business at the present time that the system is going to die a natural death . . . '[5] There was, of course, some recovery after the war, but in terms of numbers of bills things were a very different order and were producing a rapid contraction in the numbers practising parliamentary agency. Twenty-five firms handled the 113 promotions of 1910, twenty-one the 63 bills promoted in 1915, and, as appendix D shows, fifteen firms of agents dealt with the 120 bills of 1920. But if bills were fewer in number they tended to be larger in scope, more complex in their provisions, and in both their preparation and their advocacy they were much more demanding. Local government bills especially, though not only they, had to meet more rigorous criteria and were judged against the growing background

---

1   For the Society's campaign about the Welsh bill see below pp. 180-182.

2   Private memorandum by the Secretary of the Society of Parliamentary Agents, April 1905. Rec SPA.

3   Min SPA, March 1905. See below, p. 149-151.

4   Min SPA, 25 July 1905.

5   Balfour Browne, *Forty Years at the Bar*, p. 154.

of public legislation and policy. As the representatives of the parliamentary bar put it to the important Select Committee on Private Bills of 1930: 'The subject-matters of private legislation are today much more complex than they were 40 or 50 years ago. In those earlier days the majority of Bills presented to Parliament were for schemes for railways, waterworks, docks and harbours and public works of an accepted and well-recognised character . . . the Bill followed, in all main essentials, a recognised common form, and the principal question to be decided by a Select Committee . . . was the comparatively simple one — whether there was a sufficient public case to justify the authorisation of the particular scheme. . . . Nowadays . . . the Private Bills which are promoted are not the simple type of Bill. . . . They are more particularly concerned with modifications or extensions of schemes already authorised, or the amendment or extension of legislation contained in Public and Private Acts . . . the Parliamentary practitioner of today has . . . to investigate and master a mass of detail which in former days was seldom, if ever, necessary.[1] They might well have added that a growing proportion of bills, especially those promoted by local authorities, were 'omnibus' bills covering a variety of provisions. Indeed by 1930 it was the view of the Ministry of Health that local authorities should be encouraged to think ahead and to strive to include such provisions as they might need in as few bills as possible. To this end it invited the committee of 1930 'to consider whether it might not be laid down that the same Local Authority shall not be enabled to introduce Bills at shorter intervals than, say, three years' except by special leave of the House authorities to meet exceptional circumstances.[2] This, it was added, was not intended to 'restrict' the right of direct access to Parliament — , 'the question is whether that right might not be regulated'. The Ministry's principal assistant secretary, in evidence, thought such a limitation would not 'work any hardship at all', though he was 'not suggesting for a moment that local authorities would like it' and he accepted that there would have to be exceptions.[3] The Committee, accepting the desirability of encouraging local authorities 'to plan, as far as possible, in terms of long-period programmes', nevertheless felt that 'it would be inexpedient to place a barrier of time in the way of Local Authorities' access to Parliament'.[4]

It will have been seen that much of the business of agency

---

1   HC (1930) 158 p. 170. See also the statement submitted on behalf of the parliamentary bar, and reproduced as appendix 8 to the report.

2   *Ibid.* Appendix 7, para. 11.

3   *Ibid.* Qns. 1136-1153.

4   *Ibid.* Rept., p. xix.

throughout the period covered by this study had been in the hands of a relatively small number of firms for whom parliamentary agency had been their principal and in a few cases, their sole business. Changes in the climate and character of private legislation in the 1920s and 1930s, as much as the mere decline in the number of bills, increased this concentration and acted as a considerable though not complete discouragement to the occasional practitioner. From appendix D and even more from appendix E, which summarises the activities of agents in the last decade covered by this work, it will be seen that for some of the older firms, especially those who had been much dependent on railway legislation, there was now little agency business. Of the 42 firms registered in the House Register for 1890, and promoting or opposing bills, there was no registration for 25 in 1920. In some cases firms abandoned agency; more often it was a matter of absorption in, or amalgamation or some looser association with, another firm. The important amalgamation between Dyson & Co., and Bell & Co., has already been mentioned. Although in 1919, the trend of business would have been sufficient explanation, personal factors contributed. Only one partner of W. & W.M. Bell & Co., E.G.H. (later, Sir Geoffrey) Cox, survived the First World War. When, in September 1919, the partners in Dyson & Co., C.E.C. (Later Sir Charles) Browne and H.R. Cripps decided to part (the latter becoming assistant solicitor to the Ministry of Transport), a new partnership between Browne and Cox effected the amalgamation, the firm subsequently being known as Dyson, Bell & Co.

One history of amalgamation will serve to throw light on the way practices developed and connections were established. It has the interest of involving the firm of Rees & Freres, the professional heirs of John E. Dorington. Frederick Gale, solicitor, parliamentary agent (and member of the M.C.C.), promoted his first bill — impressively titled the Bombay, Baroda and Central India Railway Company Bill — in 1859, thus starting a one-man practice which continued until 1883. In that year the firm of Torr & Co., solicitors, promoted their first bill and by the time of Gale's retirement (probably in 1885) had enough parliamentary business to justify taking over his practice, thereby inheriting the great asset of experienced clerks. Torr & Co. became regular parliamentary agents. Although reference to appendix C shows that, with five promotions that year, they were not among the larger firms, their promoting business was regular and they had rather more work in conducting oppositions (17 in 1900). With the decline in the number of bills in the years just before World War One and the severe fall in 1914, an amalgamation was contemplated, and in 1914 took place with the old firm of Durnford, whose history as agents dates from at least 1837 and who in the early years had been heavily dependent on railway business. The firm was then known as Torr, Durnford & Co. Like Torr & Co., the firm of S.H. Lewin was primarily a firm of solicitors, whose first promotion took place in 1869. Its early business was almost exclusively in Lancashire and the north-west, but it quickly developed a wider clientele among local authorities. It too, rather more rapidly than Torr & Co., entered into amalgamation with an old name in parliamentary agency, that of Gregory & Co., which dated from at least 1841, practising for a year or two as Lewin & Gregory and, from 1882, as Lewin, Gregory & Anderson. Although Lewin & Co., developed a successful local authority practice its business declined steeply during World War One and post-war conditions pointed to further amalgamation. This took place in 1927 with the firm of Torr, Durnford & Co., the firm's title being Lewin, Gregory, Torr, Durnford & Co. Subsequently an association, which though in practical terms an amalgamation, left both firms practising under their own names was arranged between Lewin & Co., and the firm of Rees & Freres, who had lost the leading place once held by their predecessors Dorington & Co. In a number of ways the four firms thus brought together were complementary. Two, Rees & Freres and Durnford & Co., were primarily parliamentary agents; the other two as much solicitors as parliamentary agents. (As in similar cases there was practical separation between the parliamentary and the ordinary legal activities of these firms). To a degree, their agency business had different characteristics, Rees & Freres having special interests in south-west England and South Wales and in Dock and Harbour business, reflecting the former interests of Dorington & Co. Much of Durnford's business had come from north-east England, and Lewin & Co., still had many of its clients among local authorities in the north-west.

The firm of John Kennedy mentioned in appendices C, D and E was connected in its origins with Durnford & Co., Kennedy being either a partner or an employee of that firm. He promoted his first bill independently in 1895 and rapidly built up a practice, based to a considerable extent on Scottish business (five of his eleven bills of 1900 were Scottish), thus founding a firm which retained its separate existence to the end of our period. John Kennedy was effectively taken over by Sherwood & Co., in 1956, after the death of the sole practitioner, A.E. Carr, probably the last agent without legal qualifications.

The appearance of new names in appendices D and E deserves some explanation, for conditions in the 1920s and 1930s were not such as to attract new independent practitioners or to make it likely for them to establish viable practices.

The firm of Vizard, Oldham & Co., (appendix E) was not in fact new to parliamentary agency, though its activities, which were never great in terms of number of bills promoted, having escaped previous notice. On the contrary it was an old-established firm of solicitors closely associated with parliamentary matters especially in the early nineteenth century. It had agency business, mainly in personal bills, throughout the century, but rather more business as parliamentary solicitors instructing other agents. As solicitors and parliamentary agents to the Confederation of British Industries from 1923, its agency work was probably increased and diversified. Several of the new names are explained by what happened to the bulk of railway legislation after the amalgamation of the railway companies into the 'big four'. From appendix E, it will be seen that in the last decade covered by this study Sherwood & Co., led in the field of railway legislation, as they had nearly a century earlier, being responsible for 24 of the 50 bills promoted in the decade. It held this pre-eminent position because it handled the bills of the London & North-Eastern Railway and the Southern Railway. The firm of Beale & Co. (appendix E) were solicitors who became parliamentary agents to the London, Midland & Scottish Railway, for whom all its ten bills of the decade were promoted. The Great Western Railway preferred to have employees in its legal department as parliamentary agents, and Messrs. Hoskins and White-legge (appendix E) acted successively in that capacity.

A successful new entrant into a contracting profession may be noticed. Sir Ernest Hiley, sometime Town Clerk of Birmingham and secretary of the County Boroughs Association, turned to parliamentary agency in the early 1920s, handling his first promotion in 1925. He established a considerable local authority practice, drawing much of his business from the East Midlands. Not surprisingly, in view of the changed conditions in which the profession was working, his activities excited some suspicion and, one gathers, resentment, but he was eventually accepted as a member of the Society of Parliamentary Agents and regarded as a well-established agent by the late 1930s.

The adoption by both Houses of Parliament, after consultation with the Society of Parliamentary Agents, of new rules for parliamentary agents in the summer of 1938 ends this survey.[1] The new arrangements under which there were to be two rolls — the permanent "A" roll for agents regularly active in the conduct of both promotions and oppositions and the sessional "B" roll upon which solicitors who actually

---

[1] For the history of the adoption of the new rules see below pp. 152-54. The rules are reproduced in appendix H.

had an opposition to conduct could place themselves — went far to resolve a state of affairs which had long vexed the profession. Circumstances made the adoption of this reform comparatively easy by the late 1930s, for though it virtually eliminated the 'occasional' agents so far as promotions were concerned, there were by that time few such agents, and the bulk of the business was in the hands of a few firms. The following comparison of firms promoting bills in the Sessions 1937-8 and 1938-9, shows that the immediate impact of the new arrangements was not an upheaval, though those arrangements had created an important change in principles.

1937-8	*1938-9*
Batten & Co.	Baxter & Co.
Beale & Co.	Beale & Co.
R.W. Cooper & Sons	Dyson, Bell & Co.
Dyson, Bell & Co.	Hiley & Redfearn
Ernest Hiley	Lees & Co.
Lees & Co.	Lewin, Gregory & Co.
Lewin, Gregory & Co.	Rees & Freres
Rees & Freres	Sharpe Pritchard & Co.
Rhys Roberts & Co.	Sherwood & Co.
Sharpe, Pritchard & Co.	
Sherwood & Co.	
Vizard, Oldham & Co.	

Some individual agents

With one exception the nineteenth-century parliamentary agents were not public figures. They performed what one newspaper rather unkindly called 'the arid and lucrative function of piloting Private Bills through Parliament',[1] in decent obsecurity, leaving little record of their individual activities. But, fragmentary as it is, there is evidence to show that some had long and energentic careers, doing their work with distinction and responsibility.

J. St. George Burke, first President of the Society of Parliamentary Agents, though active as a parliamentary agent for only about twelve years, gave evidence to almost all the many select committees on various aspects of private bill procedure between 1836 and 1847 and, long after he had transferred his professional activities to the parliamentary bar, to the important Select Committee on Private Legislation of 1863. His criticism of the committee system and of the House machinery for dealing with private bills, his detailed grasp of standing orders and the case for their revision, above all, perhaps, his stern disapproval of an

1 'Glasgow Herald', 19 August 1909.

'unworthy system' of opposition which relied upon exploitation of standing orders' though not always immediately acceptable to members of committees, played both a large part in the reforms of the 1840s and in winning for parliamentary agents a status before, and the respect of, House committees. Joseph Sherwood, Thomas Moulden Sherwood's younger son, was an active partner in the firm of Sherwood & Co. from 1839 to 1878. George Pritt, who became T.M. Sherwood's first partner in 1832, practised until 1866 and his two sons, George Ashby Pritt and Arthur William Pritt, were partners in Sherwood & Co. from 1865 to 1906 and 1888 to 1911.[1] Henry William Lovett Cameron, another member of Sherwood & Co., was among the more prominent of the agents in the second half of the nineteenth century, his long career lasting from 1866 to 1920; both his brother, Francis, and his son, Edmund, were partners in the same firm. Among the partners of Dyson & Co., Thomas Coates (1843-83) was probably the best known mid-century agent. Twice President of the Society (1854-6, 1864-8), it fell to him to represent it before select committees, and he played a prominent part in the debate on the qualifications of parliamentary agents which preceded the Joint Committee on Parliamentary Agency in 1876.[2] In an anonymous letter preserved in the Minutes of the Society for 1883, when Coates died, the writer describes him as 'one of the last of the parliamentary agents who took a conspicuous part in the memorable railway mania of 1845-6. . . . I was managing clerk to a firm of solicitors who represented one of the great railroad companies. . . . Our firm had for six successive years to defend our territory against various (nominally) independent companies which really were under the wing of the broad gauge party . . . who never gave or received quarter. . . . It was war to the knife. . . . I think almost without exception Mr. Coates was the agent against us. Fierce as the battle was in the committee rooms . . . I never remember his doing an unhandsome thing . . . '.

Theodore Martin made the journey from Edinburgh to London at the age of 30 in 1846, having qualified as a solicitor six years earlier. The railway mania was at its height and agency booming. He joined the small firm of Cameron & Bain of which Cameron was the only other partner. From 1854 to 1862 he conducted single-handed a large

---

1 George Pritt told a select committee; 'I was connected with Parliament in 1825, my father having been solicitor for the original Liverpool & Manchester Railway Bill.' (HC (1857-8) 450, Qn. 592). The bill was one of Sherwood's major promotions, and this, it appears, is how Pritt came into contact with T.M. Sherwood and agency. *(See R.E. Carlson: The Liverpool & Manchester Railway Project, (1821-31), pp. 102 and 105-6).*

2 For Coates's pamphlet see below, p. 137.

practice until joined in the latter year by a fellow Scot, William Leslie. In the course of his exceptionally long career, — he was active to within a short time of his death in 1909 — Martin became 'by common consent the head of the parliamentary agents in Westminster'[1] was three times President of the Society of Parliamentary Agents and spoke for the profession before the Select Committee on Parliamentary Agency in 1876. The promotion of railways in North Wales and the adjacent part of England was an early speciality of the firm of Martin & Co., and Martin left his mark on the industrial life of North Wales, where he made his home, as a landowner and railway director, with interests in quarries and steelworks. The railways with which he was associated in that area in the 1860s eventually became part of the Great Western Railway and Martin handled the promotion of the bill which, by enabling that company to capitalise its debts, contributed to its prosperity later in the century. As agent for the London, Chatham & Dover Railway he fought in the fierce parliamentary contests between it and the South Eastern, yet lived to see and to participate in the promotion of the Working Union Bill of 1899 which brought about a virtual amalgamation of those companies. His other railway clients included the Great Central Railway, the Highland Railway and its constituent companies and the Metropolitan District Railway, and he was parliamentary agent for several Scottish cities, including Glasgow and Aberdeen. Most agents must have bills they regret losing; Martin is said to have regretted most the failure, for political reasons, of the Metropolitan Water Purchase Bill of 1880, a hybrid bill for which he was responsible as government agent. Introduced by Cross, Disraeli's Home Secretary, the bill would have set up a nominated and elected Trust to purchase the London water companies for the ratepayers on advantageous terms already provisionally agreed upon. Thus was lost for over twenty years the chance of public ownership, a victim of liberal ideology, and much more had to be paid for the companies when they were acquired by the Metropolitan Water Board in 1902.[2] Martin was described by a member of the parliamentary bar as 'sometimes a little impetuous . . . but of undoubted ability in small things'.[3] It was

---

1 *Railway News*, 21 August 1909.

2 *Ibid.*

3 Balfour Browne, p. 236. It fell to Balfour Browne, while appearing before a committee, to pay tribute to Martin at the time of his death: he did so in more generous terms than the above quotation. It must be said that Browne, who devoted less than two pages to parliamentary agents, did not seem to regard the agents as important. 'Counsel's life', he wrote, 'in committee is not a happy one, for he has not only the instructions of the country solicitor . . . to attend to, but has also the assistance, sometimes very pressing, of the parliamentary agents . . .'. *Ibid.* p. 235.

not, however, as an agent that Martin gained public notice. When he died the *Daily Telegraph* opened its obituary with the description 'essayist, scholar, poet, translator, biographer, author of the *Life of the Prince Consort'*, only referring later to his setting up as 'a Parliamentary solicitor'.[1] At the busiest period of his life Martin published essays, classical translations and a volume of satirical parodies, the *Bon Gautier Ballads,* which ran to seventeen editions by the time of his death. Later he wrote a somewhat defensive biography of Lord Lyndhurst. He found many of his friends among literary people, among them Browning and Thackeray, who was his next-door neighbour in Onslow Square, and married in 1851 the actress Helen Faucet. He was present at the reconciliation between Thackeray and Dickens in the Atheneum in 1863. It was above all the monumental life of the Prince Consort that brought Martin a measure of fame, a knighthood, and the friendship of Queen Victoria.[2] This is no place for a reassessment of those ponderous volumes. They were not welcomed uncritically, except by the Queen, in their own day and have often been dismissed as a stodgy eulogy. That his task was in some respects impossible at the time is not always appreciated as keenly as Martin himself appreciated it when he described his intention to be 'at once warmly sympathetic and austerely just'.[3] What proved possible may be described, at the least, as a substantial tribute to his mastery of detail, assembled with 'patience, accuracy, and integrity'.[4] The circumstances in which he received this commission, for which he insisted there must be no payment, were simple; he had already assisted Arthur Helps, clerk to the Privy Council, in collecting Prince Albert's letters, and it was Helps who in effect selected him for the larger task by recommending him to the Queen, to whom he had not been known previously.

In the twentieth century, and especially after World War One, agents were fewer in number but more highly regarded by authority. The old temptation to practise agency as a sideline had largely gone. Relations with government departments became closer and more complex with the growing need to relate private legislation to a more developed context of general statute law, particularly local government law. Harry Goring Pritchard, who practised for nearly fifty years from 1892, was a member of the important Royal Commission on Local Government, 1923-9, and was subsequently knighted. He twice held office as

1 *Daily Telegraph,* 19 August 1909.

2 It was to Martin that the Queen turned in 1869 for an explanation of Gladstone's Irish Church Disestablishment Bill and even more, of his explanatory letter.

3 T. Martin, *Life of the Prince Consort,* vol. III, introduction.

4 R. Fulford, *The Prince Consort,* introduction.

President of the Society of Parliamentary Agents and was, concurrently with his second term, President of the Law Society (1935-6) — a striking demonstration of the transformed relations between the two bodies. He was a frequent and much respected witness before select committees on private bill procedure, as was Charles Ernest Christopher Browne, a partner for fifty years (1902-52) in the firm of Dyson & Co., who in 1946 also received a knighthood for his work as government parliamentary agent. Edward Geoffrey Hippisley Cox originally of Bell & Co., whose entry into partnership with C.E.C. Browne in 1919 brought together Dyson & Co. and Bell & Co., practised until 1954, was a member of the Statute Law Committee during the 1920s, and was knighted in 1938 'for his services both as Honorary Secretary of the Society of Parliamentary Agents and as parliamentary agent'.[1]

---

[1]   Personal memorandum from Dyson, Bell & Co., 14 February 1973.

6

A DISTINCT PROFESSION?

The Society of Parliamentary Agents appears to have been formed by those practising parliamentary agency as their principal profession as a reaction to the activities of occasional practitioners. Up to the 1870s its members had not included the majority of those claiming to be parliamentary agents, but they had had the greater part of the business. The problem of competence and the regulation of entry into the profession had been discussed by the Society 'over and over again', and brought before the Chairman of Committees, but without result.[1]

Was parliamentary agency a distinct profession? The agents could point to Speaker Abercromby's rules of 1837, requiring a declaration registered in the Private Bill Office, and to a subsequent interpretation of them: in 1844 the speaker had ruled that 'agent' meant 'parliamentary agent' and upheld the action of a committee chairman who had refused to hear a petitioner's solicitor who was not registered as a parliamentary agent.[2] In the House of Lords there were no rules, but there was, apparently, a summary way of dealing with persons considered unsuitable: Lord Shaftesbury had a 'very ready way . . . he told the Clerk to "Tell that gentleman I cannot read his bills" '.[3] But this hardly sufficed to establish parliamentary agency as a recognised profession and to regulate its practice. In 1870 members of the Society were once again concerned. The Society's minutes record a meeting to consider 'the more satisfactory recognition by Parliament of the Society as an Institution'. A further minute refers to a proposed scheme (which does not seem to have survived) for organising parliamentary agency as 'a recognised profession', and to 'the expediency of the status of the . . . Society and of the profession being placed on a more satisfactory footing than they enjoy at present'.[4] The crucial practical question was whether the generality of lawyers could satisfactorily act as parliamentary agents.

At the annual provincial meeting of the Incorporated Law Society at Leeds in October 1874, draft letters to Mr. Speaker Brand and Lord Redesdale were read and approved, suggesting that, without excluding

---

1 Thomas Coates, *A Letter to the President of the Incorporated Law Society &c.* (1874), p. 8.

2 Parl. Deb. HC (1844) 73, cc.580-3.

3 HC (1876) 360, Qn. 228.

4 Min SPA, 7 & 9 July 1870.

any existing practitioner, none but solicitors and barristers should thereafter be allowed to act as parliamentary agents.[1] Behind this step was the Law Society's President, Francis T. Bircham, a partner in a firm of solicitors whose business had long included some parliamentary agency. Precisely what provoked the move was never explained. Bircham told the 1876 Select Committee on Parliamentary Agency that his letters to Speaker Brand and Lord Redesdale had not been based 'in any direct way' on actual cases of incompetency, but that two years earlier there had been 'very considerable discussion' by the Council of the Incorporated Law Society 'as to particular persons who were likely to be on the roll of parliamentary agents and who could not, as we felt, under the rules as they then stood, be excluded, although they would have been . . . highly improper persons . . . they were neither solicitors nor barristers'.[2] The Law Society's minutes confirm that there had been some allusions – though 'very considerable discussion' must have been off the record; they throw no light on who were the individuals. Apart from agents' clerks who set up in practice, solicitors sometimes engaged clerks experienced in agency, and some disapproving references were made to this before the 1876 Committee, the Lords' Taxing Officer mentioning a class of practitioners who, 'being entirely ignorant of the practice themselves, send their parliamentary clerks . . . '.[3]

The letters were sent on 10 November 1874, the substantive one to Speaker Brand, a copy with an explanatory letter, to Lord Redesdale. This was a tactical error for the Chairman of Committees was unlikely to take kindly to being treated as a secondary figure even though Bircham explained that the course had been adopted because 'the only offcial rules in respect of parliamentary agents appear to proceed from the Speaker alone'.   To Speaker Brand the Law Society's President observed that the House of Commons' rules for agents 'make no sufficient provision as to the qualifications of such agents . . . or for excluding unqualified practitioners'. Restriction to barristers, solicitors and writers to the signet 'would be . . . a proper protection . . . to the fitly educated and qualified legal practitioners'. This instrusion of professional self-interest evaded the awkward fact there were thousands of solicitors who had no experience of parliamentary work and no reason to have acquired a knowledge of private business standing orders, and on these points the Lord Chairman was to be seen to have strong views. Speaker Brand apparently agreed to meet a deputation,

1   Minutes of the Council of the Incorporated Law Society, 21 & 22 October 1874.

2   HC (1876) 360. Qns. 15, 16.

3   *Ibid*. Qns. 160, 289.

for at the next meeting of the Council of the Law Society a letter from him was read indicating that he would be ready to receive a deputation 'early in February'.[1] The Lord Chairman had not replied by the end of the year, and in January 1875 he assured the President of the Society of Parliamentary Agents that he would 'not give any reply to Mr. Bircham's letter' without knowing the agents' views on the subject.[2]

This assurance, and that from Speaker Brand, were in answer to the Society of Parliamentary Agents' urgent representations to the Speaker and Lord Redesdale. Bircham's move was 'unexpected' and 'without any prior communication with the Parliamentary Agents' Society'.[3] Within a few days of receiving Bircham's communication, a special meeting of the Society had instructed the secretary to write to the Speaker and Chairman of Committees. There was little disposition to fall in with the Law Society's suggestion, a motion for a committee to consider 'the best mode of carrying out the suggestion' and proposing co-operation getting only three votes.[4] The members, though the great majority were solicitors, were clearly vexed by the abruptness of the step. Subsequently the secretary asked the twenty-two members of the Society for their written views. Of those whose replies were preserved in the Society's scrapbook, two expressed outright objection to the Law Society's proposals, six thought law was an appropriate qualification, three would have given qualified acceptance — highly qualified for they insisted on the right of existing firms to admit suitable people, and one thought it expedient ot co-operate 'now that the matter had been raised' and because 'the notion that practitioners in every profession ought to have received a certificate of competence from an examing body has become so prevalent'. He took the view, though 'aware that this is contrary to the opinion of some of the more experienced members of our Society', that it was prudent to co-operate with so powerful a body who if it came to conflict were likely in time to get their way but who, 'if we co-operate . . . admitting the propriety of the qualification which they require', could not, he thought, 'refuse to

1 Minutes of the Council of the Incorporated Law Society, 20 November 1874.

2 Lord Redesdale to Joseph Sherwood 4 January 1875. Speaker Brand, who had of course already replied to the President of the Law Society, also assured Sherwood that the parliamentary agents would be heard before any decision was reached (Speaker Brand to Sherwood, 4 December 1874). Both these, it may be noted, were autograph letters sent from the writers' country homes, examples of a habit which accounts for the absence of official parliamentary records of this kind of business. Fortunately, these two letters were preserved in the Society's invaluable scrapbook of which the secretary noted in 1888, 'I have carefully kept this book for many years . . . it has never been the slightest use'.

3 Note by the secretary in the Society's scrapbook.

4 Min SPA 21 November 1874.

modify that qualification by any well considered scheme suggested by us', while if left to act independently 'may take a course disastrous to . . . our Society'.[1]

Meanwhile one of the more experienced members of the Society, Thomas Coates, added a touch of acerbity to the situation with a long published letter to Bircham, no doubt expecting, and getting, in the manner of the time a reply in similar form.[2] 'The sole motive' of the Law Society's proposal, remarked Coates, with a touch of sarcasm not wholly unwarranted, must be the desire to exclude incompetent agents; 'their suggestion will in no wise effect that purpose'. As for incompetent agents they 'are created and fostered by solicitors and solicitors alone; and they are so created and employed because they share their charges with the solicitors who employ them'. No new system was needed, for the remedy was in the hands of solicitors; 'They need not employ unfit persons to act for them'. Coates remarked that he would have 'no great objection' to adopting Bircham's proposal so long as he and other agents retained the right to admit any person they thought fit as a partner . . . 'who has passed two or three years in my office. Who can so well judge his fitness as I can?' But he was unprepared to compel such a person to pay for Articles and Admission as a solicitor, or make him undergo 'the inscrutable process' of becoming an English advocate. This was, of course, to desire one 'inscrutable process' rather than another, as Bircham did not fail to point out in his reply. But, if it was true as Coates averred that no adequate test by examination could be devised (and no convincing schemes were forthcoming) it was a point difficult to dismiss, and Bircham conceded that no examination could ensure a talented agent, though the Law Society's examinations were 'very healthy and useful tests' and might well be shaped 'to include examination in matters incident to parliamentary practice'.[3] What Bircham could seize upon was Coates's confirmation of 'an existing evil' which had not been solved in thirty years of discussion. There was, therefore, a case for doing something. But he had difficulty in meeting Coates's assertion that solicitors alone were responsible for

---

1 H.L. Cripps to H. Shrubsole, 30 November 1874. He had in mind a scheme under which qualified lawyers would have to obtain a certificate of competency from the House authorities before being admitted to the roll of agents.

2 Thomas Coates, *A Letter to the President of the Incorporated Law Society about Parliamentary Agents* (Wm. Clowes & Son, London, 1874.); Francis T. Bircham: *Reply to Letter by Thomas Coates, Esq., about Parliamentary Agents* (Metchin & Son, London, 1874).

3 Writing later to Speaker Brand, Bircham was much less guarded — 'we have never intended to suggest that taken alone any such rule would have the effect of supplying highly qualified practitioners, or of excluding incompetent agents from practice' — Bircham to Brand, 25 May 1875 (HC (1876) 360, App. A).

incompetent agents; it was impossible, he observed, to controvert this 'sweeping position'. On the division of charges Bircham, at this point and later, was content to uphold a practice which was common throughout the legal system.

The Speaker received the Law Society's deputation on 26 February, 1875, 'most or all of the points' in the Coates-Bircham letters being referred to by him.[1] From his 'interjectional observations' the Speaker had appeared in principle favourable to the Law Society's application, though he had seemed to infer that he had some practical difficulty, and 'at length . . . intimated that whatever might be his views . . . he should feel . . . unable to make the alteration . . . suggested by us', because of a paragraph in the Report of the Select Committee on Printed Papers of 1835, which had said evil instead of good would accrue 'if anything approaching a monopoly or restriction of the number of agents should be produced', and which the House had adopted.[2] Thus Speaker Brand extricated himself for the moment from an uncomfortable position. He may, of course, have been inclined to defer to the authority in this field of the Lord Chairman, whose decided opinions were soon to be made known, or he may have lacked interest in the matter. Bircham's comment on the outcome of this interview seems to reflect a measure of despair: 'a few words were said on our side expressive of our hesitation in accepting the construction at which he had arrived and which he evidently intended to retain'.[3]

Lord Redesdale lost little time in conveying his strong views. Writing to Speaker Brand on 9 March 1875, he called the Law Society's proposals of no practical use — the training of solicitors did not qualify them to do the work of parliamentary agents. Of the 263 petitions for bills that session, he noted, 179, more than two-thirds of the whole, were presented by eight firms of agents, the highest having 47, the lowest 13 bills. The remaining 84 bills were divided among thirty agents or firms, twelve having only one bill each. 'To pretend that you limit such a service by declaring between 10,000 and 15,000 persons fit for it appears to me absurd . . . '. He hoped that the Speaker would do nothing to encourage barristers and solicitors generally to consider themselves qualified to act as agents. 'The peculiar qualification is . . . a familiar I might almost say daily, acquaintance with parliamentary

1 Report to the Council by the President of the Law Society. Minutes 5 March 1875. Bircham added that having ascertained that the Speaker had possessed a print of Coates's letter 'for some time past', he had sent a copy of his reply on the day before the deputation.

2 *Ibid.*

3 *Ibid.*

rules and requirements, and a high standard of professional honour'. Agents not thoroughly conversant with practice caused unnecessary expenses to their clients and trouble to the House authorities that 'can hardly be over-estimated'; every session there were persons 'generally solicitors' who came to his office to be told what to do. 'These, after very long experience, are my views on the subject, and you may make what use you please of this letter . . . ' — if the Law Society could 'without unduly closing the door' suggest a course which would limit parliamentary agency 'to persons really qualified to undertake the business' they would benefit both Parliament and suitors.[1]

Though Speaker Brand had given the Law Society deputation the impression that he sympathised in principle with their case, he immediately sent Bircham a copy of the Chairman of Committee's forceful expression of opinion, remarking that 'the opinions expressed by Lord Redesdale have in the main my concurrence'.[2] Replying, Bircham emphasised that the adoption of the Law Society's proposals 'is due to the barrister and solicitor classes . . . who by enforced compliance with such apprenticeship and examination as the law has prescribed, and by payment of . . . fees and duties . . . have entitled themselves to be considered proficients in law . . . and have also entitled themselves exclusively to enjoy the privileges of their class'. At this point Bircham conceded that the proposal would not alone exclude incompetent agents, but this, he argued, could be looked after in the same way as other legal specialities, by examination in parliamentary practice, and by the fact that 'it would doubtless come to pass that candidates for entering the solicitor profession would, if they contemplated practice specially as parliamentary agents, cause themselves to enter the chambers of a parliamentary agents'.[3]

These exchanges form the background to the Joint Select Comittee on Parliamentary Agency, but were not its proximate cause. Speaker Brand may have told the solicitors that Lord Redesdale's views 'have in the main my concurrence'; in fact he was at loggerheads with the Chairman of Committees and his diary shows this to be the origin of the Select Committee —

> Saturday, 20 May 1876. I have had several conferences with Lord Redesdale with respect to the position of parliamentary agents. He proposes to put severe restrictions upon their appointment and I am not prepared to go to all lengths with him . . . a test examination as to fitness would be a proper provision . . . I told him that I should be willing to make such a change by my own authority; but if he

1 Lord Redesdale to Speaker Brand, 9 March 1875 (HC (1876) 360, App. A).
2 Speaker Brand to Bircham, 11 March 1875.
3 Bircham to Speaker Brand, 25 May 1875.

140

desired to carry me further, I could not act without instructions
from the House. The upshot . . . we propose to have a Joint Committee of both Houses to consider the question'.[1]

The Joint Select Committee 'to consider the expediency of making
further Regulations concerning the Admission and Practice of Parliamentary Agents, and to report . . . '[2] met on four days between 30
June and 13 July 1876 under the chairmanship of. Lord Redesdale[3] Its
membership included the current and previous Chairman of Ways &
Means (Messrs. Raikes and Dodson) and it examined two 'outside'
witnesses, F.T. Bircham on behalf of the Law Society and Sir Theodore
Martin for the Society of Parliamentary Agents, and two officers of
each House, — B.S.R. Adam Lords' Taxing Officer; J.H. Warner,
Counsel to the Chairman of Committees; G.K. Rickards, Counsel to the
Speaker; and Charles Frere, Commons' Taxing Officer.

Bircham's evidence followed very much the lines he had taken in
the correspondence already alluded to. Asked whether he would
suggest that solicitors generally should be entitled to practise or prefer
a separate class of agents, he reminded his questioner that 'the present
rule . . . admits every solicitor . . . ', and maintained the Law Society's
view by adding 'I would make it a rule that no-one should be a parliamentary agent unless he was a solicitor or barrister' (Qn.23). Agents
who misconducted themselves would then be subject to correction 'in
a manner which we find in the case of solicitors practising in other
departments of the profession exceedingly salutary and useful'. In the
absence of a test there were 'admirable men practising . . . quite first
rate men' and others whom he supposed were not so, but 'when we see
these totally unexamined, unqualified, untested persons in practice,
. . . it produces a sense of injustice'. Solicitors who had to undergo an
apprenticeship and examinations, to pay fiscal duties and conform to
the strict rules of the courts of law, found it 'a little hard' to contem-
plate 'a great body alongside us' under no such limitatins (Qn. 20).
The Law Society did not wish its proposal to be applied to any existing
parliamentary agent, but they wished to strengthen the authority of
their Society, to which Parliament had shown an 'increasing inclination
. . . to trust power . . . with regard to the education examination,
discipline and correction of our own body. . . .The more we are
strengthened in that respect . . . the better for the public'. (Qn.46).

1   HLRO Brand Diary, vol. V.
2   HC (1876) 360.
3   Motions were agreed to in both Houses, 23 June 1876. Moving in the Lords,
    Redesdale mentioned the Speaker's rules of 1837 as having given some sort of
security for proper conduct of parliamentary agency;   he hoped to secure
efficiency.

Sir Theodore Martin told the Chairman of Ways & Means that it 'would be a great mistake to confine agency to barristers and solicitors' (Qn.108); knowledge of the principles of law was advantageous for an agent, but knowledge of standing orders and their working, and a capacity 'to reduce . . . to an apt form of words' with promptitude the decisions of a committee, were far more important (Qns.109,113). Asked whether he thought there would be objection if in future parliamentary agents should be required to be solicitors or barristers, he replied 'I cannot say from my own experience that they should be so required'; the detailed education of solicitors would not help 'very particularly' in 'what I consider to be the important parts of parliamentary agency', (Qns. 91,92). He had 'occasionally' come across very unpleasant instances of incompetancy and had urged his Society that something must be done to stop a system which had become 'a discredit and a scandal'. Unfit people advised on proceedings, people who hadn't 'the experience or disposition' to see there was no unnecessary multiplication of expenses — 'One of the great duties of parliamentary agents'. Needless expense was caused particularly by the employment of 'inexpert counsel' and the use of large numbers of witnesses to give 'useless evidence'. An improvement bill 'within the last four years' which had cost £8,000 to £9,000 ought not to have exceeded £4,000 'if it had been properly conducted', and in other cases 'want of experience and knowledge had led to very disastrous results to the clients'. In some instances the incompetence had been by men who were solicitors (Qns. 98, 99, 101). He believed there would have to be some examination in future to put the profession 'on a right footing'.

B.S.R. Adam, the Lords' Taxing Officer, evidently a colourful character given to asserting everything in the strongest terms, spoke of 'the degenerate state into which . . . parliamentary agency is falling', 'the infinity of trouble given to officers of the House', charges which he considered 'a gross imposition' caused by unnecessary business, and, 'in strong contrast' to those who practise agency exclusively and in a most satisfactory manner, the activities of solicitors in ordinary practice who do parliamentary work through 'what they call their parliamentary clerks' and who from want of practical knowledge, were a great hindrance to business, lost bills unnecessarily and saddled their clients with 'heavy and fruitless expense' (Qns. 161-2-3, 167, 160).[1] He saw no

---

1 Adam was not given to qualifying his statements, and may not always have had a strict respect for facts. Opening his evidence he stated that prior to 1836 'the whole of the private business was conducted by officers of either House . . . no body of practitioners like the present parliamentary agents existing' (Qn. 135). No doubt he was expressing Redesdale's strongly held belief, but he should have

merit in confining agency to solicitors or barristers; their examinations had 'nothing whatever to do with parliamentary agency'. The true position of an agent as regards Parliament was that of 'an assistant to the officers of the House' (Qn. 160). Satisfactory agency would be achieved only if future candidates were required to serve at least three years' articles with an agent and to pass an examination 'before examiners appointed by the Clerk of the Parliaments, to whom the "sole right to nominate" to the roll of parliamentary agents "might fairly be entrusted" (Qns. 176, 199). The Speaker and clerk of the Parliaments should 'forthwith' prepare a roll of parliamentary agents, to include those existing agents 'who are known to the officers of the House as being competent' (Qn. 176). Adam's preference for a strictly limited roll, controlled by officers of the two Houses, clearly reflected the Lord Chairman's views. He would have allowed solicitors not on the roll to present petitions against bills (on merits only) and conduct oppositions (Qns. 219, 220). J.H. Warner, Counsel to the Lord Chairman, supported Adam's suggested test for agents but attached more importance to 'actual practice in a competent agent's office'. Though he would not place a strict limit on numbers he thought about forty agents would suffice (Qn. 293-4), a view which clearly would have eliminated the generality of solicitors and which reminds one of Speaker Brand's note of the 'severe restrictions' on appointment of agents desired by Lord Redesdale.

In contrast Counsel to the Speaker, G.K. Rickards, while believing that 'some qualification, or some certificate of fitness, should be required', would have included in an initial roll of agents 'all those who are or have been recently in actual practice' and would have recognised the claims of solicitors. He wasn't ready to exclude this 'vested interest', but would have excluded all those who had not passed any examination whatever and 'have brought some degree of stigma on the profession . . . some of them have been clerks to parliamentary agents'. He thought that such evils as had arisen had been through people practising who were not lawyers. Not surprisingly he was taxed by Redesdale, who did not want to hear this, about having a roll 'with 10,000 persons' at least on it and asked whom he would exclude. 'The grounds', he answered, 'would not be incompetency, but character', adding 'I cannot make up my mind to exclude solicitors who have gone through a legal training from practising in Parliament' (Qns. 324-363). Rickards may or may not have been expressing Speaker Brand's views: they were certainly views which would explain the Speaker's earlier hesitations. The other Commons witness, Charles Frere, the Taxing Officer, took a more

known better having been there at the time. He was first appointed a Lords' clerk in 1833.

independent line. He had certainly met 'evils' resulting from incompetent agents, though 'the leading members of the profession are distinguished by . . . integrity, uprightness of character, zeal and ability', (Qn. 434). Frere disagreed with the Law Society's proposals, wanted a body recognised 'as a distinct profession from that of solicitors', and said, 'certainly', when the Lord Chairman asked him, 'is it necessary that the number . . . must be very limited? He thought both an examination and an apprenticeship were necessary for agents, and agreed with the former Chairman of Ways & Means that the prohibition of profit-sharing would 'tend greatly to take away . . . means of practice (from incompetent agents)' (Qns. 408-10, 446-9).

The same witness thought that a society of agents might be given legal status by Act of Parliament, and the Lord Chairman's counsel believed that the agents could well be given a corporate constitution and allowed to regulate entry into their profession. Early in his evidence the Law Society's witness was questioned on this matter and said that he would 'scarcely like' to give the Society of Parliamentary Agents, 'a body which is wholly without legal position', control of entry (Qn. 20). On this both the views of the Society of Parliamentary Agents and the nature of that society were of some importance. Sir Theodore Martin was examined on the second point by the Chairman, and answered at length. The character of the Society, he said, was 'difficult to express' but he defined it as 'a voluntary association of gentlemen who have practised for a considerable number of years as parliamentary agents. . . . Originally composed of men, many of whom had been officials of one or other of the Houses of Parliament, who used in those days to take charge of private bills. When they resigned . . . they seem to have formed a society among themselves. . . . They have no written rules[1] [but] . . . an understood code . . . that every gentleman practising before Parliament shall thoroughly know the profession. . . [and] that he shall practice it upon . . . strictly honourable principles. . . '. Important transactions, Martin explained, had to be concluded hurriedly, 'by mere word of mouth' and trust was essential. This 'tacit code', he added, worked exceedingly well. 'We have one rule . . . really the only tangible and fundamental rule of the

---

[1] This was not correct, except in the sense that there may have been no separate document reciting the rules. As has been seen, rules were approved and written in the minutes of the Society from the mid-1840s (See p. 117), and the Society's scrapbook contains the rules of the Society, written out in the secretary's hand, undated but from their context apparently written in the first half of 1873. They are entitled 'Copy of Existing Rules of the Parliamentary Agents' Society', which suggests that an earlier version may have existed, and a note after Rule 2, which stated the annual subscription, reads 'altered in 1871'. The first surviving printed set of rules is dated January 1877.

Society . . . we shall all practise the profession upon an equal footing: that is . . . we shall communicate no interest in our emoluments to the solicitors or to anybody else. We charge according to the scale of fees settled by the House and . . . will not share them with anybody'.[1] For this there were two reasons: first, 'we consider the remuneration is no more than is necessary', second, if it was not adhered to 'we should place ourselves in a false position towards the solicitors, which might destroy our independence and bias our judgment which very often may conflict with their pecuniary interests'. The Society recruited its members by observing other practitioners; 'when the body seems generally satisfied that they are proper persons . . . an invitation is generally extended . . . ' (Qns. 87, 105). He had not known any applicant refused. (Qn. 106). The Society could form an efficient examining body, especially with the assistance of the officers of the House 'in settling the principles of the examination'. He envisaged a 'moderate' examination to test a liberal education, but 'not such as I sometimes see for the Civil Service', and one on the Principles of Law, but laid great emphasis on experience as assistant to an agent in the management of bills, which was 'quite indispensible' before anyone could be considered qualified (Qns. 95, 97, 111). Martin believed that the Society should be constituted and given powers by Parliament similar to those of the Incorporated Law Society (Qn. 116).

In the course of his evidence counsel to the Lord Chairman offered an exposition of the responsibilities of parliamentary agents which lent powerful support, on grounds of public interest, to the view that parliamentary agency should be confined to a small class of practitioners. To their clients, Warner argued, agents owed a duty analagous to that of barristers and solicitors — and it did not seem 'creditable to Parliament' that they should go untested. But that duty was modified and extended by their public duty. In this respect there was an important difference between the position of parliamentary agents and that of barristers and solicitors who, if incompetent, could inflict injury only on the parties to an action. In contrast, agents were responsible for bills in which in most cases the public generally, as well as the promoters and opponents, had a direct interest. That the tolls specified in a railway bill or the height of an embankment in a waterworks bill were correct was a matter of public concern and the parliamentary agent's responsibility. Every local bill 'affects, more or less nearly, a large number of persons who have no *locus standi* before a committee' and it was for their

---

1 This rule was not included in the rules referred to in the previous footnote, but had existed in written form for a long time in the minute book of the Society (Min SPA, 20 February 1847).

protection that a system of practice had been established, 'embodied partly in the standing orders of the two Houses, partly in the model bill, but principally in the unwritten law of Parliament'. A thorough acquaintance with that system of practice and a willingness to see that his bills did not deviate from it without sanction were the first duties of an agent. But that duty in itself did not go far enough: the 'rules of private bill legislation' were 'necessarily very elastic' and founded on 'the supposition that agents . . . are men of integrity and ability who will properly discharge their duty both towards their clients and towards the public'. It was the agent's duty 'not to strain unduly' the rules in the interests of his client. Implicit, and occasionally explicit, in the detailed examples which Warner went on to give the Committee of the agent's public duties, is the view that an agent should have the public interest in mind as well as that of his clients, and exercise a 'fair discretion' in protecting that interest. It was not enough to fulfil the letter of the rules; the agent must regard their intentions even to the extent of taking positive action to prevent their possible frustration. For example, when the agent had seen that the plans and sections for a waterworks bill were consistent and the powers to deviate were within the limits laid down, he had not fulfilled his duty: he must satisfy himself that the powers of deviation 'could not be used by the undertakers to the detriment of the public' and, if they could be so used, 'he should take care to insert a proper clause to prevent the possible mischief'.

Warner remarked upon four major aspects of private bill procedure in which the agents had important public duties: the framing of Newspaper notices, drawing the bill, the preparation of plans and sections, and the conduct of the bill through Parliament. In respect of the first 'great latitude' had always been allowed, 'stringent rules' were impossible, and trust had to be placed in the discretion of agents. It was the agent's duty to see that the bill was drawn 'properly and fairly', that recitals did not conceal material facts and that clauses were 'correctly framed', that particular objects were not hidden under 'vague generalities', and that there was 'no omission of clauses usually insisted upon in bills of a similar character'. On this point Warner added that he had known a solicitor acting as the agent for the bill of a large railway company 'ignorant of the very existence of the model bill. . .' and he lost much valuable time correcting bills, though these if badly drawn could 'seldom be brought into a thoroughly satisfactory form'. But it was in the conduct of the bill through Parliament that he most appreciated the difference between a capable and incapable agent, and among incapable agents in this respect he 'must reckon even solicitors of position and ability . . . ' for 'they naturally think of their clients only', and even if they had the will to assist had not the knowledge of practice.[1]

The Lord Chairman's Counsel concluded that the only real security for Parliament to adopt was to entrust the conduct of private bills 'to a limited number of practitioners of honour and integrity'. But it was important that they had the status of quasi-officers or assistants of the two Houses; if that principle were adopted there would be no difficulty in regulating things in practice. The only effectual alternative — and one not likely to protect the public as well as it would be protected 'by a really competent and trustworthy class of agents' — would be to give the Chairmen of Committees and Ways & Means 'much more stringent powers than they now possess', add considerably to the legal staff of the Houses, and make an inflexible rule that every bill should be revised by an officer of the House at each stage in its progress (Qn.286).

The select committee's report opened with the unqualified assertion that 'before 1836 the whole of the private business of Parliament was conducted by officers of the two Houses' and that those who then elected to retire 'established the firms by whose representatives the greater part of private business has been conducted'.[2] Indeed, the draft report had gone further and named Dyson, Sherwood, and Dorington, as firms established by retiring officers in 1836. This inadequate history seems to have been inspired by Adam, the Lords' Taxing Master, and welcomed by Lord Redesdale, who clearly wished to believe that the generality of lawyers had no historical claim to practise as agents and liked the idea of a small band of agents under the strict control of the House authorities.

Not surprisingly, the Committee concluded that parliamentary agents practised a profession 'at least as distinct from those of a barrister and solicitor as those two professions are from each other', and was not prepared to recommend that barristers and solicitors should be 'exclusively eligible' to become parliamentary agents or have a right to practice as such without further tests.[3] Wishing to give full protection

1 During this evidence Warner showed the extent to which he regarded the Lord Chairman of Committees as the ultimate authority. Speaking of various stages of a bill's progress through both Houses he emphasised the importance of an agent submitting the bill as amended to the Chairman before a committee met and when amended by a committee, before it was considered. This was the 'primary rule of practice in the House of Lords'. Warner thought the system worked 'only because of the careful supervision and great authority' of the Lord Chairman.

2 HC (1876) 360, p. iii.

3 *Ibid*. pp. iii, iv, v.

to what may possibly be considered as 'existing rights', the committee could not ensure 'that all incompetent agents will be at once excluded from practice' but believed that the adoption of its recommendations would ensure that 'before long' agency would be confined to those who could be trusted to conduct business in a manner helpful to Parliament, and efficiently and economically. A Roll should be kept, and published annually, by the Clerk of the Parliaments, of those exclusively entitled to practise as agents. Included in it initially should be all who during the current or previous Parliaments had introduced and conducted any private bill through both Houses, and such others as the Speaker and Chairman of Committees had 'special reason' for including, but, subsequently, 'fitness for office' should be tested by special examinations to find persons 'thoroughly qualified by actual practice'. Barristers, solicitors, graduates, and those 'who shall have passed a general examination to be conducted by the Civil Service Commissioners' should be allowed to present themselves for a special examination. Successful candidates should be admitted to the roll at the discretion of the Speaker and Chairman of Committees, who would nominate the examiners and have authority to strike off agents 'for neglect of rules or professional misconduct of any kind'. For the future all private bills should be marked with the agent's name and 'any partnership'. As to the contentious question of fee-sharing or division of profits, the committee considered it desirable to 'forbid altogether' any division of charges of a parliamentary agent on pain of summary removal from the Roll. And the committee thought that the expediency of restricting all business relating to Provisional Orders and Certificates to agents on the new roll deserved 'serious consideration' — a suggestion which would have confined to parliamentary agents a class of business which was rapidly growing in importance and was, with the development of diverse forms of delegated legislation to assume a scope which could not have been foreseen at the time.

The Society of Parliamentary Agents found the report gratifying and rapidly resolved to petition the Commons 'acquiescing in the suggestion . . . and praying the House to carry into effect the recommendations . . .'.[1] In the event, the report was to have rather more effect on the Society than on the House. The Society's secretary was authorised to invite such non-member agents as he and the President thought fit to concur in and sign the petition, and subsequently it was decided to invite 'Wyatt and others who had signed the petition' to joint the Society.[2] In this way thirteen 'outsiders' were admitted to

1   Min SPA 31 July 1876.
2   *Ibid.* 28 October 1876.

membership, after the Society had relaxed its rules to ease the election of agents who were not partners of existing members. The admission of so many outsiders no doubt strengthened the Society, though the new admissions did not include any partners of the firm of Bircham & Co., a firm of some importance, or Sharpe & Co., not yet but later to become a leading firm in the profession. They were both very much outsiders, the first having done much to provoke the controversy just described and the second having been commended by the Council of the Incorporated Law Society for its zeal in reporting on the close relations between the Society of Parliamentary Agents and Lord Redesdale.[1] Possibly because of the increased membership, it was felt desirable, by the beginning of 1877, to have printed rules. The profit-sharing issue was a delicate one, especially after Parliament had failed to act on the joint select committee's recommendations, and it was decided that 'whilst adhering strictly to this practice (of not sharing with solicitors), which has always been the *lex non scripta* of the Society, it was not expedient to make any express rule on the subject'.[2]

The report of the joint select committee was considered in the Lords on 24 and 28 July 1876,[3] and in the Commons on 2 August.[4] Its recommendations were opposed by the Lord Chancellor, who could see no reason for distinguishing between solicitors and parliamentary agents in respect of fee-sharing, or how any rule against it could be enforced. Nevertheless, Lord Redesdale successfully urged the Lords to agree to the report. It was equally strongly, but unsuccessfully, commended to the Commons by H.C. Raikes, the Chairman of Ways & Means. The House does not seem to have been very interested and the field was left to opponents of the report. All nine speakers to Raikes's motion seized upon the lateness of the session to urge postponement. Raikes then withdrew his motion, Speaker Brand noting in his diary that, 'Mr. Raikes judiciously abstained from asking the House to go beyond a preliminary discussion on the present occasion'. The Brand diaries show that Raikes had agreed to withdraw his resolutions in the event of opposition. Speaker Brand wanted no trouble, though he expected that 'the country attorneys will give us trouble next session on this matter'.[5] The attorneys never had occasion to. The only parliamentary action resulting from the report was that which Lord Redesdale was

1 Minutes of the Council of the Law Society 10 March 1876.
2 Min SPA, 3 January 1877. For the rules see appendix G.
3 Parl. Deb. HL (1876) 230, p. 1767 and 231, p. 3.
4 Parl. Deb. HC (1876) 231, p. 319.
5 HLRO, Brand Diaries, vol. V, 2 August 1876.

able to urge on his own authority as Chairman of Committees; — the adoption by the Lords of the rules for agents hitherto made by the Speaker of the House of Commons.[1] But the report, with its historical inaccuracies, was recalled by officers of the two Houses and the Society of Parliamentary Agents whenever the question of fee-sharing or qualifications for agents was raised later.

In the long run, failure to act on the recommendation that a distinct qualification for parliamentary agents should be introduced was not so much a cause of serious damage to the profession as of resentment among those whose principal business was parliamentary agency — a resentment which amounted to a sense of grievance when private business was slack. The continuance of profit-sharing threatened, by the end of the century, to become a scandal for reasons for which little account had been taken in 1876. That the practice was not likely to make solicitors zealous in minimising costs of parliamentary proceedings, and that it might encourage touting for business was obvious enough, and perhaps reprehensible enough when the solicitors concerned were private practitioners. But in the last decade or so of the nineteenth century a growing part of private parliamentary business came from salaried town and other local authority clerks, to whom the same practice was extended. The local authorities, when they knew of the practice, could of course provide that sums so received by their chief officers be paid into the borough funds, and many of the larger authorities did so; some smaller authorities, whose clerks may not have been full-time employees, did not.

In 1900 the Joint Select Committee on Municipal Trading[2] heard the town clerks of three major authorities on this practice. The town clerk of Birmingham, having explained that division of profits was a well-known practice where the London solicitor happened also to be a parliamentary agent, said that in the case of large corporations the allowances were paid into the borough funds, no town clerks receiving them personally.[3] The town clerk of Leeds confirmed that this was so 'in most cases', adding that certain parliamentary agents who were primarily solicitors made an allowance of one-third of their fees though there was a tendency 'now' not to make that allowance if it went to the town and not to the town clerk. Leeds received no such allowance.[4] The town clerk of South Shields explained that he was prohibited by the

1 Parl. Deb HL (1876) 231, p. 1061 (11 August 1876).
2 HC (1900) 305.
3 *Ibid.* paras. 2075-2077.
4 *Ibid.* paras. 3166-3168.

terms of his appointment from receiving any commission. He had been offered one-third of their charges by a firm named to the Committee, 'assuming the town clerk is authorised to accept the allowance'. Nevertheless he did not think the allowance made by parliamentary agents was large enough to be a temptation to town clerks.[1] This was not a view held universally; two years later the House of Lords' Taxing Officer told the Joint Select Committee on Private Business that the system of dividing profits which prevailed amongst certain agents was 'conducive to promoting bills' and led to it being no one's interest in particular to reduce fees on taxation. He believed that in some cases the town clerk paid over what he received to the town council.[2] The town clerk of Wolverhampton gave evidence to this committee on lines similar to that given by his fellow clerks to the committee of 1900, and Mr. G.A. Pritt, on behalf of the Society of Parliamentary Agents, explained his own Society's firm rule on the subject. Neither Committee made recommendations but the Earl of Morley who was chairman of the Committee on Municipal Trading (and Chairman of Committees) reminded that committee of the recommendations of 1876, expressed strong dislike of the practice and wished for its abolition.

What years of talk had failed to achieve came about as the result of the conviction at Bow Street in February 1905 of the unfortunate town clerk of Holborn on a charge of misappropriating borough funds. A representative, ironically enough, of Bircham & Co. gave evidence of the payments his firm had made to the clerk over the previous four years. The evidence of a member of the Council's finance committee suggests a state of affairs that can hardly have been unique to Holborn Town Council — that local authorities may not always have been aware of the practice — for he stated that it had never occurred to him that the firm 'would treat their salaried town clerk as though he were a country solicitor'.[3] There was, of course, no question of the firm of agents having acted criminally. Indeed, in the view of the Society of Parliamentary Agents, that these charges were associated 'with the name of an eminent firm of solicitors and parliamentary agents . . . who appear to have acted in perfect good faith . . . ' served to confirm the opinion that the division of profits 'is a bad system, exposes the

1   *Ibid.* paras. 3235-3242.

2   HC (1902) 378 paras. 1040-1044. Considering the matter in 1905, the authors of a memorandum on the subject for the Society of Parliamentary Agents noted that small local authorities had recently been very active promoting bills and 'it is a matter of common repute that one of the contributing causes has been the encouragement offered to their legal advisers by the division of profits'. Rec SPA.

3   These details of the Holborn case are taken from a memorandum among the records of the Society of Parliamentary Agents.

client to great temptation, and leads to grave abuses'. Not only was the reputation of parliamentary agents impugned, but a reflection was cast on the Speaker and the Chairman of Committees 'for allowing a system to continue which encourages dishonesty and extravagance'.[1]

During May 1905, the matter was aired on the floor of the House of Commons as a result of persistent questioning by the Member for Devonport.[2] On the first occasion, the Prime Minister, after deploring the use of the expression, 'secret commission', to describe what was 'an agency payment recognised as such amongst solicitors', said that the firm of agents was of the highest reputation, but commissions of this kind were 'engaging the attention of the Lord Chancellor . . . the Chairman of Committees, and the Law Society'. The Member's subsequent attempt to move the adjournment 'to discuss a definite matter of urgent public importance' failed, the Deputy-Speaker rejecting the view that, because a member of the firm concerned was the Government parliamentary agent, the firm was 'a servant of the Government'. In a fuller answer on 15 May, the Attorney-General observed that the former Holborn clerk's offence had been to conceal from his Council the payments he had received and which by the terms of his engagement he had been bound to hand over to the Council; but Messrs. Bircham & Co., the parliamentary agents, had not been aware of this. The clerk, not the Council, he said, had employed the parliamentary agents upon agency terms, a common practice in the legal profession.[3] After reminding the House of 'the great division of opinion on this subject' in 1876, he said that the propriety of such terms was being considered by the authorities of both Houses. Doubtless the Holborn case, and these exchanges moved those authorities to end profit-sharing. In August 1905, Speaker Lowther and the Lord Chairman issued new rules for parliamentary agents to replace those made by Speaker Brand in 1873. Rule 13 provided that 'a Parliamentary Agent shall not divide with or pay to any client, or any solicitor, clerk, officer, or servant of any client, any moneys which the Agent at any time receives in respect of his costs, charges, and expenses in promoting or opposing or otherwise dealing with any Bill or Provisional Order, or give any commission or gratuity to any person in respect of his employment as a Parliamentary Agent'.

1 Memorandum 'Division of Profits with Solicitors and Town Clerks', Society of Parliamentary Agents, April 1905.

2 Parl. Deb. HC (1905) 146, cc. 57-59, 286, 287-9, 736, and 962.

3 As the President of the Local Government Board pointed out to the same questioner on the same day, Bircham & Co. had expressed this view in a letter to *The Times*. They maintained that they had never held any appointment or

The recommendation made in 1876 that would-be parliamentary agents should be subject to some examination or test of fitness was never acted upon in any sense that would occur to the reader. When the question of qualifications was seriously discussed again there were far fewer agents, all of them well known to and in frequent contact with the House authorities and members of a handful of firms whose competence was not in question. They had acquired, or re-acquired, that status of quasi-officers of the House talked about in 1876 by their close involvement in the work of Parliament and their competence, not by any formal process. And for the ordinary legal practitioner the attraction of undertaking the promotion of private bills had virtually gone. On 30 May 1930, a committee consisting of Counsel to the Speaker and to the Chairman of Committees, the Principal Committee Clerk of the House of Lords, and the President and Secretary of the Society of Parliamentary Agents, met to consider the status of parliamentary agents. They unanimously agreed that a roll of agents should be established, consisting of (a) those qualified to conduct both promotions and oppositions, and (b) those qualified to conduct oppositions only, and practice limited to those on the roll. Experience during the previous five years was to be the test for the initial constitution of both classes. This proposal, which obviously recalled some of the ideas mooted in 1876, formed the basis of the rules eventually adopted, though some other suggestions went further than was found acceptable.

No immediate action followed. But in March 1937 there was a resumption of discussions, for which Edward Vigors, Principal Clerk of Committees, House of Lords, prepared a memorandum. Although he had participated in the unanimous conclusions of the 1930 committee, second thoughts had supervened and he saw 'some difficulty' in asking the Society of Parliamentary Agents to act in an advisory capacity, 'so long as that Society is a body which has no corporate existence but consists of a body of gentlemen consisting of any persons whom they see fit to admit to their ranks and without any definite status'. As parliamentary agents were, with few exceptions, 'either solicitors or barristers', he thought the Law Society, 'as suggested by Mr. Bircham sixty years ago' would be able to act in an advisory capacity 'by seeking the advice of the Society of Parliamentary Agents or those members of its profession who act as such agents', and the Inns of Court might so act as regards barristers. An examination 'as suggested by Mr. Bircham' might or might not be necessary.[1] Edward Vigors, some of whose

retainer from the Council, but had for eighteen years acted for Mr. Jones, the clerk.

1 Edwards Vigors, *Memorandum: Status of Parliamentary Agents,* (17 March

communications to the Society of Parliamentary Agents suggest an authoritarian temperament, was not to succeed in turning the wheel full circle. The most likely result of his suggestion for a somewhat clumsy advisory arrangement is that, when new rules were adopted the following year, the composition of the advisory committee was left undefined. Of the meeting which followed on 19 March 1937, there is no direct record, but within a few days Counsel to the Speaker had forwarded for consideration to the secretary of the Society of Parliamentary Agents what he called, 'a rough draft, in which, with Vigors' help, I have endeavoured to reduce to writing the decisions arrived at . . .'.[1] This document, undated but presumably prepared between 19 and 22 March 1937, and headed 'Recommendations', reaffirmed the desirability of restricting parliamentary agency 'to persons who are properly qualified', and of providing for the two classes of agent noticed already — for which the terms "Roll A" and "Roll B" were used. Much of what followed must have gone unrecorded, but clearly there was close co-operation between the secretary of the Society and the House authorities: by June the Society's copy of the 'Recommendations' had undergone extensive amendment — in four colours. Comparison of the document with the rules eventually made suggests that the Society did most to shape the formula for protecting the right of existing agents to continue in practice. Of Vigors's suggested advisory committee to be provided by the Law Society and the Inns of Court there was no trace, but possibly his influence may be seen in the provision that, in addition to satisfying the Speaker and Lord Chairman as to knowledge of standing orders and practice, an applicant for entry on roll "A" must be or have been a solicitor or barrister'. This final suggestion that parliamentary agents be required to have legal qualifications went unamended in the Society's copy of the Recommendations. Surprising as that may seem, it is perhaps an indication of the extent to which agreement was reached informally: at some stage the notion was dropped in a manner unrecorded.

On 21 March 1938 a meeting of the Society of Parliamentary Agents was held to consider the new rules which were about to be made. Only minor verbal alterations were suggested and the meeting approved them with an expression of appreciation for having been given the opportunity

1937) (Rec SPA). Vigors evidently had been reading the report and evidence of 1876. He reviewed what some of the witnesses had said, and his memorandum began with a repetition of the myth made official by that Report — 'Before the year 1836 the whole of the Private business of Parliament was conducted by the Officers of the two Houses'.

[1] Manuscript letter, Sir Frederick Liddell to Colonel Cox, 22 March 1937, Rec SPA.

to consider them in advance[1]. The Lord Chairman's rules were issued on 29 March, the Speaker's on 4 April 1938; they were, of course, effectively identical, and came into operation at the end of the current Session. As the text of the Speaker's version is given in full in appendix H, it will suffice to note here the innovations which established the modern basis on which parliamentary agents are entitled to practise. The principle of the "A" and "B" Rolls (though they are not so described in the rules) was adopted. Registration on the "A" Roll — that is of agents entitled to practise both in promoting and opposing bills — was put on a permanent, not a sessional, basis; registration on the "B" roll, for conducting oppositions only, was to be on a sessional basis, as all registration had previously been, and dependent upon the applicant having an opposition to conduct. Enrolment was clearly placed on a personal basis. On this it may be remarked that the earlier rules appeared to imply that enrolment was an individual matter, but examination of the registers shows, at least in the case of firms of solicitors, that it had been common practice for one partner to register the names of all the members of a firm and subscribe the required declaration in their behalf. The point is brought out by the opening words of a Practice Note issued in connection with the new rules 'enrolment as a Parliamentary Agent becomes an individual matter. A written application . . . must therefore be made by each person wishing to have his name registered, and not on behalf of a firm'[2]. Finally there was the positive power entrusted to the Speaker and Chairman of Committees to control admission to Roll A. They had to be satisfied of the applicant's 'practical knowledge of the Standing Orders and procedure of the House of Commons regulating Private Business (House of Lords, 'relative to Private Bills'). But no formal machinery for testing fitness was provided, nor, however much weight might be given to it, was a legal qualification required. The quality of those admitted was to depend upon the integrity of the firms admitting them to partnership, the judgment of the officers of the Houses, and the discretion of the Speaker, the Lord Chairman of Committees, and their Counsel. Theoretically, the arrangement may be thought indefensible — or very British. It could work only with the small number and the close relationships of those involved.

---

1 Min SPA, 21 March 1938.

2 Undated Practice Note issued by the Committee & Private Bill Office, circulated by the secretary of the Society of Parliamentary Agents, 23 May 1938, Rec SPA.

7

THE THREAT OF CHANGE

'Of Select Committees we have had an infinity . . . and very little
has come of it . . . Private Legislation calls for the attention of Her
Majesty's Government and requires reform'. — J.G.Dodson, Chairman of Ways & Means, 1872.

'It would lay on the Government too great a burden in matters
which are not its primary or exclusive concern'. — Chichester
Fortescue, President of the Board of Trade, 1872.

'I repeat my conviction, shared, I believe, in the main, by all my
professional brethren, that the existing system is satisfactory to the
suitors in Parliament'. — Theodore Martin, Parliamentary Agent,
1872.

In terms of procedural development the late 1860s and early 1870s
may have seen the end of 'the formative period'[1] For the parliamentary
agents those years marked the start of a period during which they felt
more keenly the need to defend the system of private legislation from
the advocates of change. The schemes and suggestions put forward, the
accompanying reasons, and the remonstrations of the parliamentary
agents and others, savour of a protracted, if intermittent, wrangle rather
than a great debate; they did not constitute an attempt to examine
'the system of Private Legislation' as a political institution, or to think
creatively about the nature of the role it could or ought to perform in
rapidly changing times. In the main, the reformers were concerned to
find expedients to meet the criticisms to be found in the reports of
that 'infinity' of select committees, to relieve the supposedly excessive
burden on the House of Commons, or to change something they
considered inordinately costly. Expedients designed to curtail the
activities of private bill committees or, even more, to transfer proceedings to tribunals which might sit in distant parts of the country could
not but present something of a threat to parliamentary agency as a
compact and distinct profession.

In July 1869 members of the Society of Parliamentary Agents were
concerned about a plan to have opposed private bills considered once
only in committee, before committees composed of Members of both
Houses. Such tribunals, it was unanimously resolved, 'would be in-
pedient . . . (and) unsatisfactory to suitors in Parliament'.[2] Having

---

1 *HistPBProg*, I, 175.

2 Min SPA 19 July 1869. It was an old idea of which the Society had disapproved
much earlier. (Min SPA 19 June 1858).

sought unsuccessfully to give evidence to the Joint Select Committee on the Despatch of Business, then sitting, officers of the Society had 'certain interviews' with the Lord Chairman and other members of the select committee with results considered to be satisfactory.[1] Nevertheless, the joint select committee included in its recommendations for simplifying and speeding up proceedings the establishment of joint private bill committees for opposed bills and the treatment of such bills, after they had undergone in other respects the normal stages in the House of origin, as unopposed in the second House. That recommendation was neglected. Within three years came the boldest of the schemes for reform, put to the House of Commons by its Chairman of Way & Means, J.G. Dodson, and debated briefly on 15 and 22 March 1872.[2]

The first of Dodson's four resolutions — 'That in the opinion of this House, the system of Private Legislation calls for the attention of Her Majesty's Government, and requires reform' — sought to place upon the government the responsibility for initiating change; the outcome of that will be noticed presently. His other resolutions outlined a far-reaching scheme to transfer to a permanent judicial tribunal, sitting in London, Edinburgh, Dublin and possibly other major cities, the consideration in the first instance of virtually all private business. Dodson envisaged the end of local and personal Acts — 'no such thing would remain' if his scheme were adopted; everything would proceed by provisional orders obtained on application in many cases to government departments, and in others by application to the external tribunal, who would hear counsel and witnesses in open court. He was not, however, inviting Parliament to part with its ultimate control of any part of legislation. To safeguard this all such provisional orders, whether made or refused, should be laid before both Houses. From the decisions of the tribunal, appeal would lie to a joint committee of both Houses, constituted as recommended by the joint select committee of 1869. The Chairman of Ways & Means was somewhat obscure on this important matter, speaking at one point of appeal as 'a matter of right' and at another making it conditional on the decision of either House, who would consider and, he believed, usually acquiesce in the report of a standing committee established to decide whether a *prima facie* case for appeal existed. But he was clear about the practical

---

1 *Ibid.* 26 July 1869. The Committee (HC (1869) 386) was concerned with expediting parliamentary business generally, with special regard to relations between the two Houses. The only witness, Erskine May, urged joint private bill procedure.

2 Parl. Deb. HC (1872) cc.27 & 507 ff.

effects he foresaw: the number of appeals, he believed, could be measured by the number of bills which under the existing system were opposed in both Houses, (40 to 60 annually), and those appeals could be dealt with by 20 or 25 Members of each House, compared with the 180 to 250 Members required to man the existing private bill committees. Dodson also proposed ending the 'very cumbrous and inconvenient' method of confirming provisional orders by bill; they should be laid on the table and if not petitioned against, or an adverse motion made, held to have received the assent of the House.

The Chairman of Ways & Means previously had opposed suggestions for extra-parliamentary tribunals on the grounds that they must necessarily aim at consistency and would not change with the times, whereas Members of Parliament reflected changes in public opinion.[1] But he had come to believe that a private bill committee was 'generally a bench much weaker than the bar before it', that the system was 'costly, uncertain and mostly unsatisfactory' in its results, and that the tribunal he was proposing would be cheaper and more efficient. One must note his conviction that local proceedings would be cheaper, apart from those exceptional cases in which the need to bring eminent counsel and witnesses from London would add to the cost. Parliamentary agents, assuming that what Dodson regarded as the exception must be the rule, were to emphasise the opposite. When Dodson's reasons for putting forward his plan are looked at as a whole they are seen to be mixed, though he seems to have been much concerned with the need to provide parliamentary time for other matters. He spoke of the 'difficulties and inconveniences, occasionally much aggravated by the fluctuating nature of our parliamentary tribunals', of the congestion of business into a few weeks which he saw as the chief cause of expense in private legislation, and of the advantages to Parliament in providing more time for public business 'which was yearly increasing' and relieving it of an immense amount of work which he had come to believe Members were not best qualified to perform.

Some hostile press comment may be noticed. The *Saturday Review*[2] observed that the Court of Referees had 'illustrated by its notorious failure the inconvenience of a fixed tribunal to determine mixed issues of fact and expediency'. The *Pall Mall Gazette*,[3] in advance of Dodson's explanations and 'setting aside' the concession it would be to the advocates of Home Rule in Ireland, thought the suggested decent-

1 Parl Deb. HC (1867-8) 190, cc 190 ff., and (1871) 207, cc. 686 ff.
2 16 March 1872.
3 8 March 1872.

ralisation 'a serious evil', saw the scheme as inapplicable to railway bills, feared rigidity of decision where what was required was concern with expediency not precedent, and believed there would always be 'a more or less valid reason' for allowing appeal to Parliament. But it was an organ closer to the largest interest involved with private legislation, the *Railway News*,[1] which appears to have made most of the possibility of a tribunal in Dublin. A leading article tendentiously headed '"Home Rule" in Private Bill Legislation' referred to the 'political considerations' involved and the strenuous attempts which had already been made to have Irish bills inquired into and possibly settled in Ireland; 'It would be a direct concession to the "Home Rule" party to grant this. . . "'. In more judicious vein, the *Railway News* surveyed 'the efforts hitherto made to relieve Members of Parliament from the heavy tax on their time' from the Preliminary Inquiries of the late 1840s onwards and noted they had failed 'because Parliament clung tenaciously to its powers and privileges'. Whether Mr. Dodson's ideas were workable in relation to bills 'in circumscribed localities' remained to be seen, concluded the *Railway News*; they were 'certainly inapplicable to railways generally'.

Well before Dodson moved his resolutions the Society of Parliamentary Agents held special meetings and set up a committee to prepare its views and 'to communicate with the parliamentary bar and other persons and bodies interested'. Meetings were arranged with the President of the Board of Trade, and opposition leaders. In due course, the Secretary noted with satisfaction that the House was far from adopting a scheme 'which practically involved delegation by Parliament of their jurisdiction in private bills to an outside tribunal', and it was resolved to prepare a statement 'in vindication of the present system of private legislation'.[2] This task fell to Theodore Martin. His fourteen pages of vigorous assertion were not a critique of Dodson's proposals and certainly made no attempt to do justice to the tentative way in which Dodson had set forth some of the possible details, but what may be taken as a standard statement of the agents' defence of the existing arrangements, repeated for the most part in pamphlets published by other parliamentary agents over the next thirty years.[3]

As a parliamentary agent, Martin began, he could say with authority that 'the present agitation of the subject' was not due to the dissatis-

1   March 1872.

2   Min. SPA, 6, 19, 22 & 25 March 1872.

3   Theodore Martin: *Notes on the Present System of Private Legislation*, J.B. Nichols & Sons (1872).

faction of those bodies 'who as Promoters or Opponents of Private Bills are most frequently in Parliament'. They viewed 'with apprehension' the suggestion that Parliament should divest itself of its private bill functions. Committees of Parliament were 'high courts of arbitration' reconciling private rights with public interest and performing, 'wisely and promptly' a duty 'which they cannot without mischief delegate to others'. Turning to the three specific charges against the system — that it was uncertain in its results, time-consuming and costly, he found the first inherent in the subjects dealt with, and a virtue which would be absent from any alternative permanent tribunal. Unlike parliamentary committees who, in changing circumstances, would 'this year grant . . . what last year they denied', the members of a permanent tribunal 'must . . . incline to be governed . . . by definite rules or presupposed principles or recorded judgements in what many be deemed analagous cases'. The freedom and elasticity of judgement which in legislative matters the ever-shifting conditions of social wants and industrial development demand, would be sacrificed. Far from being time-consuming, inquiries before parliamentary committees were 'conducted with greater promptitude than before courts of law', nor were there any 'heart-sickening *remanets*'. Martin denied that time was wasted by superfluous evidence before committees, though the opposite was often held. Cost, he argued, was common to all litigation on matters of sufficient importance 'to justify the employment of eminent counsel and skilled witnesses'; expense could not be lessened and might well be increased if local tribunals were resorted to, and certainly would be greater if appeal were allowed to Parliament as of right. Provisional orders he dismissed as having 'not been found to be acceptable' other than for simple and uncontested matters, not involving encroachment on property rights and joint private bill committees on the grounds that, given the asumptions Martin made about their size they would not lighten the work of Members and more particularly because they would remove the existing element of appeal and the opportunities for promoters and opponents to judge each others' cases and come to terms between the hearings in the first and second Houses. There was, maintained Martin, notwithstanding all that had been said upon the point. no serious problem in manning private bill committees. Opposed private bills in the Session of 1871 had required the appointment of 37 committees involving 166 Members of the Commons; if each committee were reduced to three, the number of Members required would be reduced to 129, and it could 'scarcely be contended that it would tax the resources of the House . . . to find this number . . .'. It was, he concluded, his conviction, 'shared, I believe, in the main by all my professional brethren, that the existing system is satisfactory to the suitors in Parliament . . . if the House Fees are somewhat reduced, and if all the committees shall consist of three Members who of course alone should vote, there will be no need to resort to any new tribunals'.

These 'Notes' were circulated on behalf of the Society of Parliamentary Agents, copies being sent to and acknowledged by the President of the Board of Trade, Gathorne Hardy, E.P. Bouverie, and others. Bouverie, with whom the President of the Society of Parliamentary Agents had already had 'a very satisfactory interview'[1] was selected presumably because he was a prominent Liberal Member who was disposed to take an independent line towards the Liberal government's policies. Acknowledging the pamphlet, he wrote, 'I am satisfied that the difficulties attending any material change are so great, and the possible good to arise from such a change, so problematical, that I do not think the profession need feel any apprehension on the subject'.[2] This was realistic, for on the resumed debate (22 March), after some support had shown itself for Dodson's first resolution but considerable dissatisfaction had been expressed about his plan, the President of the Board of Trade had relegated the scheme to the sphere of things that might be done but were not practicable. He had at once concurred in the idea of substituting a system of provisional orders for private bills and declined to admit that 'the present tribunal has been very unsatisfactory'. He had doubted 'whether it was safe, even if possible, to make so great a change', and had gone on to approve of joint private bill committees and a 'limited extension' of the provisional order system. Most important of all, he had both said that he would not oppose Dodson's first resolution 'as taken by itself and not in its terms' — a truly Gladstonian phrase — and had objected to it because 'it would lay on the government too great a burden in matters which were not its primary or exclusive concern'. To meet this expression of the government's unwillingness to initiate change Dodson's first resolution had been amended to read 'private legislation calls for the attention of Parliament and Her Majesty's Government . . .' and agreed to in that form. His other resolutions he had then withdrawn with the intention, unfulfilled, of re-introducing them 'sometime after Easter'.

As noticed, some satisfaction was recorded by the Society of Parliamentary Agents with the unreadiness of the Commons to adopt Dodson's scheme. Further comfort could be taken from a speech made a month later by the Prime Minister to a highly interested audience. Gladstone

---

1   Min. SPA, 25 March 1872.

2   E.P. Bouverie to the President of the Society of Parliamentary Agents, 19 April 1872. Rec. SPA.

told the Institution of Civil Engineers that he had noticed 'a change creeping over the habit of mind of the people of this country with respect to the interference of government'; he trusted that the duties of government would always be chiefly negative ones and hoped that they would take care 'not to hand over to the Executive Government the charge of functions which they can perform much better for themselves'. Judging from the emphasis with which the agents' secretary marked this passage, it was taken as indication of the government's unwillingness to encourage changes the Society deprecated. Whether or not it was an allusion to the subject, there could be no doubt about what followed. Speaking immediately after the Prime Minister, the President of the Institution of Civil Engineers regretted 'a tendency at the present moment to remove from the Houses of Parliament that jurisdiction which they have so ably exercised over the engineering projects of this country'. They judged every bill by 'the principles of common sense'; he was satisfied no other tribunal could be substituted which would be equally advantageous to the country. And another guest, the Lord Chairman of Committees, whose influence in these matters was probably greater than that of any other individual, declared that 'if the question is fairly considered, it will be found that none but a parliamentary tribunal can deal satisfactorily with those important matters that are brought before us . . . '.[1]

Though the threat appeared to be receding the Society of Parliamentary Agents remained watchful. We find its secretary recording a meeting held to discuss 'the crucial question' should a government department be allowed to determine whether or not application should be made to Parliament for a local bill?[2] The occasion was a set of resolutions put down in June 1872 by a back-bench Member, F.S. Powell, the most significant of which called for the prohibition of private bills except when it had been proved to the satisfaction of a government department that the circumstances were exceptional and could not otherwise be provided for. This radical proposal was debated briefly in terms which showed that neither the House nor the President of the Local Government Board were ready for what its mover called 'so drastic a proposition'. Powell was concerned not so much with private legislation generally as with the lack of uniformity in sanitary provisions in local bills. He was subsequently mollified by the President of the Local Government Board's statement that he was considering with the House authorities the extension of the standing order relating

1   Report of Speeches. Annual dinner of the Institution of Civil Engineers, 24 April 1872, pp. 14-18.
2   Min. SPA 8 June 1872.

to the deposit of bills with government departments to ensure that his department had adequate opportunity to report upon them.[1] On the day Powell moved his resolutions J.G. Dodson, no longer Chairman of Ways & Means, asked the President of the Board of Trade what the government was proposing to do about the reform of private bill legislation.[2] He was told that it was impossible to say when positive information could be given, but so far as the Board of Trade was concerned the matter was one of examining how far the provisional order system could be extended. The first part of that answer suggests that the government were at least contemplating something being done other than the considerable development of provisional order-making powers for which the first Gladstone administration (and its successors) were responsible, but nothing happened.

O.C. Williams remarks of the 1880s that 'it was now from local authorities, not from private undertakers and private owners, that complaints of cumbrousness and expense began to be pressed against the system of private bill legislation'.[3] This was markedly true of Scottish complaints. The Scottish petitions preserved by the Society of Parliamentary Agents date from 1872, though as usual with petitions they are undated; with one exception they are from local authorities.[4] Several express support for J.G. Dodson's resolutions; all dwell on the expense of private bill procedure, and the desirability of an extra-parliamentary tribunal to take evidence once for all on behalf of both Houses. They are the precursors of that persistent Scottish pressure for reform which provided the background for the next parliamentary campaign in the mid-1880s. The petition of the Scottish solicitors, which drew attention to 'the enormous expense attendant on taking witnesses from Scotland to England', though expressing support for the principles of Dodson's resolutions, called for separate tribunals for England, Scotland, and Ireland (which Dodson had dismissed on the

1   Parl. Deb. HC (1872) 211 cc. 1666-9. The extended requirement for deposit of Bills with the Board did not come until 1882, in which year growing objections to the variety of sanitary provisions led to the establishment of the Police & Sanitary Committee. No record of the parliamentary agents' views at the time on what turned out to be an important innovation in private bill procedure has come to light. For the standing order on deposits see *HistPBProc.*, II, 54-6; for the Police & Sanitary Committee, *Ibid.* I, 211-12.

2   Parl. Deb. HC (1872) 211 cc. 1853-4.

3   *HistPBProc,* I, 177.

4   Petitions of The Royal Burghs of Scotland, of North Berwick, Inverness, Inverurie, Town Councils of Greenock & Brechin, and the Incorporated Society of Solicitors in the Supreme Court of Scotland. Non-Scottish petitions included those of the Association of Chambers of Commerce of the United Kingdom and Leeds Chamber of Commerce.

grounds that there would be insufficient work to occupy distinct Scottish and Irish tribunals). It foreshadowed the schemes put forward by the Scottish M.P. A. Craig Sellar, almost annually between his election in 1883 and his death in 1890. The Scottish desire for change was emphasised in the deputation from the Convention of Royal Burghs to the Lord Advocate and Lord Rosebery in January 1882. On that occasion Lord Rosebery held out little hope of the government initiating change. He remarked — with Ireland in mind? — that 'local tribunals . . . afford a dangerous precedent . . . not in this country, but which if established in this country might be held to be required elsewhere, and there might be strained to a pitch not consistent with the security of the Empire'[1] That the government, while prepared to contribute sympathetic noises, was not disposed to reform the system of private legislation unless circumstances compelled it to was apparent both at that time and in the reception it gave to Craig Sellar's schemes. More notice might have been taken of the brief but pointed reply Joseph Chamberlain had already made to Commons questions as to whether the government contemplated extending the scope of provisional orders. 'Every possible opportunity', he had answered, would be taken; the provisional order system had two distinct advantages over local legislation. 'It certainly relieves Parliament of a great deal of unnecessary legislation, and . . . helps to reduce the cost of litigation'[2] Significantly, the leading radical figure in the administration kept aloof from the debates raised by Craig Sellar. He was more interested in ensuring that the legislation for which he was responsible as President of the Board of Trade gave scope for provisional orders rather than for private bills.

A. Craig Sellar first put forward his plan for reforming private legislation within a month of entering Parliament in 1883. His ideas may be sufficiently appreciated from the debates on his resolutions in 1883 and 1884, and on his Private Legislation Bill of 1884-5[3]. To his plan as distinct from the accompanying arguments, we need pay only brief attention for it was not such as to command significant support, nor did the parliamentary agents feel called to criticise it. Less radical than J.G. Dodson's proposals, Craig Sellar's scheme would have retained existing private bill procedure up to and including second reading, but would have substituted for the committee stage a hearing before

1 *The Scotsman*, 31 January 1882.

2 Parl. Deb. HC (1881) 259, cc 427-28.

3 Parl. Deb. HC (1883) 276 cc 1611-47; (1884) 285 cc 1554-89; (1884-85) 294 cc 1264-1309 and 1520-21. The remarks and references which follow are confined to those occasions.

external commissioners or judges. In 1883 he called for the establishment of distinct commissions in England, Scotland and Ireland. Subsequently he abandoned the idea of separate English, Scottish, and Irish commissions or courts. It was, as he explained in 1883, a plan to remove 'the expense, uncertainty, and unprofitable waste of time' associated with private bill committee proceedings. Two years later, during the debate on his Private Legislation Bill,[1] he described it as one 'to set free . . . the time but preserve the control of Parliament . . .' by delegating Parliament's judicial but not its legislative functions. Craig Sellar, though he supported parliamentary control and was, therefore, opposed to the provisional order system, believed that once confidence was established in his tribunals, their decisions would usually be acquiesced in by parties to private bills, and by Parliament. Therefore appeals to the joint committee of both Houses, which his plan provided for, would be exceptional. That the opposite was at least equally possible and, if so, there was likely to be increased debate on private bills on the floor of the House was a weakness of his scheme. Nor did Craig Sellar demonstrate, or even try to show, that in practical terms it was possible to separate the legislative and judicial aspects of private bill procedure. Moreover, the advantages he saw were largely based on a mixture of faith and assertion. There would, he declared in 1883, 'undoubtedly be a great saving of expense' for no one would dream of taking parliamentary counsel, accustomed to drawing large fees, before local tribunals. The view, reiterated by the parliamentary agents whenever local tribunals were suggested, that parties would wish to do just this, and at increased expense, was perhaps more realistic, except in cases where the issues were comparatively unimportant. Craig Sellar believed that local tribunals would 'greatly tend to elicit the truth' and provide opportunities for a hearing to those precluded from appearing 'before committees in London'.

The parliamentary reception of Craig Sellar's early attempts showed that there was some support for reform, especially among members with responsibilities connected with private bills, but little for Craig Sellar's scheme. Sir John Mowbray, Chairman of the Committee of Selection, took the opportunities offered by the 1884-5 debates to lament the growing difficulties of manning private bill committees, and the former Chairman of Ways & Means, H.C. Raikes, who had most radical views on this question, strongly supported the need to change the existing 'dilatory, costly, and uncertain' system (1883), though he thought that Craig Sellar's scheme would not command public confid-

---

1   Bill 25, Sess. 2, 1884-5.

ence. Raikes believed that whatever steps were taken, 'the services of that meritorious body, the parliamentary agents, to whom the House owed so much as regards the transaction of its business', should be retained. In 1885 he allowed his name to appear on the back of Craig Sellar's bill, though in debate he dissociated himself from the details of the scheme. Some such change as that proposed by the bill, Raikes pointed out, had been 'countenanced' by every Chairman of Ways & Means for the previous twenty years. Both Raikes and the Chairman of the Committee of Selection were interested principally in pressing the government into taking the initiative. The former observed in 1884 that debate would be time wasted unless the government was prepared to take the lead, and, on the same occasion, Sir John Mowbray urged the House to say it was the duty of the government to come forward with a definite scheme. Craig Sellar himself, at times during these debates, appears primarily to be attempting to provoke government action.

Ironically, in 1883 and 1884, it fell to J.G. Dodson as Chancellor of the Duchy of Lancaster to indicate that the government favoured change, but not immediately. On the first occasion he said Sellar's plan did not go far enough (and persuaded the House to reaffirm his resolutions of 1872), on the second that he was for 'root and branch' reform, and on both that the government was unprepared to act during the current session. By the time Craig Sellar's bill had its second reading in February 1885 Dodson had gone to the Lords as Lord Monk Bretton, and the Chancellor of the Exchequer (H.C.E. Childers) dismissed the scheme as similar to the unsuccessful Preliminary Inquiries of the late 1840s, and one which would have the bad effect of causing private bills to be contested on the floor of the House.[1] He urged withdrawal of both the bill and an amendment in favour of joint private bill committees; it was, he went on, the last session of Parliament and the matter was better left to a new one when, if that government was still in office, they would 'afford facilities for considering the matter fully'. Craig Sellar's Bill was defeated in a division in which the Prime Minister and other members of the government voted with the 'Noes'.[2]

Craig Sellar's campaign coincided with the introduction of the large

1 In due course, Clifford criticised Craig Sellar's scheme on the same grounds; it would be 'prolific of discussion in both Houses', and little more than a revival of the old Preliminary Inquiries, which produced doubled inquiry and expense. Clifford II, 908.

2 Parl. Deb. HC (1885) 294 c. 1309.

Commons standing committees on Law and Trade, which between them required 160 members, and talk of more such committees. Such innovations lent some force to the old argument that the Commons were overburdened and required relieving of private legislation. Craig Sellar made some use of this point, but his principal achievement was to raise to a new pitch that rarely-absent sense of sin at the alleged costliness of private legislation, by a pugnacious and somewhat specu-lative use of statistics, official and otherwise, of private bill costs. He had, he remarked early in his first speech in 1883, intended to confine his purpose to Scotland, and this both his use of figures and the sub-sequent course of events suggested he would have been wiser to have done. He could claim to know Scotland and its constituencies, and the 'very deep dissatisfaction in that country with the present system of private bill legislation'. More particularly, he was on his strongest ground when he spoke of the special problems of small burghs — of, for example, the 'small Scotch burgh' with a rate income of £3,500 *per annum* which 'within the last year or two has had to spend £2,500 on parliamentary costs relating to a Bill to supply the burgh with pure drinking water'.[1] But he had concluded that what was bad for Scotland was bad for Ireland and could not be good for England. So his attack upon the system, and particularly its cost, became a general one. From the feast of rather stale figures he offered in 1883, we may note that, according to Craig Sellar, law and parliamentary expenses for railways 'before the crisis of the railway mania' averaged £1,500 per mile and there were cases of companies having 15% to 17% of their capital eaten up by such expenses. He did not attempt to analyse such figures, or to take into consideration important elements of cost, such as those incurred in the preparation of plans and other data, and advertise-ments, which might be held to be unavoidable under any system where public control and private objection was to be provided for. Nor were underlying political considerations touched upon. Neither Craig Sellar

---

1 Craig Sellar did not identify the burgh, and it is not possible to say whether it proceeded from choice to promote a bill instead of applying for a provisional order. But it has to be remarked that local authorities sometimes chose to pro-mote bills when provisional order procedure was available. One may note the following evidence given by J.W. (later Speaker) Lowther in 1904 — 'Our experi-ence is that in many cases local authorities are fond of coming for a Bill when they could really get all they want by Provisional Order. What they dislike is the control of the Local Government Board: and by coming to Parliament for a Bill they obtain sanction to all sorts of enactments which give the go-by to the Local Government Board and relieve them from the responsibility which they are under to that office. That is very often the reason why they come to Parliament for the powers rather than go to the Local Government Board for a Provisional Order.' Select Committee on the Private Legislation Procedure (Wales) Bill, 1904. HC (1904) 243, Qn.421.

nor other contributors to the debates questioned whether, in a society which attached central importance to individual rights, especially property rights, and accepted the provision of public utilities by commercial venturers, there could be any standard or limit against which the expenditures of promoters and opponents of schemes could be judged excessive. And though the point to emerge most clearly in these debates was the burden private bill costs could be to small local authorities, there was no disposition to consider whether to them, as representing the public interest, different principles were relevant.

The costs mentioned above and the 'rather more than £2 million spent by Railway, Gas, and Water Companies' between 1855 and 1861, were figures expected to speak for themselves, and to demonstrate that by some undefined standard the system was inordinately extravagant. The unphilosophical nature of the argument was emphasised by Craig Sellar's readiness to clinch his point by a comparison with the state of affairs under a regime which was hardly an appropriate object for admiration by a Gladstonial liberal. Yet it seemed to him proof that the system deserved to be condemned that, according to evidence given to the Royal Commission on Railways of 1867, the 'various preliminary expenses' incurred in railway promotion in the United Kingdom amounted to 'nearly the whole cost of the Prussian railway system'.[1] The cost, asserted Craig Sellar was due to the procedure, a procedure which 'great companies' were interested in keeping expensive to prevent small companies interfering with their monopoly. The main causes of expense were 'the enormous charges' for professional assistance which had grown up in connection with parliamentary committees.

After his initial sally based on old statistics Craig Sellar was assiduous in calling for returns. In addition to returns of fees paid to both Houses, three returns of expenses incurred in connection with private bills were made at his instance, covering the eleven years 1872-82 inclusive.[2] Their compilation depended upon the willingness and ability of the

---

1 Craig Sellar cited this during the debate of 6 March 1883. It was a statement easily improved upon; the following day the *Morning Post,* after agreeing with Craig Sellar that 'a Private Bill Committee is the most expensive tribunal that exists anywhere in the world', told its readers that 'the preliminary expenses incurred in England in connection with the promotion of Railway Bills cost more than the whole Prussian railway system'.

2 (i) Expenses incurred by each Railway, Gas, & Water Company, (HC (1883) 299, pp. 71/ (Accounts & Papers 1883 LXI, p. 207 ff). (ii) – by Canal, Tramway Co., Dock, Harbour, Navigation, Pier & Port Authorities, HC (1883) 303, pp. 35 (Accounts & Papers 1883 LIV p. 63 ff.); (iii) – by each Town Council, Local Board, Improvement Commissioners, Police Commissioners & Commissioners of Supply in Scotland, Town & Township Commissioners in Ireland, HC (1883) 351, p. 60 (Accounts & Papers 1883 LIV, p 83 ff.).

companies and local authorities to provide the information, and those relating to tramways particularly, and to a lesser extent to railways, were incomplete. For all their considerable length, they provide no information beyond the gross figures for the promotion of and opposition to private bills. There is no breakdown of costs and, of particular significance in relation to local authority bills, no distinction between the expenses strictly attributable to the system and those incurred as a result of the habit of sending official deputations to watch parliamentary proceedings, a custom which parliamentary agents were to describe as neither necessary nor helpful. In the round figures as used by Craig Sellar in the debate of 15 March 1884, expenditure over the eleven years covered by the returns was as follows:

	£
Railway Companies	3,900,000
Gas Companies	356,000
Water Companies	380,000
Canal Companies	40,000
Tramway Companies	375,000
Harbour, Dock &c. Authorities	360,000
Local Authorities	1,300,000

Comparing these with the miscellaneous figures he had used the previous year Craig Sellar concluded that private bill costs were increasing, and asked the House to relieve the public by establishing another tribunal which would do the work 'at half the cost and twice the efficiency'. What efficiency implied in this context (unless it was another way of referring to cost) he did not examine or explain. The following year, during the debate on his bill, he described these costs as 'a tax imposed by the present system in getting parliamentary sanction to a series of useful industrial undertakings', a remark which shows his tendency to over-state and over-simplify his case. However, he gave less attention on that occasion to his usual general arguments, preferring to make a good deal of the current *cause célèbre,* the Manchester Ship Canal Bill, upon which promoters and opponents incurred costs estimated at £250,000 in 1883 and 1884. In the former year that measure spent 49 days and in the latter 69 days before committees, and was rejected by the second House on both occasions. To Craig Sellar it was not so much an exceptional case as 'a flagrant example of the uncertainty and caprice of the tribunals'.[1]

---

[1] To some parliamentary agents it was a good example of the magnitude of the interests sometimes involved in private legislation, of the conflict of interests,

The principal reaction of the parliamentary agents was the circulation, in March 1884, by the President of the Society of Parliamentary Agents of a printed statement on private bill legislation prepared by the agent J.M. Clabon[1]. Its main purpose was to show that the returns obtained by Craig Sellar suggested not an extravagant but an economical system. Somewhat selectively, Clabon extracted from them the expenditure by English railway companies − £3,098,000 over eleven years − and comparing it with the paid-up capital of the same companies − £615,000,000 − showed that their private bill costs were under one shilling per £100 of capital. He asserted that 'speaking generally' the companies were 'well satisfied' with the tribunal, defended the system as one of arbitration, and gave the usual case against fixed external tribunals. For any problem of parliamentary time there were, he said, two remedies; the constitution of private bill committees of three members instead of four, and greater determination on the part of chairmen 'in stopping superabundant and irrelevant evidence'. The former remedy, often advocated, has never been adopted, and the latter suggested a state of affairs strongly denied by Theodore Martin in 1872. Clabon concluded: 'It is equally the opinion of the suitors of Parliament and those by whom they act that the present system is satisfactory, and can only be amended with advantage to the public by doing all that is possible to make it less burdensome to Members of the Legislature'. His *Notes* contained no explicit reference to local authorities or to any special problems some of them may have had. In his letter to *The Times* Clabon claimed that 'whatever reasons may be alleged . . . with reference to expense . . .' the movement for change was 'mainly designed for the relief of Members'.

Many years before, the Conservative leader, Lord Salisbury, had shown considerable impatience with a system which required Members of Parliament 'returned to attend to great Imperial questions' to spend their time 'listening to trifling litigation' upon matters which they were not competent to judge[2]. After he became Prime Minister in 1886 there were indications of possible reform. The Speech from the Throne, 1887, mentioned a measure 'to cheapen and improve the process of private bill legislation'. About this the Society of Parliamentary Agents

and of the regard paid by Parliament to that conflict.

1   J.M. Clabon, *Notes on Private Bill Legislation*, (1884). A note in the Society's records lists 48 members of the Commons to whom this statement was sent. But the agents were of course well-placed to approach Members and officers of the House informally and one cannot expect to find their activities recorded fully. At the same time a letter to *The Times* (14 March 1884) by J.M. Clabon made publicly many of the same points.

2   Parl. Deb. HC (1857-58) 150, cc455 ff.

sent a deputation to the First Lord of the Treasury, W.H. Smith. Subsequently, its secretary noted, 'this bill was never introduced, though it was generally understood that, if brought in, it would be on the lines of Mr. Sellar's bill . . .'.[1] The following year the Royal Speech again foreshadowed a proposal 'for diminishing the cost of private legislation'. The position in the speech of this indication, though not its terms, suggests that the government's intentions were now confined to making special arrangements for Scotland, where agitation, especially among legal bodies, was growing. Craig Sellar continued his campaign. On 17 December 1887, *The Scotsman* reported a long and rousing speech to his constituents in which Craig Sellar, now a Unionist, after some sallies at his erstwhile leader's Irish policy, spoke of private bill costs as 'a grievance to everybody except the parliamentary agents and counsel, and the directors of the great opulent companies . . '. A memorial, supported by twenty-eight public bodies was presented to the Secretary for Scotland in December 1887; it urged the adoption 'of a system of local inquiry with reference to Scottish private bills . . . in lieu of the present system'. Subsequently the Secretary for Scotland received a strong deputation from these memorialists. There came, on March 1888, not legislation but yet another joint select committee which, despite his deprecation of committees, Lord Monk Bretton (Dodson) was persuaded to chair. Its Commons' members included such strong critics of private legislation as Craig Sellar and Raikes, a milder complainant − the Chairman of the Committee of Selection (Sir John Mowbray), and a stalwart defender of the system, Sir Joseph Pease. It was required to examine and report in what manner without prejudice to public interests the system of private legislation might be modified in the interests of suitors, the economy of the time of Parliament, and the reduction of costs and charges.

The Joint Select Committee on Private Bill Legislation sat, intermittently, over four months. Its report and minutes of evidence[2] extend to over 600 pages, and its deliberations excited considerable activity among the parliamentary agents. Sir Theodore Martin gave extensive evidence.[3] A Memorandum which showed keen appreciation of some practical problems and suggested detailed procedural changes was

1 Min SPA, undated, 1887.

2 HC (1888) 276.

3 *Ibid*. Qns. 498-695. Martin was, for a second time, President of the Society of Parliamentary Agents, but did not claim to be giving evidence on the Society's behalf. The only other 'agent' to give evidence was James Beale, the solicitor to the Midland Railway Company, who conducted oppositions to but not promotions of bills. He expressed satisfaction with the existing system (Qns. 1354-56).

submitted by the Society of Parliamentary Agents.[1]   And at least two
of the published pamphlets on private legislation preserved in the
records of the Society of Parliamentary Agents were produced.

Sir Theodore Martin reminded the committee of his pamphlet of
1872, which 'really expresses my opinions now' (Qn.566).   Apart
from his general defence of the system as it existed there were other
points deserving attention in his evidence.   Two, though he did not
associate them, may be noticed together.   He remarked early in his
examination on the great transition he had seen in over forty years of
practice 'since the days of the great contests' (Qn.530), and on the
'very extravagant and wasteful style' of the system in the 1840s, 'and
even after', — a wasteful system that was 'dead long since' (Qns.535-37).
Then, following a long sequence of hostile questions from Craig Sellar,
he denounced as fallacious the returns of expenditure on private bills;
they afforded, he said, 'no material for analysis', were 'most misleading',
and did not discriminate between 'the actual cost of the tribunal',
which 'would be found to constitute but a small proportion of these so-
called parliamentary expenses', and what was 'due to the particular
questions which came before the tribunal'.   They were, he added,
swollen by 'the cost of unnecessary deputations . . . especially from
local authorities, who come to London and think they are indispensible' (Qns.683-4).   He was touching here upon another and later
wasteful style which was an extravagant concomitant rather than an
essential feature of the system.   Martin submitted to the committee the
'costs' of thirteen Scottish bills, taken from his firm's books.   These are
confined to agents, charges and disbursements for House fees, counsel,
evidence, and printing, and may be thought too circumscribed to be
regarded as private bill costs.   But he was concerned with costs strictly
attributable to the tribunal.

Invited to comment on the nature and quality of Commons' private
bill committees, Martin expressed himself cautiously.   He had seen in
former years stronger committees 'than we sometimes see now',
committees that faced 'bigger questions . . . and longer inquiries', but
he thought allowance must be made for the 'tremendous pressure' and
long hours faced by the House of Commons (Qn.546).   The fluctuating
composition of Commons committees was, he believed, 'inherent in an
elected assembly', and should be counterbalanced by choosing
experienced and strong chairmen (Qns.694-95).   On two further points

[1]   Memorandum to the Joint Committee on Private Bill Procedure by the Society
of Parliamentary Agents, June 1888, Rec SPA.   Most of its text is reproduced at
Appendix S to the committee's proceedings.

he was both critical and constructive. First, any scheme of delegation 'which did not delegate the whole function of private legislation to some external tribunal' carried with it the danger of a return to the canvassing to end which open committees had been abolished, and of bills being debated on the floor of the House; a practice analagous to the old 'mischievous' one of throwing them out upon Report or third reading might be revived, and instead of judicious consideration 'it would be a question of who could bring the most influence . . .' (Qns. 553-54). Of course, he did not favour any external tribunal (Qn.556). Second, he emphasised the practical necessity for those in charge of bills to be in close touch with the House authorities, which provincial inquiries would render difficult. The valuable expertise built up by the Lord Chairman of Committees, the Chairman of Ways & Means, and 'their considerable staff', would become less readily available and much would be lost (Qn.585). He suggested amendment of the existing system — which was otherwise best preserved — by the adopting of a joint standing orders committee for both Houses, the possible abolition of the Court of Referees for which he had little liking, and a reduction in the number of simultaneous private bill committees to be achieved by beginning committee proceedings earlier in the Session (Qns. 571, 597-8). In the face of growing clamour for change from some Scottish interests, Martin assured the committee that he 'had never had a complaint' from Scotland about the expense and difficulty of proceedings in London (Qns.588-9).

Of much of the lengthy evidence given to the 1888 committee the late Dr. Williams provided an excellent summary.[1] He remarks (rightly, if we except the strong views of the then Chairman of Ways & Means, L.H. Courtney, in favour of complete delegation) that 'the witnesses with the most intimate knowledge of practice were united in arguing that no radical reforms were called for'. But, like the members of the committee, the witnesses represented strongly conflicting viewpoints, and the Society of Parliamentary Agents wisely waited until June 1888, by which time many of the witnesses had been heard, before submitting its written evidence. It then concentrated on detailed ways for diminishing expenditure under the existing system. The Society's four-page Memorandum had a severely practical tone, over half of it being devoted to the expense stemming from practices which had developed in the drafting of newspaper and gazette notices, and notices to be served on landowners, lessees and other occupiers. The 'great expense' of the former, the Society held, was a consequence of 'excessive minuteness of detail . . . calculated to embarrass and bewilder,

---

1   *HistPBProc.* I, 186-8.

rather than to convey to the general public clear impressions of what is intended . . .; the evil could be corrected if Examiners of private bills were instructed to hold that notices 'set forth in broad, clear, general terms' met the requirements of standing orders. 'The use of broad, general language which all can understand, divested of all formal and technical phraseology . . . will, it seems to the Society, answer every purpose for which the standing orders were framed'. It revived a suggestion made by a President of the Society as early as 1864 for the amendment of standing orders to permit less repetition of newspaper advertisements. Also urged was a simplification and abridgement of the onerous advertising requirements when lands in more than one county were to be taken.[1] So as to allow private bill committees to start earlier in the parliamentary session, the Society urged the adoption by the Commons of the Lords' practice requiring promoters to proceed with the second reading of their bills within a limited and defined time. And they pointed to the savings possible if more was done by the House of Lords to ensure that witnesses and solicitors did not have to attend until 'they are pretty sure they are wanted'. In this respect practice might profitably be assimilated to that of the House of Commons, where the authorities made careful attempts to estimate how long the first bills in a group were likely to be in committee, watched their progress, and 'starred' other bills in the official list to show that two days would elapse before their consideration. Criticising the 'tradition, rather than any established rule' under which opponents of bills endangered their freedom to oppose a bill as a whole at a later stage if they attempted to get clauses in their favour in the first House, the parliamentary agents' Society recommended that 'discussion of clauses in the First House should not prevent opposition to the preamble in the Second'. These somewhat technical and strictly practical suggestions deserve detailed description not only as showing the approach made by the Society of Parliamentary Agents to the deliberations of the 1888 Committee, but also because they foreshadowed and influenced important changes in standing orders made before the end of that year. The right of petitioners to discuss clauses in the first House and subsequently oppose the preamble of a bill was embodied in standing orders, 'due', Williams notes, 'to representations made by parliamentary agents before the Joint Committee on Private Legislation of 1888' (Hist. PBProc.II, p. 162). Much of what the Society had recommended

---

1 Standing orders relating to publications of notices in newspapers involved in such cases what the Society called 'very heavy and, in many cases, a very needless, expense', and their suggestion was made in the knowledge that the Lord Chairman approved of it. For the history of this aspect of the standing orders see Williams's historical note on standing orders 10 & 11 *(HistPBProc.,* II, 26-8).

relating to notices was also incorporated in standing orders in 1888. It seems no exaggeration to say that the Society's Memorandum had more impact than the committee's report was to have.

There was by this time a sense among some parliamentary agents that the tide of private legislation was ebbing, and the joint select committee of 1888 marked, as it turned out, the climax of the movement for general change. Throughout that movement four characteristics may be discerned: a belief among Chairmen of Ways & Means and other officials of the Commons concerned with private legislation in the supposedly intolerable burden it imposed on the House, an inability to agree precisely on a substitute, the unwillingness of governments to shoulder responsibility for change, and a conviction, as strong as any held to the contrary by Commons' officials, among the officials and officers of the Lords that the existing system presented no insuperable problems. The majority of the select committee clearly were impressed by the first, concluding that, though it must be experimental, some form of commission 'presents the best hope of an adequate solution'.[1] But they shirked a firm resolution of the second, and failed to heed the lesson of the third. The committee had had before them two schemes, put forward by E. Stanhope, a former President of the Board of Trade, and by E.H. Courtney, then Chairman of Ways & Means. Stanhope's plan, based on the belief 'that Parliament ought to retain effective control over the principles of private bill legislation, while delegating to others the examination of details' bore resemblances to the schemes which had been promoted by Craig Sellar, being essentially a variant of the notion of delegating the Committee stage to a commission, while preserving to the Houses the other stages of procedure. And it sought to preserve a connection between such a commission and Parliament by making the Lord Chairman and Chairman of Ways & Means ex officio members of the commission. But the plan of the Chairman of Ways & Means, who had no 'suggestions for the improvement of the present system', was grounded on the view that 'the association of private bill committees with parliamentary life . . . was an incurable defect'. He was for an external tribunal, the members of which he would have excluded from either House of Parliament, to consider applications for private bills and take all their stages. Successful bills would become law subject to negative resolution by either House, but those rejected by the tribunal would not even be reported to Parliament.[2] The select committee, or rather the majority which was

1 HC (1888) 276, Rept p. viii, para 24.

2 *Ibid*. Qns. 4300, 4347, 4390, 4308, 4479, 4313. Both this and Stanhope's Commission were to deal with Provisional Order Confirmation Bills, and it is

responsible for its report, confined itself to expressing the opinion that Stanhope's scheme would provide 'a substantial accomplishment of the chief objects immediately aimed at with the least disturbance of existing interests and arrangements'. Glossing over the constitutional radicalism of the Chairman of Ways & Means' scheme, it went on to opine that if the Stanhope Plan was a success it might at some future time be 'extended and simplified' on the lines of Courtney's scheme. But the great weakness of the committee, appointed 'to report how far and in what manner' the existing system could be modified, lay in the previous paragraph of the report, where, after having suggested a commission, the majority went on to say that precise method 'can only be determined and carried through by a Government . . . and on its responsibility'[1]. To recognise that the assistance of the machinery of government would be needed to effect parliamentary change may have been realistic, but to place upon the government the whole responsibility was, in the light of what had gone before, abject.

Such a report was not likely to make much impact, the more so as it was accompanied by an incisive draft report written by Lord Balfour of Burleigh and favoured by four members of the select committee, of whom three were peers. Lord Balfour noted that 'if the House of Commons decided that they are no longer able or willing to find efficient committees . . . it will . . . be necessary to find some other method of dealing with private bill legislation . . . ', but so important a question was one to be settled by that House itself after formal discussion. He invited the committee to consider the public interest and that of the parties to private bills, unaffected by any seeming desire 'to get rid of an irksome and thankless duty'[2]. Apart from this consideration, Lord Balfour evidently was unimpressed by the alternatives which had been suggested. 'It appears', he remarked, 'that the remedy of creating a new tribunal far outstretches the evil complained of'[3]. He suggested that the burden of expense was caused sometimes by

---

interesting to question what would have been the constitutional position of a Minister whose departmental orders were rejected, especially under the Courtney scheme where Parliament would have no cognizance. The point does not appear to have been considered before the select committee.

1   *Ibid*. Rept, p. viii (paras 26 & 27).

2   *Ibid*. pp. xiii, xiv.

3   *Ibid*. p. xvi. Some years later when, as Secretary for Scotland, Lord Balfour received a deputation of Scottish reformers, he explained that 'I was much more impressed then (i.e. in 1888), and to some extent I am still, with the difficulties of finding a satisfactory substitute for the present system than of desiring to be regarded as altogether a supporter of the system . . .'. – report in *The Scotsman*, 21 October 1896.

committees sitting at a distance from the localities concerned, and in no inconsiderable degree by the sending to London of unnecessary deputations and witnesses. While, he continued, it was by no means certain that any saving of expense would be affected by local inquiries except for comparatively unimportant bills and those affecting a narrow locality, there was scope for an extension of the provisional order system especially for municipal and improvement legislation, gas, water, and short tramway bills, which 'would relieve promoters and Parliament'. The committee, he proposed, should conclude 'that the main features of the present system . . . should be retained', that 'almost everything complained of could be remedied by improvements' in it, and therefore no new tribunal 'to take the place of Committees of Parliament which they believe in the main command the confidence' of the business world and of the country generally' should be recommended. Included among seven specific detailed improvements suggested were the recommendations submitted by the Society of Parliamentary Agents in its Memorandum, as well as a virtual halving of House Fees, extended powers to award costs, the assimilation of the standing orders of both Houses, and the avoidance of concurrent sittings of private bill committees. The scope of provisional orders, he suggested should be extended, and opposed provisional order confirmation bills taken by a single tribunal — a joint committee or a committee of one House.[1]

It is small wonder that Lord Balfour's draft report became referred to as a 'Minority Report' — and was so spoken of by Balfour himself. The actual report was left unconsidered by either House, though before the end of 1888 a government spokesman mentioned that private bill legislation would receive the earnest attention of the government in the following session. The detailed procedural changes already mentioned were made, amongst others unconnected with the proceedings of the committee, and, in what were to prove the closing months of his life, Craig Sellar introduced one more reform bill. In retrospect, it can be seen that, with the subsequent decline in the volume of private legislation, any serious threat of general change passed. As O.C. Williams put it, 'the House of Commons got over its anxieties and proceeded, with some grumbles and readjustments, to tackle its work, while the House of Lords continued to function with unperturbed serenity. The private business . . . did not break down, (and) no radical alteration was made in the private bill system . . .'. More strictly he might have written, 'no general alteration', for he adds, 'the one tangible result of the various proposals for reform was the gradual shaping, in

1   *Ibid*. pp. xv-xviii.

the course of ten years, of the Private Legislation Procedure (Scotland) Act, 1899'.[1].

The parliamentary agents could look upon the outcome of the proceedings of 1888 with some equanimity. When, in 1889, the secretary of the Society of Parliamentary Agents noted that 'the interests of the Society had not been affected by legislation', he could have had in mind not only that no action followed the report of the 1888 joint committee but also the changes which the major Local Government Bill of 1888 had undergone during the course of its enactment. For the authors of that measure had envisaged a grand scheme of devolution under which order-making powers, including those of government departments under the Pier and Harbour Acts, Gas and Waterworks Facilities Acts, the Tramways, and Electric Lighting Acts, and the Public Health Acts, would have been transferred to the new County Councils. As a result of amendment the practical likelihood of legislative and rule-making decentralisation largely receded, there remaining as Section 10 of the Local Government Act no more than what Redlich and Hirst describe as 'a statutory basis for future devolution', the difficulty of making use of which had already been demonstrated by 1889.[2]

The series of abortive Private Bill Procedure (Scotland) Bills introduced by the government each year between 1889 and 1892 — and adequately described by the late Dr. Williams in his long section on the evolution of the Scottish Procedure Act — were noted by the Parliamentary Agents' Society, but there is no evidence of any overt action or protest against them. Put forward amidst a clamour of conflicting Scottish opinion ranging from a desire for complete legislative devolution to opposition to any devolution of parliamentary powers, they were unlikely to satisfy any shade of opinion and were in turn withdrawn. The bills of 1889, 1890 and 1891 were each denounced in substantial articles in the *St. James' Gazette* by 'A Correspondent' whom the records of the Society of Parliamentary Agents identify as Sir Theodore Martin.[3] The bill of 1889 he sees as inspired rather by an anxiety 'to catch the votes of a few clamorous Scotchmen than to propound a measure called for by public necessity and founded on a sound principle'. He asserts repeatedly that Craig Sellar was 'at least

1   *HistPBProc.* I, 191.

2   Redlich & Hirst, *English Local Government*, II, 72-3 and *Hist.PBProc.* I, 182. For the devolutionary aspects of the Local Government Act see *ibid.* I 180-2; for an unsuccessful attempt in 1889 to endow the new local authorities with order-making powers see *ibid.*, I, 191-2.

3   *St. James Gazette* 6 May 1889; 25 April 1890; 14 January 1891.

logical' in maintaining that change, if needed, 'was no less needed for England and Ireland', and finds 'objectionable' the fact that the substitution of an external commission for private bill committees will revive the obsolete device of discussing in the House matters on which it has not heard the evidence. He wonders at a Conservative administration proposing the 'revolutionary' delegation of 'purely legislative functions to a weak outside tribunal'. The constitution of the tribunal was indeed the least satisfactory feature of each of these bills. The inclusion of a judge of the Court of Session – in the 1889 bill as president of the tribunal – was a contentious feature; Martin thought that 'a worse selection could scarcely be made . . . as president of a body to deal not with questions of law but of public expediency'.

'May they let us alone is all we ask'. Thus wrote the Secretary of the Society of Parliamentary Agents upon the formation of a new Conservative government in 1895.[1] But two years later he was recording as inimical to the Society's interests the consideration in the Lords of 'Lord Balfour's Provisional Order Scotland Bill',[2] the measure which foreshadowed the Private Legislation Procedure (Scotland) Act, 1899.[3] Balfour of Burleigh, the author of the so-called minority report of 1888, had become Secretary for Scotland in 1895. In October 1896 he had received a very numerous deputation of the Scottish Private Bill Legislation Association, the introducer of which, Sir John Stirling Maxwell M.P., had said that he knew of no particular piece of Scottish legislation so much wished for as that to deal with the procedure of private bills.[4] Lord Balfour had assured that deputation that he would press upon the Government the desire that this question be taken up 'as a matter of practical legislation', dwelt on the long history of the attempts to bring about change and on the particular difficulty of finding a satisfactory substitute tribunal – which he saw as the explanation of the failure of earlier bills – and undertaken to do his best 'to devise some scheme which may minimise the inconveniences which you labour under' while retaining the general control of Parliament. The Private Legislation Procedure (Scotland) Act of 1899 was, for the most part, the product of that undertaking. Its evolution need not be examined in detail here, having been sell described elsewhere.[5]

---

1   MinSPA, August 1895.

2   *Ibid*. (undated) 1897.

3   62 & 63 Vict. c.47.

4   Report in *The Scotsman* 21 October 1896. The further references to this occasion are taken from the same source.

5   See *HistPBProc*. I, 195-205. As Williams shows, the bill of 1899 was subjected to considerable amendment, and the final provisions were not in all respects what

Under its provisions persons and public authorities desiring to obtain parliamentary powers in regard to any matter affecting public or private interests in Scotland were required to proceed by presenting a petition to the Secretary for Scotland praying him to issue a provisional order in accordance with the terms of a draft order submitted to him.[1] Thus the provisional order concept was at once extended to cover virtually the whole field of private bill legislation so far as Scotland was concerned and made a required, not an optional, mode — a considerable constitutional innovation. Upon the Chairmen of Committees and Ways & Means the measure placed the responsibility of deciding whether or not a draft order related exclusively to Scotland or had provisions of such character or magnitude or raised any such question of policy or principle that they ought to be dealt with by private bill, in which case the Secretary for Scotland was to decline to make an order and the promoters would be at liberty to proceed by what came to be known as a substituted bill.[2]

The Scottish Secretary was required, if there was opposition to the draft order, or he considered it otherwise necessary, to direct an inquiry by four Commissioners sitting in Scotland. The measure provided for the formation of an extra-parliamentary panel of Commissioners, nominated by the Chairman acting with the Secretary for Scotland, and, should the two Houses of Parliament so decide, the provision by standing orders of the Houses of parliamentary panels, in which case Commissioners would be selected from the extra-parliamentary panel only if members of the parliamentary panels were unavailable. Though all provisional orders made by the Secretary for Scotland had to be confirmed by bill, no absolute right to a parliamentary hearing for petitioners against such a bill was given. Only in the event of a motion being moved and carried would petitioners have a second, and parliamentary, hearing before a joint committee. Such were the main features of the one radical change to emerge from all the proposals for reform alluded to in this chapter. Nothing has remained

Lord Balfour desired.

1 Such provisional orders must be distinguished from the departmental orders made by government departments under the provisions of particular public enactments, for example, the Public Health Acts. The powers of the Scottish office to make orders of the latter kind were unaffected by the Scottish Procedure Act.

2 As the Scottish Procedure, as amended by an Act of 1933 (23 & 24 Geo. to c.37) and the consolidating Private Legislation Procedure (Scotland) Act, 1936 (26 Geo. 5 & 1 Edw.8, c.52), has remained a feature of private legislation it is to be noted that different criteria were eventually laid down for the exercise of this discretion. For this and other amendments see May (17th edn.) ch.XL, and *HistPBProc*, I, 252-3.

on record of the efforts which parliamentary agents presumably made to encourage opposition to the measure before it was passed, but, undoubtedly, it was unwelcome to them. There is a note of chagrin and even annoyance in the minute of a meeting held in January 1901 by the Society of Parliamentary Agents 'on the Private Bill Procedure (Scotland) Act and the evident intention of the authorities to send all possible business to Edinburgh for decision'.[1] That the measure was prepared, enacted, and for sometime administered without formal consultation with the agents is probable. When some years later their Society was consulted on Scottish procedure by the Lord Chairman's Counsel, its secretary described the occasion as 'an important departure in administering the Scotch Act, as heretofore agents had not been consulted and their advice would have been regarded with suspicion'.[2]

On the second reading, 25 March 1904, of a private members' bill 'for improving and extending the Procedure for obtaining Parliamentary Powers by . . . Provisional Orders in matters relating to Wales', the President of the Local Government Board supported the view that further devolution to other parts of the United Kingdom might be desirable and that its consideration should be preceded by an inquiry into the working of the Scottish Act.[3] Accordingly, the following month, the select committee on the Welsh bill was instructed (before going through the bill) to inquire and report upon the working in Scotland of the scheme, and the expediency of extending it, with or without modifications, to other parts of the United Kingdom. For what was to prove to be the last time a select committee examined the possibility of a general, if partial, substitute for private bill legislation, this time against the background of an existing system in Scotland and the demand from Wales.

The Society of Parliamentary Agents 'took steps to oppose' the Welsh bill, not by appearing 'actively in opposition' but by collecting evidence and securing the calling of witnesses'.[4] A special committee of the Society was established for the purpose immediately after the second reading of the Welsh bill. By the time the select committee was appointed on 26 April 1904, the Society's 'Welsh Committee' had met several times, conferred with representatives of the parliamentary bar, obtained a promise of co-operation from the Railway Association in

1   Min SPA, 7 January 1901. No details of the discussion were recorded.

2   *Ibid.* (undated) 1907.

3   Parl. Deb. (HC (1904) 132, cc.750-794. Bill 19 of 1904 — Private Legislation Procedure (Wales) Bill.

4   Min SPA, March, 1904.

opposing the Welsh bill and, 'by arousing the interest of the older and more experienced Members of the House of Commons', had been 'to some extent successful', as it believed, 'in preventing the inquiry . . . being relegated to a small and biassed select committee dominated by the advocates of the Bill'.[1] It may also have influenced the terms of reference of the select committee for it found the width of these 'a matter of congratulation . . . as it may facilitate obtaining a report against the proposals of the Bill, and for the maintenance of the present system' (1st rept.p.4). Its influence appears to have been in other respects rather limited, for of the eight suggested witnesses it put forward only four were acceptable to the select committee, and only three gave evidence. Moreover, it was faced with 'an intimation' that the parliamentary agents would not be invited to give evidence on the question of any extension of the Scottish system. However the Scottish parliamentary agent, Andrew Beveridge was invited to give evidence on the working of the new system in Scotland. He took the opportunity to condemn it outright as 'unnecessary' and 'inconvenient'.[2]

The parliamentary agents' Welsh committee, 'being impressed with the want of knowledge among younger Members of Parliament', also invited 'the historian of private bill legislation' to write on private legislation and the Scottish Act, and, according to the committee's records, the cost of printing and publishing that work was met by the parliamentary bar. Thus was published F. Clifford's *Local and Private Bills – 1904: Some Remarks on Pending Legislation*.[3] This essay was in no sense that up-dating of the subject matter of private legislation the absence of which the late Dr. Williams regretted, but a demonstration that Clifford's opposition to any delegation of parliamentary authority had not changed in the seventeen years since the completion of his *History of Private Bill Legislation*. Clifford put forward an uncompromising plea for the retention of the system as it existed or rather had existed before the introduction of the Scottish procedure. The agents' committee believed the publication to have had a 'useful effect'.[4]

The select committee on the Private Legislation (Wales) Bill reported the bill without amendment, but it was never proceeded with. However,

---

1 SPA Committee on the Private Legislation Procedure (Wales) Bill 1904; 1st Report, pp. 3 & 4, Rec SPA. The committee made two reports, on 6 May & 12 July 1904; they were considered sufficiently important to be printed and placed among the records of the SPA.

2 HC (1904) 243, Qns. 2461-2681.

3 Eyre & Spottiswoode (London, 1904), 28 pp.

4 SPA Committee on the Private Legislation Procedure (Wales) Bill, 1st Rep., p. 7; 2nd. Rept. p. 10. RecSPA.

in its special report the select committee noted that 'Wales stands in a different position to (sic) Scotland on the one hand, or England on the other' and concluded that it 'did not think the precise procedure which had been found to work successfully in Scotland would be well adapted to Wales', but its wants and wishes should be met by some adaptation of the principle of local inquiry.[1] In England the committee found no 'widespread or matured desire' for change that could not be met by extending the provisional order system.[2] The committee's chairman, in a rejected draft report, had wished merely to report 'that the Scottish procedure could not with advantage be applied to Wales nor be extended to England'.[3]

The parliamentary agents' Welsh committee hoped that the Society would find the result 'fairly satisfactory', though they would have liked to have seen the adoption of the chairman's draft report, and considered that the committee's report had been 'based not so much upon the evidence submitted to them as upon the preconceived opinion of members'.[4] In fact, though private legislation was to be questioned from time to time, the long argument was being overtaken by events. The growth of departmental provisional orders was eroding the sphere of private legislation. For that and other reasons the annual number of private bills had fallen considerably and was about to decline more markedly, alleviating the special problems which had turned so many Chairmen of Ways & Means into radical, though ineffective, reformers. The Scottish procedure had satisfied for the most part clamour from Scotland, and Irish Nationalists had set their sights higher.

Not that private legislation was entirely below the notice of Irish nationalists in Parliament — they provide an epilogue. In July 1905 the then secretary of the Society of Parliamentary Agents wrote:

> During this Session the obstructionists in the House of Commons have made use of private bills as a means of embarrassing the Ministry by wasting time and preventing parliamentary business being done.

Subsequently he wrote:—

> "Later in the Session the Nationalist party snapped a division and beat the government late of a Thursday evening. Next morning, because the Premier declined to make any statement indicating dissolution, the Nationalists blocked all private bills standing on the notice paper at 2 o'clock. The Session was far advanced; the

1   HC (1904) 243, p. iii.

2   *Ibid*. p.v.

3   *Ibid*. p.xi.

4   SPA Committee on the Private Legislation Procedure (Wales) Bill. 2nd Rept, pp. 11-13. Rec SPA.

government had no time to spare, and private bill promoters were anxious to avoid delays. The block continued from day to day, the number of bills gradually swelling. Most opportunely a Dublin Tramways Bill was amongst them and this the Nationalists desired to pass, but the Unionist members retaliated by blocking it.[1]

It was felt necessary on 25 July, he tells us, to send a deputation of agents to the Chairman of Committees and the Lord Chairman to protest against a hint that all bills might be suspended until the following Session, but:—

The only suggestion which these gentlemen seemed disposed to accept was that local influence should be brought to bear on Members . . . Most opportunely local supporters of the radical Members were in attendance the following day as promoters of bills before unopposed Committees, and it is reported that they openly threatened their Members with the loss of their seats if the block were not removed. This, added to protests from the constituencies, . . . led to a withdrawal of the block on 27 July, after a good deal of theatrical display in the House .

It was not only 'bad for business' and unseemly 'that the agents should be obliged to stir up the constituencies because the House cannot conduct its business in a businesslike way'; the secretary feared most that it might bring about what that infinity of committees had failed to effect, 'for if private bills are to be used for obstructing Government business, both front benches will insist on their removal'.

Though he records the removal of the general block:—

it was continued on the Rathmines Improvement Bill, which had been persistently opposed by the Dublin Members . . . The closure was here first applied to a private bill debate, but the motion to agree was allowed to be carried over to a subsequent day, and when the Irish Members had succeeded in having the bill appointed for . . . the last available evening, they withdrew all opposition to Government business in the afternoon (knowing that the Government would not make a House for discussing a private bill) and so brought the Session to a close except for the formal business of the Royal Assent.[2]

The formation of Campbell-Bannerman's Liberal Government in December 1905 and the general election of the following month have often been treated as landmarks in modern British history. So they were for the parliamentary agents, not only because of the vigorous policies of public legislation which followed and which were in part responsible for the contraction of private legislation. That, perhaps, could not be foreseen at the time. But the election of a House of Commons nearly half of whose Members were new to Parliament was

1   Min SPA July 1905.

2   *Ibid.*

not from a practical point of view a matter for rejoicing. Most of his professional colleagues probably would have agreed with the Secretary of the Parliamentary Agents' Society when he lamented the result of the general election for the loss of 'many good Chairmen of Committees'.[1] Whether they all would have shared his terse opinion of the new administration as 'a red hot radical, socialistic combination . . . the men who have done the most shouting have been chosen in preference to others more worthy of office'[2] — or appreciated its inclusion in the minutes of the Society — is another matter.

1 Min SPA, January 1906.
2 *Ibid.* December 1905.

8

'OFFICERS OF THE HOUSE'
1906 — 1939

The Society of Parliamentary Agents never formally claimed to represent every practitioner or became in the fullest sense a professional body, controlling the profession or governing entry to it. A definition offered by its secretary early in the period with which we are now concerned described the Society as a social institution designed to maintain the profession of parliamentary agency by the high standard of honourable conduct of its individual members and by concerted action in protecting the general interests of suitors and agents and in facilitating the progress of business.[1] But as the number of agents, and especially of occasional agents, declined the Society spoke more confidently for the profession. Its representative character towards the end of our period may be gathered from the following exchange between the Chairman of the Commons Select Committee on Private Bills (Local Legislation Clauses) of 1937 and the President of the Society:

> I see you start by saying that your Society consists at present of 30 members who conduct the very large proportion of the business of promoting and opposing Private Bills in Parliament. Are there Parliamentary Agents outside your society — A few, yes.
>
> How many would there be? — Perhaps four or five firms, who practise fairly regularly, are not members of the society, and, of course, there are Parliamentary Agents, in the sense that they are professionally representing petitioners, whom we do not regard as regular practitioners at all. Occasionally, a solicitor presents a petition, and acts as Parliamentary Agent. He, of course, is not a member of our Society in that way.
>
> But I imagine there is no reason to suppose that any views you put forward would not be the views of all those who practise? — I think that may be assumed.[2]

Seen through the eyes of successive secretaries of the Society, the period 1906 to 1912 was one of some tension, a certain disenchantment, but also of some development in co-operative relations with the authorities of the two Houses. 'The new House (of 1906)' one noted, 'is largely composed of new men', and that, as we have already seen, meant for the agents the loss of many experienced committee chairmen.[3] A member of the Society reported having been taken to task

---

1 The definition, made in 1909, is quoted on p. 116.

2 HC (1936-37) 112, Qns. 506-508.

3 Min SPA February 1906.

by the Lord Chairman for not having marked precedents on bills; the Society reacted by agreeing that 'a slavish following of precedents is not desirable, as precedent was frequently bad'.[1] But, having mentioned that, we must note that the Lord Chairman (Lord Onslow), on resigning a few years later, sent through an agent a message of appreciation to the members on the way they had helped him and the way he could trust them.[2] In 1906 the Society, presumably through its secretary, had discussions with the Chairman of Ways & Means, during which the Chairman indicated that the Committee on Unopposed Bills intended to be more critical, and the secretary subsequently noted, 'the Unopposed Committee in the course of the Session became a much more formidable undertaking; the members showed themselves very keen critics and created a precedent by rejecting an unopposed gas bill for bad finance'.[3] This new rigour may have been one result of the creation of the salaried post of Deputy Chairman of Ways & Means to assist and relieve the Chairman of Ways & Means in respect of private business. This step, and others to strengthen the Unopposed Bills Committee, notably the inclusion of Counsel to the Speaker on it, had been taken in 1903 upon the recommendation of the Select Committee on Private Business of 1902'.[4] With the Deputy Chairman, the Secretary of the Society of Parliamentary Agents apparently did not get on too well in 1906, on one matter at least, for he writes of inconclusive discussions on obstruction, in which 'the new deputy chairman showed that his sympathies at least were all on the side of the obstructionists. . . .'.[5] The following year he records that 'the Session showed a considerable falling off in private bill business, but not much abatement in obstruction' and complains of 'a disinclination by the Chairman of Ways & Means (under pressure from the government whips) to give opportunities for debate'.[6]

But there were also matters on which the Society's secretary expressed satisfaction or qualified satisfaction. Though it has been referred to before, we may notice again the pleasure expressed at the new tendency in 1907 for the House authorities to consult the Society on Scottish procedure 'an important departure in administering the Scotch Act, as

---

1   *Ibid.*

2   *Ibid.* April 1911.

3   *Ibid.* 1906.

4   HC (1902) 378, I have not included an account of this committee's proceedings in the course of which several parliamentary agents gave evidence. O.C. Williams dealt with it at length (*HistPBProc.*,I, 226-34).

5   Min SPA, 1906.

6   *Ibid.* 1907.

heretofore agents had not been consulted and their advice would have been regarded with suspicion'.[1] That year, too, it was recorded that the Society had established a standing committee on standing orders, though in consequence of some amendments to standing orders being announced 'when most private business was over and many agents on vacation', the secretary felt it necessary to write that, 'if the Society wants an opportunity of considering amendments they should make their own suggestions early in the session'. The much more satisfactory opportunity parliamentary agents had, at the end of our period, in this respect will be seen presently. In 1911, the Society received much satisfaction from the House of Commons Standing Orders Committee who at its request altered their rules in two senses desired by the Society, the more important of which related to the hearing of agents by the committee in opposed cases.[2]

The period after World War One was one both of further reduction in the number, but not the complexity, of private bills and one in which parliamentary agency had to adjust itself to changed ways of doing many of the things with which agents had been concerned. New forms of legislative delegation and their associated procedures both restricted the field of private legislation and brought the agents into closer contact with public legislation and the departments of government responsible for it — as, indeed, did the growing tendency to gear private legislation to public policy and to standardise provisions, especially those relating to local legislation. The years 1919 and 1920 brought major public legislation relating to the supply of electricity and gas and the Special Order procedure to replace, in those fields, provisional orders with their attendant confirmation bills. The Society of Parliamentary Agents appears to have been able to take influential steps to see, at least as respects gas, that the new procedure included positive parliamentary control: the minutes record that 'as a result of action taken by the Society, the Board of Trade had consented to move an amendment to the Gas Regulation Bill, that special orders made thereunder should not become operative until they had received the affirmative sanction of both Houses of Parliament. . . .'.[3] But as regards railway legislation, once the major field of parliamentary agency, the end of an era had to be recognised. The Railways Act of 1921 brought about the reduction of the number of railway companies from well over 100 to four. In face of the bill it had been decided that 'the

1 *Ibid.*
2 *Ibid.* February 1911.
3 Min SPA, 16 July 1920.

Society as a Society' could not usefully object to proposals in the Railways Bill as to the preparation and confirmation of amalgamation schemes without reference to Parliament, or take steps in regard to the question of compensation for parliamentary agents.[1] Nor was any vision of the motor age repeating the lucrative glories of the railway age to be realised, though some such vision seems to have flashed momentarily across the scene. In January 1924, the Society's President drew attention to a Private Member's Bill (introduced by J.R. Clynes) which sought to empower the Minister of Transport to make orders authorising the construction of motor roads and the compulsory acquisition of lands therefor. The President referred to the great alteration in procedure (presumably, no private bills) which would be effected in case such a bill received the sanction of Parliament. It was decided that the committee of the Society should be prepared to offer effective criticism to any similar bill which might be deposited, and to take action to oppose it.[2] Two further matters may be noticed briefly. In 1921 the Society unanimously resolved (a new member having raised the point) that applications for ministerial orders where the confirmation of Parliament was not required should be regarded as Parliamentary agency and not ordinary legal business.[3] And in 1929, when the House of Commons made an order to enable a more expeditious procedure to be applied to private bills whose passage was certified by the Lord Privy Seal as likely to lead to the reduction of unemployment, the Society resolved that its members should take all possible steps to co-operate.[4]

The problems of local authority legislation brought, at the end of the 1920s, the one major parliamentary inquiry into private legislation in the period now under review. In 1904 a Welsh Member of the Select Committee on the Private Legislation Procedure (Wales) Bill had sought to draw a distinction between bills promoted by local authorities, who ought to be representing the public interest only, and bills promoted by 'commercial adventurers'.[5] Had another Welsh Member, Aneurin Bevan,

---

1 *Ibid.* 23 May 1921.

2 *Ibid.* 8 January 1924. There is no sequel that I know of to this, and I record it merely as an indication of the pains of adjustment. There is evidence in the minutes & records of the Society that the agents regarded as excessive the special order-making powers already possessed by the Minister of Transport and other Ministers, and were concerned at the lack of uniformity in special order procedures.

3 *Ibid.* 5 January 1921.

4 *Ibid.* 19 December 1929. For Certified Bills and the subsequent Public Works (Facilities) Act, 1930, see *HistPBProc.*, I, 237-40.

5 HC (1904) 243, Qns. 81-84.

read this passage and was he recollecting it when in November 1929, he successfully moved, 'that in the opinion of this House, inquiry should be instituted into the desirability of so amending the Standing Orders relating to Private Business as to facilitate and shorten proceedings on legislation promoted by local authorities and to lessen the heavy costs now incurred'.? In the debate,[1] Bevan emphasised that he was concerned to cheapen things for local authorities coming to Parliament 'under the pressure of public need', rather than for promoters seeking powers in order to make profits. He suggested among other things that Government departments might provide such services as would enable local authorities to dispense with the need to employ parliamentary agents. A Select Committee on Private Bills — the Dunnico Committee — was subsequently appointed to consider and report 'whether any, and if so what, alterations are desirable in the practice and procedure of this House with a view to facilitating proceedings on Private Bills and lessening the expense at present incurred'.[2] It will be noticed that the terms of reference did not quite reflect Aneurin Bevan's interest in local authority bills. But the committee, which sat on nineteen days, examined very thoroughly and methodically the matters referred to it, especially in relation to local authority bills. It did not pursue the possibility of parliamentary agents being dispensed with in respect of such bills.

The Dunnico Committee's inquiry had three main aspects:— the timetable of private legislation, expense, and the problems posed by the Local Legislation Committee. Upon these the two parliamentary agents who represented their Society (Sir Harry Goring Pritchard and Mr. (later Sir) Charles E.C. Browne) had a good deal to say, and, as will be seen presently, the Society of Parliamentary Agents made a rather special contribution, very much in the spirit of quasi-officers of the House, to the discussion of expense. In addition to giving evidence on two days, the agents submitted a long statement, which was not printed with the proceedings and to which some attention must be given. But it seems desirable first to attempt to elucidate the nature of the problem presented by the Local Legislation Committee.

The committee dated from 1909, but was a continuation of the Police and Sanitary Committee first appointed in 1882 and re-appointed in all but a few sessions between then and 1909, after which the newly named committee was appointed sessionally. . . . The Police and Sanitary Committee's original terms of reference were 'to consider, and report on any provisions in private bills promoted by municipal and

1 Parl. Deb. HC (1929-30) 231, cc. 2125-84.
2 HC (1929-30) 158, Rept. p.iv.

other local authorities by which it is proposed to create powers relating to police or sanitary regulations which deviate from, or are in extension of, or repugnant to the general law', and the committee was required to make a special report to the House, with reasons and precedents whenever it recommended such powers.[1] The aim was to secure some degree of uniformity especially in public health regulations through reference of all such clauses to a single committee relatively fixed in membership and, in time, expert — a special private bill committee considerably larger than a normal committee but with power to divide. In practice all local authority bills containing 'local government' or 'local legislation' clauses, or powers to borrow, were referred to this committee; 'local legislation' clauses originally meant in this context clauses relating to police and sanitary matters. In 1909 the order of reference was extended so that it included police, sanitary or other local government regulations in conflict with, deviation from, or in excess of provisions of the general law. The new category of 'local legislation' clauses was hardly precise, so it is worth seeing what practice had become by 1920. An official of the Committee and Private Bill Office told the Dunnico Committee that 'local legislation' then included:—

> Control of markets and fairs, street trading, weighing machines and petrol pumps: control of construction of streets and buildings, sewers and drains; control of infectious diseases, sanitary arrangements and other matters relating to public health; police licensing of hackney carriages; regulation of traffic; grant of powers to local authorities to acquire land to provide and let public halls, bathing pools, and charges for admission; control of river traffic, clearing of rivers; powers to carry out town planning schemes, control of common lodging houses; and regulations concerning the sale of coke and ice cream.[2]

Thus there was a wide range of 'local Legislation' subjects which had to go before the Local Legislation Committee — one reason why the committee had become a bottleneck. Delays were attributed to the committee's careful procedure, but also to its unwillingness to use the powers it had to refer non-local legislation parts of local authority bills to ordinary committees. In the decade 1919-29 the Local Legislation Committee considered twenty per cent of all private bills.[3] Apart from two bills in 1920 and one in 1923 it wholly neglected its powers to refer non-local legislation parts of bills elsewhere,[4] though these were often the contentious and time-consuming parts. Of the eighteen

1 *HistPBProc.*, I, 211.
2 HC (1929-30) 158, Qn.209.
3 *Ibid.* Rept. p.xl.
4 *Ibid.* Appendix 2.

bills referred to it in 1927 only one consisted more than half of local legislation clauses and one bill had only one such clause;[1] the average of local legislation clauses in these bills was 29 per cent. The Local Legislation Committee's insistence on taking the whole of a bill, including hotly-contested boundary revisions and water schemes, was probably the chief cause of difficulty and pointed to one possible remedy. As the witness on behalf of the Committee and Private Bill Office, already quoted, put it, 'we suggest . . . the present procedure should be reversed . . . instead of all Bills having Local Legislation clauses passing to the Local Legislation Committee, only the Local Legislation clauses of all Bills should pass to that committee . . . ' the rest going to an ordinary committee or, if unopposed, to the Unopposed Committee.[2]

This was a solution acceded to by the Parliamentary agents, provided both parts of a bill were not taken at the same time. As their memorandum put it, 'the Society . . . agree that the Local Legislation Committee has owing to the growth of the number of bills promoted by Local Authorities, become somewhat congested and that it would tend to lighten the labours of that Committee if such parts of a bill promoted by a Local Authority as do not deal with local legislation provisions should stand automatically referred to an ordinary Private Bill Committee.[3] This view was almost certainly put forward in a spirit of acquiescence rather than one of enthusiasm, for parliamentary agents were usually aware of the inconveniences attending any division of bills between committees. When the question of special committee treatment for local legislation clauses was revived a few years later the same witnesses emphasised these inconveniences. In the event, the Dunnico Committee recommended in 'the cause of expedition and economy' that the Local Legislation Committee should not be reappointed.[4]

The Dunnico Committee, in the interest of facilitating procedure, gave general consideration to the preliminary stages through which a private bill must pass and its stages in the House.[5] The Parliamentary agents offered the committee detailed evidence in support of their view (with which the committee agreed) that obtaining a Private Act of Parliament did not take unduly long and the time taken compared favourably with that needed for Special Orders.[6] The following, based

1 See *ibid*. Appendix 3.
2 *Ibid*. Qn.211.
3 Statement pp. 19-20, Rec SPA.
4 HC (1929-30) 158, Rept. p.xliii.
5 *Ibid*. Rept, paras 5-8, and 10-18.
6 *Ibid*. Rept. p.v, and Qns. 331, 409.

on the experience of one firm, is adapted from the agents' statement.[1]

Average period for bills in session 1927, 1928, and 1929, from date of deposit in Parliament to Royal Assent (26 bills)	172 days
Average period for bills in sessions 1927 and 1928 (ignoring session 1929 on account of special expedition that session), from date of deposit to Royal Assent (18 bills).	196 days
Average period taken for the last 18 Gas Special Orders from date of lodging with Board of Trade to date of final confirmation by Parliament	209 days
Average period taken for the last 18 Electricity Special Orders from date of lodging with the Electricity Commissioners to date of final confirmation by Parliament	455 days

The agents also gave convincing evidence against proposals to permit the introduction of bills at any point in the session, or on two or more different dates, and the emphasis they laid on the importance of having the maximum possible time between the deposit of a bill in Parliament and its consideration in committee, to allow for negotiations, may have led the Dunnico Committee to stress the same point.[2] In both oral evidence and their memorandum the parliamentary agents gave valuable and detailed evidence relating to the simplification of advertisements and the possibility of advancing the parliamentary timetable for private bills. The considerable changes in the dates for notices and deposits recommended by the committee and subsequently accepted by the House were bolder than those suggested by the agents. The date for the deposit of bills was brought forward from 17 December to 27 November (at which it has remained) and other dates adjusted accordingly. The consequent task of drafting the amendments to standing orders was undertaken by the secretary of the Society of Parliamentary Agents and Counsel to the Speaker.

An outstanding feature of the Dunnico inquiry — and the one to which the parliamentary agents made a special contribution — was an investigation of the costs of private bills. At the beginning of a survey of expenditure which occupies over twenty pages of their report the committee referred to 'the most frank and extensive assistance' they had received from the Society of Parliamentary Agents.[3] In fact, the basis of this aspect of the committee's inquiry was an elaborate docu-

---

1 Proof of Evidence, pp.4 and 5, Rec. SPA.

2 HC (1929-30) 158. Qn. 334; Rept, p.xv.

3 *Ibid*. Rept. p. xix.

ment drawn up by the Society with the co-operation of individual agents and their clients, which showed in total and in detail the costs incurred in respect of each of 55 bills promoted in 1927, down to overtime payments to clerks in the offices of promoters.[1]   Some indication of the scope of the exercise undertaken by the Society on the committee's behalf, as well as of the categories of cost liable to be incurred in promoting a bill, can be gained from a description of the Society's analysis, but it is not possible to reproduce the extensive document itself.   In addition to an indication of the amount of opposition, if any, particulars of the costs of each bill were given, as applicable, under the following heads, viz.:

1   Professional charges or emoluments of Town Clerk, County Clerk, Clerk, or Solicitors

2   Costs of Notices to Owners, etc.

3   Parliamentary Agents' Professional charges.

4   Counsel's Fees.

5   Fees of and disbursements to Experts.

6 and 7   House of Commons and Lord's Fees.

8   Shorthand Writers' Fees.

9   Advertising.

10   Printing of Bill, Evidence, and other documents.

11   Miscellaneous expenditure, including −

    I   Preparation of Book of Reference

    II   Lithographing deposited Plans, etc.

    III   Maps.

    IV   Expenses of taking a Poll of Electors.

    V   Travelling and other expenses of officials and others.

    VI   Other payments to officials, including clerks' overtime.

    VII   Other expenses.

12   Amounts credited for sale of Bills and Evidence.

1   82 bills were promoted in the Session 1927, according to a return by the Committee and Private Bill Office (*ibid.* Appendix 2); the 55 analysed by the

Extremely wide variations in costs, and the differences between one private bill and another, prompt caution in striking averages. But it is possible to extract from the Society's document a reasonable indication of the extent to which the costs related to parliamentary agency:—

1	2	3
Total cost of the least costly bill to pass all stages	Parliamentary agents' professional charges	2 as a percentage of 1
£451.5.10	£126.0.0	27.9
Total cost of the most costly bill		
£16,441.8.8	£1,569.18.1	9.5
Aggregate total costs of the 55 bills		
£192,125.7.5	£31,490.1.11	16.39

The belief in some quarters that the abolition of the Local Legislation Committee had removed a valuable instrument for securing uniformity in local legislation provisions led to the appointment of the Commons Select Committee on Local Legislation Clauses in the Session 1936-37. The Chairman of Ways & Means told that committee that 'Of late years . . . Local Legislation Bills or clauses dealing with local Legislation matters have sometimes not been dealt with very satisfactorily'; consequently, he said, certain Members of the House had been giving special attention to private bills, a number of which had been opposed in the House. He spoke of the need in local legislation matters to give special attention to see 'that when such powers are given to Local Authorities, they should be given upon some uniform system, so as to avoid varying forms'. He reminded the committee of the Local Legislation Committee, which, he said, had dealt with these matters much more satisfactorily, but rightly had been 'regarded as causing a good deal of unnecessary time and expense', and therefore had been done away with. What appeared to be needed 'is some greater co-ordination in the Committee procedure on Local Legislation Bills or . . . clauses, by some method not involving additional expense or delay'. The Chairman of Ways & Means proposed that opposed private bills containing local legislation clauses should be divided by the Chairman of Ways & Means assisted by Counsel to Mr. Speaker. Ordinary private bill committees should deal with the preamble and opposed portions (not being local legislation matters) of such bills, and the

Society of Parliamentary Agents presumably were those handled by its members, or in respect of which the Society was able to collect the details.

unopposed portions and opposed local legislation clauses should be referred to the Unopposed Bill Committee or preferably, for the latter was overworked, a special committee working in a similar way to the Unopposed Committee, though it would have to be set up in two branches for opposed and unopposed local legislation business. The special committee would be chosen from a panel of Members and chaired by a Member nominated by the Chairman of Ways and Means.[1]

This proposal to re-establish a modified form of local legislation committee had strong support, especially from witnesses representing the Ministry of Health (which, in 1930, had urged not the abolition but the extension of the functions of the old Local Legislation Committee), but was held to be unnecessary by the Clerk of the House, the Principal Clerk of the Committee and Private Bill Office (O.C. Williams), and the parliamentary agents.

The Society of Parliamentary Agents was represented before the Select Committee on Local Legislation Clauses by the two agents who had given evidence to the Dunnico Committee. But on this occasion they dwelt on the inconveniences and what they believed to be the additional expense and loss of time insepaarable from any plan to divide bills between two committees. Moreover, though recognising the proposal before the committee 'presents certain advantages' (upon which they did not enlarge either in their written statement or oral evidence) they doubted whether the proposed change was 'really essential' to ensure uniformity in regard to local legislation clauses. That was to be achieved by making full use of the reports which the Government departments concerned made whenever they thought necessary on the provisions of private bills, and in respect of which private bill committees were required under standing orders to report to the House on the manner the recommendations therein had been dealt with and the reasons for dissenting from any such recommendations. There was also the advice of Counsel to Mr. Speaker to be had, and it was thought that 'if advantage were taken more frequently of his services by committees considering opposed bills it would conduce to better co-ordination'.[2]   In his oral evidence Sir Harry Pritchard referred to the representatives of Government departments at committee hearings, observing, 'I feel sure that they have only to assert themselves, as we know they can, to bring quite clearly before the committee the point which the report raises'.[3]   A related point of

1   HC (1936-37) 112, Qns. 1 and 8.

2   Statement on behalf of the Society of Parliamentary Agents HC (1936-37) 112. Qn. 504.

3   *Ibid.* Qn. 571.

importance to the practice of parliamentary agency was made by his fellow agent – 'Quite often . . . the Government departments are in the habit of communicating with us, in an informal way, long before they draft their formal report on the bill, raising all sorts of points and criticism, showing that they have gone very carefully into, one might say, every clause in the bill. That correspondence very often leads to arrangements between the parties and the departments to which effect is given by amendments made in committee. If there is any trouble about it, the department put in their report dealing with those matters which have not been settled in that informal way by correspondence or interview'.[1] Of this by no means new but developing practice, corroboration may be seen in the following passage from the Annual Report of the Ministry of Health for 1937-8. 'The number of reports would have been much greater but for the success of negotiations with the agents for the bills. These negotiations not only reduce the scope of the Minister's reports to Parliament, but also result in a reduction of the time required for the committee stage, so reducing both the pressure upon the members and the labour and expenditure of the promoters'.[2]

The recommendations of the Select Committee on Local Legislation, though in some respects a compromise between two conflicting views, favoured the advocates of a special committee for local legislation clauses, but were not found acceptable and little came of them. But though the secretary of the Society of Parliamentary Agents minuted that the committee had not adopted the recommendations made on behalf of the Society,[3] the sequel was in at least one respect in accordance with those recommendations. Among four sessional orders made by the House in the following session (and renewed thereafter until made standing orders in 1945) one provided that committees on opposed bills containing local legislation clauses should have, when considering such clauses, the assistance of the Counsel to Mr. Speaker.[4]

There had been another device for furthering uniformity to which the agents had referred to in their statement to the Committee on Local Legislation Clauses. 'The Report of the Committee on Common Form Clauses in Local Legislation Bills appointed last session', they had written, 'was only published at the end of the session and its effect on the work of the committees is not yet apparent. It is generally considered, however, that it must result in securing greater uniformity'. Here

1 *Ibid.* Qn. 593.
2 Cmd.5801 of 1937-38, p. 142.
3 Min SPA, 13 July 1937.
4 *HIST.PBProc.,* I, 318.

that device, or rather its development, must be referred to principally as an outstanding example of close collaboration between parliamentary agents and officers of the House and, in this case, Members of the House, and officials of Government departments, and others. Early in 1936 two members of the Society of Parliamentary Agents were invited by the Chairman of Ways & Means to participate in an unofficial committee 'to consider clauses included in recent private bills as clauses of common form to which objection has been taken, with a view to forming an opinion whether or to what extent such clauses or any of them are necessary or expedient and whether or to what extent they go further than is requisite for dealing with the mischief they are intended to remedy: and to report what action should be taken thereon'.[1] The unofficial committee on Common Form Clauses eventually consisted of the Deputy Chairman of Ways & Means, two other Members of the House, the Speaker's Counsel (Sir Frederick Liddell), the Principal Clerk of the Committee and Private Bill Office (O.C. Williams), two parliamentary agents (Sir Harry Pritchard and Mr. , later Sir, Geoffrey Cox) and the town clerk of Croydon. With the assistance of officers of government departments the committee reviewed a large number of clauses; its report was ordered to be printed by the House.[2] and was followed by the publication of the first edition of *Standard Clauses* consisting of: —

1 Clauses normally acceptable without special proof;
2 Clauses similarly acceptable with certain amendments;
3 Clauses not acceptable without proof of local need;
4 Clauses not acceptable except in very special circumstances.

There was also a fifth category which would become unnecessary with the passing of the Public Health Act 1936. Thus the committee devised a way of securing a degree of uniformity in local legislation matters, easy to revise (a revised edition was issued in the following session). 'Common form' or 'standard' clauses were to be of considerable importance in connection with future local legislation.

In the course of this history no works have been cited more frequently than those of the late O.C. Williams. Fittingly, the study ends with reference to a collaboration between parliamentary agents and officers of the two Houses which he did much to initiate. In April 1943, Williams, as Principal Clerk of the Committee and Private Bill Office, informed the Chairman of Ways & Means that his history of the

1 Rec SPA, February 1936.
2 HC (1935-36) 162.

private business standing orders was complete, and suggested 'the careful revision of the standing orders . . . by a competent select committee or alternatively an unofficial drafting committee'.[1] The second method was chosen. The Society of Parliamentary Agents was invited to co-operate and its acting honorary secretary became a member of the unofficial committee which, between December 1943 and October 1944, thoroughly revised the standing orders. As a result of that committee's 'valuable and arduous work'[2] the Select Committee on Private Business Standing Orders was able to report the major revision of standing orders of 1945. In the same session the House of Lords revised its private business standing orders, and the select committee of that House referred both to the work of the unofficial Commons' committee, 'whose work forms the basis of this revision', and to the special thanks due to Mr. C.E.C. Browne, the parliamentary agent, 'for his assistance in adapting their work for the use of this House'.[3] The small band of parliamentary agents at the end of our period practised a profession involving complex collaboration with officers of central and local government, solicitors, financial advisers, engineering and other technical consultants, and parliamentary counsel. But their participation in the revision of the standing orders serves to emphasise that it is as 'officers of the House' — a historic status defying definition and formal fact — that these legal practitioners in a legislative setting, and their present-day successors, doubtless would wish to be remembered.

1 HC (1944-45), appendix.

2 *Ibid*. Rept. p.4.

3 HL (1945) 28, Rept, p. vi.

APPENDICES

A

PETITIONS FOR PRIVATE BILLS (Commons) 1847-51

Sixty-six firms or individuals handled the promotion of 1,262 petitions for private bills in the period from 1847 to 1851. According to the main subject matter of the related bills, the petitions are classifiable as follows:—

1	Railway	(669)
2	Canal, river, navigation	(36)
3	Dock, harbour, bridge	(75)
4	Improvement, market	(114)
5	Paving, lighting, water, sanitation	(141)
6	Inclosure, drainage	(31)
7	Other	(196)

(1,262)

A schedule, using the above classification, of 47 of these firms and the 872 petitions they handled in the sessions 1847, 1847-8, and 1849, is given on the following pages. Agents named in the schedule also dealt with 361 petitions in the sessions 1850 and 1851. In those two sessions nineteen other agents promoted a further 29 petitions; one dealt with 6 petitions, no other with more than 2.

(Sc) and (Ir) indicate practices originally Scottish or Irish.

Agent	1847							1847-8							1849							Total 1847-49
	1	2	3	4	5	6	7	1	2	3	4	5	6	7	1	2	3	4	5	6	7	
Bainbrigge, Wm. A.	1																					1
Baine, Geo.													1									1
Baker, T. (Ir)			1								1	1				1	1					5
Bell, Stewart & Lloyd	2		1	1				1										1	1			7
Bonner, J.						1																1
Bower & Son	1											1										2
Browne, M. & Son			1	1								1		3							1	9
Bryden, Wm. (Ir)				1	1				3													9
Bulmer, Durnford & Co.	5		3	1								2			1		1				1	14
Cameron & Martin	3		1	1	1										2						1	8
Cleobury, Thos.		1																				1
Coppock, J.			1											1				1			1	4
Deans, Dunlop & Hope (Sc)	10		5		5	1	4	9						1	2		1	1			1	23
Dodds, J. (Sc)	3			1									1					1				3
Dorington & Co.	43	3	5	6	5	1	4	19		2	6	4	2	6	8			3	1	3	5	128
Drew & Shadwell					1									1								1
Dyson & Co.	62	1	1	9	6	3	3	19	3	5	1	3	3	1	7	2	1		3	1	4	137
Everest & Co		1					2							1								3
Fallows, J.							1															1
Fearon & Clabon								1		1	1			1			1				3	9
Grahame, Weems & Grahame (Sc)	12						2	7			2		1	1	5		1	1			1	31
Gregory & Co.	3			3			1	3				2		2	1				1		1	18
Gurney, John (Sc)			1	3																		4
Johnston & Co. (Sc)													1									1
Jones & Walmisley	2		2	1	1			2				2		3								13

Agent	1847							1847-48							1849							Total 1847-1849
	1	2	3	4	5	6	7	1	2	3	4	5	6	7	1	2	3	4	5	6	7	
Lang, G.H. (Sc)	8							6							2							16
Law, Anton, Holmes & Turnbull	12		1					6							2				1			22
Macdougall & Youall				1			2			2												5
Norris, Allen & Simson											1											1
Parkes, J	5			2	1																	8
Parkin, Wm	1																					1
Parratt & Walmisley	1		2		1										1							6
Pritt & Co. (Sherwood & Co.)	145	1	8	2	18		2	43		2	3			3	23				5	1	6	264
Richardson, Connell & Loch (Sc)	3		1		2	1	3	1	1	1		2	1	1	1		1		1		2	23
Smythe, George Lewis (Ir)	3		1			1	1				1		2		1			1	1			12
Smythe, Wm.																					1	1
Spottiswoode & Robertson (Sc)	1		1				1	2	1			1		1			1				1	12
Sudlow & Kingdon											1	1										2
Toogood, H. & W.								1			1								1			3
Tyrell, E. (City Remembrancer)				4					1		1								1		2	9
Walmisley & Son												1						1	2		3	8
Webster, G. & T.W. (Sc)	12						3	8		1		1		1		1	1		5	1	1	33
Williams, C.R.							1															1
Williamson, Hill & Co.														2				1				3
Wright & Bonner														1								1
Wright, Smith & Shepherd	3			1															1			5
Yates, T.				1																	1	2

B

PETITIONS FOR PRIVATE BILLS – 1875

Key – 1 Railway & Tramway
2 Canal, River, Navigation
3 Dock, Harbour, Bridge
4 Improvement, Market
5 Paving, Lighting, Water, Sanitation
6 Inclosure, Drainage
7 Other

Agents	1	2	3	4	5	6	7	Total
Ashurst, Morris & Co	1							1
Baxter & Co.	3	1		1			2	7
Bell, Wm.	12		1	1	2		1	17
Byrnes					1			1
Clabon & Fearon			2					2
Cooper, R.W.	1				4			5
Cruse & Sandes	2			1	1			4
Dickson & Co.					2			2
Durnford & Co	3	1		1	3			9
Dyson & Co.	18		4	8	11		5	46
Gedge, Kirby & Millett	1							1
Gough & Co.	1							1
Graham, John					2			2
Grahames & Wardlaw	3				3		3	9
Hargrave, Fowler & Blunt				1				1
Holmes & Co.	1			2				3
Hirst, A.				1				1
Lewin, S.H.	1			3				4
Lydall, J.H.							2	2
Loch & Maclaurin	1		2	1				4
Marriott & Jordan	1		2		1		1	5
Martin & Leslie	9			2	3			14
Norton, G.					3			3
Pead, R.J.				1				1
Porter, G.T.	1							1
Rees, J.C. (Dorington)	10	4		3	11		1	29
Robertson, Wm.							1	1
Sharkey, P. Burrowes	3	1						4
Sharpe & Co.	1				2			3
Sherwood & Co.	15	1		3	6	1	2	28
Simson, Wakeford & Simson	3		2	2	6		2	15
Tarhoudin & Hargreaves	1				1			2
Taylor, Hoare, Taylor & Cooke					1			1
Toogood, W.	2							2
Toogood & Ball	11		1	2	2			16
Wainright, G.W.R.	1							1
Walker, Chas.					1			1
Wyatt, Hoskins & Hooker	7			1	4	1		13

| | | | | | | | | 262 |

C

PETITIONS FOR PRIVATE BILLS – 1900

Key – 1 Railway
2 Tramway
3 Canal, River, Navigation
4 Dock, Harbour, Bridge
5 Local Authority, Improvement
6 Paving, Lighting, Water, &c.
7 Drainage
8 Other

Agents	1	2	3	4	5	6	7	8	Total
Baker, Lees & Co.	3	1·		1	2	13			20
Ball, J.C.						2			2
Batten & Co.						1			1
Bell, W. & W.M.	8	2		2	1	4			17
Beveridge, A. & W.					2	2		1	5
Bircham & Co.	1								1
Brown, Ringrose & Co.								1	1
Clay & Close						1			1
Cooper, R. W. & Son	1			1	2	2			6
Durnford & Co.	1	1			2	4	1		9
Dyson & Co.	9	4	1		15	7	1	2	39
Faithfull & Owen								1	1
Flux, Thomson & Flux								1	1
Fowler & Co.						1		1	2
Grahames, Curry & Spens	3				1			2	6
Hargreaves & Co.					1	1			2
Holmes & Co.	1				1	1			3
Kennedy, J.	4	2	1			2		2	11
Lewin & Co.		1			5	2		1	9
Martin & Leslie	5	1	1	1	3				11
Rees & Freres (Dorington)	4	4		4	4	12		3	31
Robbins, Billing & Co.						1			1
Roberts & Co.						1			1
Robertson, Wm. & Co.	1			1	1				3
Sharpe & Co.	1	7		1	11				20
Sherwood & Co.	19	5		2	7	5		8	46
Speechley & Co.					1				1
Tarhoudins & Hitchcock		3							3
Tetley, J.D.	1					1			2
Torr & Co.	1					4			5
Warwick Webb		1							1
Wilde, W.G.								1	1
Wyatt & Co.					2	3		1	6

269

D

PETITIONS FOR PRIVATE BILLS – 1920

Key – 1 Railway
2 Tram & Transport
3 Canal, River, Navigation
4 Dock, Harbour, Bridge
5 Local Authority General
6 Lighting, Water
7 Drainage
8 Other

Agents	1	2	3	4	5	6	7	8	Total
Baker & Sons					3				3
Bircham & Co.	2					1		1	4
Dyson, Bell & Co.	3	5	1	7	6	4			26
Grahames & Co.						1	1	1	3
Kennedy, J.	1						1		2
Lees & Co.					7	4			11
Lewin, Gregory & Anderson					4	1			5
Martin & Co.					1	1			2
McDonnell & Jackson					1				1
Rees & Freres	1	1	1	1	3	1		1	9
Sharpe, Pritchard & Co.					16	4			20
Sherwood & Co.	1	1		1	6	6		5	20
Torr, Durnford & Co.		1	1		2	5		1	10
Vizard, Oldham & Co.				1					1
Wyatt & Co.				1		1		1	3
									120

E

PETITIONS FOR PRIVATE BILLS, 1928-9 to 1937-8

Key — 1 Railway
2 Tram & local Transport
3 Canal, River, Navigation
4 Dock, Harbour, Bridge, Tunnel
5 Local Authority general
6 Electricity, Gas, Water, Sanitation
7 Other

Agents	1	2	3	4	5	6	7	Total
Batten & Co.						2		2
Baxter & Co.	4							4
Beale & Co.	10						1	11
Bircham & Co.		1		3	1		1	6
Blyth, Dutton & Co.						3	2	5
Burchells			1					1
Cooper, R.W. & Son					1	4		5
Dyson, Bell & Co.	2	7	4	7	38	34	11	103
Grahames & Co.			3				2	5
Hiley, Sir E.				1	16		2	19
Hoskins, H.F.A.	5							5
Kennedy, J. & Co.		7	1	1	2	2	1	14
Jackson, J.M. McDonnell, & Co.					1			1
Lees & Co.		4			57	13	2	76
Lewin & Co.		2	2	1	30	18	7	60
Martin & Co.			1	1	1	3		6
McIntyre, J.						1		1
Rees & Freres		13	14	2	8	30	5	72
Rhys Roberts & Co.					2			2
Sharpe, Pritchard & Co.	1	2	5	7	110	15	4	144
Sherwood & Co.	24	2	1	5	41	46	13	132
Vizard, Oldham & Co.			1			2	3	6
Whitelegge, C.H.	4							4
Wyatt & Co.				1				1
	50	38	32	30	308	173	54	
								685

F

VACHER'S 'PRIVATE BILLS'

The Westminster firm of Vacher & Sons, though an outside firm of printers and stationers, had some official status in the mid-nineteenth century, having been given the running of the Copying Office. Until it was abolished in 1864, the principal function of that office was to copy evidence given before private bill committees.

Vacher & Sons issued their annual *Lists of the Petitions for Private Bills* from 1847 until the parliamentary session of 1938-39. 115 numbers, with minor variations of title, were published, additional numbers in some years showing the progress of bills up to Easter. Two lists are always given, (i) alphabetical. (ii) the order in which petitions are numbered in the Examiners' lists. The title of each bill, the parliamentary agent, associated engineers or surveyors (from 1860) and solicitors (from 1878) are shown. Some early numbers record the composition of committees on opposed bills and of certain other committees, titles of bills introduced in the House of Lords, orders relating to private bill proceedings, and sundry other items. From 1870 applications for provisional orders and special orders under specified Acts are listed. Other miscellaneous information occasionally given includes lists of petitions relating to disputed elections, with the names of Members involved, and the names of Members of Parliament who were directors of railway companies.

When this work was started no complete set appeared to have survived outside the offices of parliamentary agents, though the British Library has a broken set and the Bodleian Library a few numbers. It has now been possible to make available a photographic copy of a complete set in the House of Lords Record Office.

G

FIRST PRINTED RULES OF THE SOCIETY OF PARLIAMENTARY AGENTS

That the appointment of President of the Society be determined by ballot, without previous nomination.

That the President of the Society hold his office for two years, and that he do not fill the same office until the expiration of two years from his previous presidency.

That in the ballot for the office of President, each Member present shall put in a list of the Members' names, with the name of the person whom he desires to fill the vacant office marked thereon: and that the ballot be renewed between the two persons having the greatest number of votes, unless one of them has an absolute majority of the votes of the persons present.

That the appointment of Secretary of the Society be determined by ballot, without previous nomination.

That the Secretary of the Society hold his office for three years, and that he be always re-eligible.

That the same form be observed in the election of Secretary as of President.

That the Annual Subscription be Three Guineas.

That the Subscription of every Member elected by payable immediately on his election; but that any Member elected at the Summer Meeting be only required to pay half a subscription.

That all future Members elected do pay an entrance fee of 5 guineas, in addition to their annual subscription for the year wherein they may be elected.

That no motion to regulate the practice of the Members of the Society or to alter any of the rules of the Society be put from the Chair, at any Meeting of the Society, unless the Chairman of such Meeting is satisfied that due notice of such motion has been given to each Member of the Society at least one clear day before the day of such Meeting.

That no person shall be proposed as a Member of the Society who shall not have *bona fide* practised as a Parliamentary Agent two years at least previously, and have conducted Bills through Parliament in that capacity; but this rule shall not apply to any partner in any firm of which every other partner is a Member of the Society.

That the name of any Candidate be transmitted to the Secretary and President 15 days at least prior to one of the half-yearly General Meetings, and at such Meeting the Society may proceed to the election of such proposed Candidate.

That the Secretary do send to each Member of the Society the name of the Candidate, together with those of the proposer and seconder, at the same time that he intimates the day appointed for the half-yearly Meeting at which such election shall take place.

That every election shall be by ballot, and that three black balls shall exclude; and that no ballot be valid unless ten Members at least shall vote.

January 1877.

H

RULES FOR PARLIAMENTARY AGENTS

Between 1837 and 1938 four sets of rules were issued by the Speaker of the House of Commons under the Commons' resolution of 16 August 1836 (CJ(1836)819), viz. in 1837, 1873, 1905 and 1938. Three sets of rules were issued by the Lord Chairman of Committees up to 1938, the first being in 1876.

Reproduced here are —

(i) The original rules made by Speaker Abercromby in 1837;

(ii) The 1938 rules, which placed parliamentary agency on its modern basis by introducing two types of registration and giving the Speaker positive control over registration.

(i)

IN pursuance of the Authority vested in me by the RESOLUTION of The HOUSE of COMMONS of the 16th day of August 1836, I hereby establish the following RULES to be observed by the OFFICERS of the HOUSE, and by all PARLIAMENTARY AGENTS and SOLICITORS engaged in prosecuting Proceedings in the HOUSE of COMMONS upon any PETITION or BILL:—

1.   THAT every Agent conducting Proceedings in Parliament before the House of Commons shall be personally responsible to The House, and to The Speaker, for the observance of the Rules, Orders and Practice of Parliament, as well as any Rules which may from time to time be prescribed by The Speaker, and also for the payment of the Fees and Charges due and payable to the Officers of the House of Commons.

2.   THAT no person shall be allowed to act as such Agent until he shall have subscribed a declaration before one of the Clerks in the Private Bill Office, engaging to observe and obey the Rules, Regulations, Orders and Practice of the House of Commons, and also to pay and discharge from time to time, when the same shall be demanded, all Fees and Charges due and payable upon any Petition or Bill upon which such Agent may appear;   and after having subscribed such declaration, and entered into a recognizance or bond (if hereafter required), in the penal sum of *500 l.* conditioned to observe the said declaration, such person shall be registered in a book to be kept in the

Private Bill Office, and shall then be entitled to act as a Parliamentary Agent: provided that upon the said declaration, recognizance or bond and registry, no Fee shall be payable.

3. THAT the declaration before mentioned, and the recognizance and bond, if hereafter required, shall be in such form as The Speaker may from time to time direct.

4. THAT no Notice shall be received in the Private Bill Office for any proceeding upon a Petition for a Bill, or upon a Bill brought from the Lords (after such Bill has been read a first time), until an Appearance to act as the Parliamentary Agent upon the same shall have been entered in the Private Bill Office; in which Appearance shall also be specified the Name of the Solicitor (if any) for such Petition or Bill.

5. THAT before any party shall be allowed to appear or be heard upon any Petition against a Bill, an Appearance to act as the Parliamentary Agent upon the same shall be entered in the Private Bill Office; in which Appearance shall also be specified the Name of the Solicitor and of the Counsel who appear in support of any such Petition (if any Counsel or Solicitor are then engaged), and a Certificate of such Appearance shall be delivered to the Parliamentary Agents to be produced to the Committee Clerk.

6. THAT in case the Parliamentary Agent for any Petition or Bill shall be displaced by the Solicitor thereof, or such Parliamentary Agent shall decline to act, the responsibility of such Agent shall cease upon a Notice being given in the Private Bill Office, and a fresh Appearance shall be entered upon such Petition or Bill.

7. THAT any Parliamentary Agent who shall wilfully act in violation of the Rules and Practice of Parliament, or of any Rules to be prescribed by The Speaker, or who shall wilfully misconduct himself in prosecuting any proceedings before Parliament, shall be liable to an absolute or temporary prohibition to practise as a Parliamentary Agent, at the pleasure of The Speaker: provided that upon the application of such Parliamentary Agent, The Speaker shall state in writing the grounds for such prohibition.

8. THAT the above Rules shall commence upon Monday the 13th day of March 1837.

J. ABERCROMBY, SPEAKER

(ii)

RULES to be observed by the OFFICERS of the HOUSE, and by all PARLIAMENTARY AGENTS engaged in prosecuting Proceedings in the HOUSE of COMMONS upon any PETITION or BILL:—

1. There shall be kept at the Committee and Private Bill Office a register of the persons entitled to practise as Parliamentary Agents distinguishing those entitled so to practise both in promoting and opposing Bills and those entitled so to practise in opposing Bills only.

2. No person shall be entitled to practise as a Parliamentary Agent unless he is so registered:

Provided that a person so registered, if a member of a firm, may carry on his business as Parliamentary Agent under the name and style of the firm notwithstanding that one or more other members of the firm are not so registered, but partnership with a person who is so registered shall not entitle any partner not so registered to practise as a Parliamentary Agent.

3. No person shall be registered until he has subscribed before one of the Clerks in the Committee and Private Bill Office a declaration in such form as the Speaker may prescribe engaging to obey and observe the Orders and practice of the House of Commons and any Rules prescribed by the Speaker, and also to pay and discharge from time to time when demanded all fees and charges due from the Promoters or as the case may be the Opponents for whom he shall act.

4. Any person either before or after his name has been entered in the register shall, if required by the Speaker, enter into a recognisance or bond in a penal sum not exceeding £500, with two sureties each for half the penal sum, to observe the said declaration.

5. In the case of a firm, it shall suffice if one member of the firm subscribes the required declaration and enters into the required recognisance or bond on behalf of the firm.

6. No fee shall be payable in respect of the said declaration, recognisance, bond or registration.

7. No applicant shall be qualified to be registered as a Parliamentary Agent entitled to practise both in promoting and opposing Bills unless he satisfies the Speaker that he has practical knowledge of the Standing Orders and procedure of the House of Commons regulating Private Business:

Provided that any person shall be entitled to be registered if before or within six months after the date when these rules come into operation he makes an application for the purpose, and proves that within the five preceding years he either

(i) *bona fide* practised as a Parliamentary Agent and in that capacity conducted the promotion of two or more Bills which have passed into law or of two or more Provisional Orders under the Private Legislation Procedure (Scotland) Act, 1899, or the Private Legislation Procedure (Scotland) Act, 1936, which have been confirmed by Parliament; or

(ii) being a member of a firm which *bona fide* practised as Parliamentary Agents, was concerned in the conduct of two or more such Bills as aforesaid or two or more such Provisional Orders as aforesaid.

8. The Speaker may, if he thinks fit, appoint an Advisory Committee and refer to that Committee for advice any question arising as to the qualifications of any applicant for registration.

9. No person shall be qualified to be registered as a Parliamentary Agent entitled to practise as such in opposing Bills only, unless he is actually employed in opposing a Bill or Special Order, and the registration shall cease to have effect on the close of the session in which it was effected.

10. Any person possessing the required qualifications shall be entitled to be registered unless the Speaker otherwise directs:

Provided that unless he is a solicitor or has been registered as a Parliamentary Agent before the date when these Rules come into operation he must on his first application for registration produce to one of the Clerks of the Committee and Private Bill Office a certificate of his respectability from a Member of Parliament, a Justice of the Peace, a Barrister, or a Solicitor.

11. Every application for registration must be in writing.

12. No person's name shall be printed on any Private Bill, as Parliamentary Agent for such Bill, unless and until his name has been duly inscribed upon the Register of Parliamentary Agents.

13. No Notice shall be received in the Committee and Private Bill Office for any proceeding upon a Petition or Bill, until an Appearance to act as the Parliamentary Agent upon the same shall have been entered in the Committee and Private Bill Office; in which Appearance

shall also be specified the name of the Solicitor (if any) for such Petition or Bill.

14. Before any person desiring to appear by a Parliamentary Agent shall be allowed to appear or be heard upon any Petition against a Bill, an Appearance to act as the Parliamentary Agent upon the same shall be entered in the Committee and Private Bill Office; in which Appearance shall also be specified the name of the Solicitor and of the Counsel who appear in support of any such Petition (if any Counsel or Solicitor are then engaged), and a Certificate of such Appearance shall be delivered to the Parliamentary Agent, to be produced to the Committee Clerk.

15. Except in cases where a Bill is promoted or a Petition is presented by two or more companies bodies or persons separately interested, one Parliamentary Agent or firm of Agents only shall be allowed to appear and to be heard in the proceedings on the Bill on behalf of the Promoters or the Petitioners.

16. In case the Parliamentary Agent for any Petition or Bill shall be displaced by the Solicitor thereof, or such Parliamentary Agent shall decline to act, the responsibility of such Agent shall cease in respect of any Fees incurred after that time upon a Notice being given in the Committtee and Private Bill Office, and a fresh Appearance shall be entered upon such Petition or Bill.

17. No written or printed statement relating to any Private Bill shall be circulated within the precincts of the House of Commons without the name of a Parliamentary Agent attached to it, who will be held responsible for its accuracy.

18. The sanction of the Chairman of Ways and Means is required to every Notice of a Motion prepared by a Parliamentary Agent, for dispensing with any Sessional or Standing Order of the House.

19. A Parliamentary Agent shall not divide with or pay to any client, or any solicitor, clerk, officer, or servant of any client, any moneys which the Agent at any time receives in respect of his costs charges and expenses in promoting opposing or otherwise dealing with any Bill or Provisional Order, or given any commission or gratuity to any person in respect of his employment as a Parliamentary Agent.

20. Every Parliamentary Agent and Solicitor conducting Proceedings in Parliament before the House of Commons shall be personally responsible to the House, and to the Speaker, for the observance of the Rules, Orders, and Practice of Parliament, as well as of any Rules which may from time to time be prescribed by the Speaker, and also for the payment of the Fees and Charges due and payable under the Standing Orders.

21. Any person registered as a Parliamentary Agent who shall act in violation of the Orders and practice of the House of Commons or who shall be guilty of professional misconduct of any kind as a Parliamentary Agent shall be liable to an absolute or temporary prohibition to practise as a Parliamentary Agent at the discretion of the Speaker.

22. No person who has been suspended or prohibited from practising as a Parliamentary Agent or who otherwise than at his own request has been struck off the Roll of Solicitors or disbarred by any of the Inns of court shall be allowed to be entered or retained on the register without the express authority of the Speaker.

23. For the purposes of these Rules —

"Bill" shall mean —

(a) any Private Bill;

(b) any Public Bill with respect to which the Examiners have reported that Standing Orders relative to Private Bills are applicable;

(c) any Bill so far as it relates to the confirmation of a Provisional Order opposed on petition;

and except as respects the proviso to Rule 7 includes a Special Order opposed on petition.

"Solicitor" includes a solicitor in England, Scotland or Northern Ireland and a Writer to the Signet.

24. These Rules shall come into operation at the close of the present Session of Parliament.

Provided that an application under Rule 7 may be made at any time before that date.

(Sgd.) E.A. FITZROY,
Speaker.

House of Commons,
4th April, 1938

I

PRIVATE BILLS DEPOSITED

in the
Sessions 1971-2, 1972-3.

(i) – SESSION 1971-2

SHORT TITLE OF BILL	PARLIAMENTARY AGENTS
Bath Corporation	Dyson, Bell & Co.
Bath Side Bay Development	Sherwood & Co.
British Railways	Sherwood & Co.
British Transport Docks	Sherwood & Co.
Burnham River Company	Vizards.
Congregational Chapel and Trust Property Deptford	Martin & Co.
Cornwall River Authority	Sherwood & Co.
Coventry Corporation	Sharpe, Pritchard & Co.
Derby Corporation	Sharpe, Pritchard & Co.
Devon County Council	Dyson, Bell & Co.
Devon River Authority (General Powers)	Dyson, Bell & Co.
Essex River Authority	Dyson, Bell & Co.
Friends of the Clergy Corporation	Sharpe, Pritchard & Co.
Glamorgan County Council	Lewin, Gregory & Co.
Great London Council (General Powers)	Dyson, Bell & Co.
Hampshire County Council	Dyson, Bell & Co.
Kensington and Chelsea Corporation	Sharpe, Pritchard & Co.
Liverpool Corporation	Sherwood & Co.
Lloyds & Bolsa International Bank	Dyson, Bell & Co.
London Transport	Sherwood & Co.,
Mersey Tunnel	Sherwood & Co.
Milford Docks	Dyson, Bell & Co.
Neath Corporation	Dyson, Bell & Co.
Oxford Corporation	Sharpe, Pritchard & Co.
Oxfordshire and District Water Board	Sharpe, Pritchard & Co.
Port Talbot Corporation	Lewin, Gregory & Co.
Railway Clearing System Superannuation Fund	Sherwood & Co.
Reigate Congregational Church	Sharpe, Pritchard & Co.
Rhondda Corporation	Lewin, Gregory & Co.
Saint Andrew's, Hove, Churchyard	Sharpe, Pritchard & Co.

Salop County Council	Sharpe, Pritchard & Co.
Seaham Harbour Dock	Dyson, Bell & Co.
Selnec (Manchester Central Area Railway, etc).	Dyson, Bell & Co.
Sheffield Corporation (General Powers)	Sherwood & Co.
Solihull Corporation	Sharpe, Pritchard & Co.
Stoke-on-Trent Corporation	Lewin, Gregory & Co.
Sunderland Corporation	Sharpe, Pritchard & Co.
Thames Barrier and Flood Prevention	Dyson, Bell & Co.
Thames Conservancy	Sherwood & Co.
United Kingdom Oil Pipelines	Dyson, Bell & Co.
United Reformed Church	Martin & Co.
University of London, King's College (Lease)	Lewin, Gregory & Co.
Upper Avon Navigation	Martin & Co.
West Sussex County Council	Sherwood & Co.
Westminster Abbey and Saint Margaret	
Westminster	Sharpe, Pritchard & Co.
Whiteley Bay Pier (Extension of Time)	Martin & Co.

(ii) – SESSION 1972-73

SHORT TITLE OF BILL	PARLIAMENTARY AGENTS
Ashdown Forest	Sherwood & Co.
British Transport Docks	Sherwood & Co.
British Transport Docks (Hull Docks)	Sherwood & Co.
City of London (Various Powers)	Sherwood & Co.
Cornwall River Authority	Sherwood & Co.
Dee and Clwyd River Authority	Sherwood & Co.
Derby Friar Gate Chapel	Sharpe Pritchard & Co.
Forward Trust	Dyson Bell & Co.
Greater London Council (General Powers)	Dyson Bell & Co.
Harwich Harbour	Sherwood & Co.
Hull Tidal Surge Barrier	Sharpe Pritchard & Co.
Humber Bridge	Sharpe Pritchard & Co.
King's Lynn Corporation	Sharpe Pritchard & Co.
Langston Marina	Sherwood & Co.
London Transport	Sherwood & Co.
Medway Ports Authority	Dyson Bell & Co.
Mercantile Credit	Martin & Co.
Metal Society	Sharpe Pritchard & Co.
North Wales Hydro Electric Power	Dyson Bell & Co.
Queen Mary College	Dyson Bell & Co.

Rhondda Corporation	Lewin Gregory & Co.
Ryde Corporation	Sharpe Pritchard & Co.
Salford Corporation	Dyson Bell & Co.
Slough Estates (Utility Services) Limited	Dyson Bell & Co.
Southampton Corporation	Sharpe Pritchard & Co.
Trent River Authority	Dyson Bell & Co.
Tyneside Metropolitan Railway	Sherwood & Co.
Upper Mersey Navigation	Sharpe Pritchard & Co.

INDEX

Note: (1) Peers are indexed under peerage. (2) In order to save space firms and individuals mentioned only in Appendices A-E are not indexed.